THE RECONCILIATION OF PEOPLES

THE RECONCILIATION OF PEOPLES

Challenge to the Churches

Edited by
Gregory Baum
Harold Wells

WCC PUBLICATIONS
1211 Geneva 2, Switzerland

ORBIS BOOKS
Maryknoll, New York 10545

34.52

Queries regarding rights and permissions should be addressed to: Orbis Books, P.O. Box 308, Maryknoll, New York 10545-0308.

Published jointly 1997 by Orbis Books, P.O. Box 308, Maryknoll, New York 10545-0308, and WCC Publications, 150 route de Ferney, 1211 Geneva 2, Switzerland
Manufactured in the United States of America
Manuscript editing and typesetting by Joan Marie Laflamme

Library of Congress Cataloging-in-Publication Data

The reconciliation of peoples : challenge to the churches / edited by
  Gregory Baum, Harold Wells.
    p. cm.
  Includes bibliographical references.
  ISBN 1-57075-107-2 (alk. paper)
  1. Reconciliation—Religious aspects—Christianity. 2. Peace—
Religious aspects—Christianity. I. Baum, Gregory, 1923- .
II. Wells, Harold.
BT736.4.R43   1997
261.8'09—dc21   96-45029
                                                CIP

WCC Publications ISBN 2-8254-1217-1
ORBIS/ISBN 1-57075-107-2

Contents

Preface

GREGORY BAUM AND HAROLD WELLS

The colossal tragedy of Rwanda and then the raging violence in Bosnia formed the shocking background out of which this book was conceived. These are just two of the most dramatic instances of the ethnic conflict that plagues our late-twentieth-century world as never before.

As Christian theologians we felt constrained to reflect upon the responsibility of Christian people and the resources of Christian faith for the great task of reconciliation. Almost all Christians would agree immediately that reconciliation and peacemaking are part of the Christian calling, both for churches and Christian organizations and for Christian individuals. That the churches and Christian people have failed in their efforts almost entirely is all too evident. That Christian people and even Christian beliefs and practices have been a contributing presence in many circumstances of violent conflict is a painful truth that we must face.

This book is a modest attempt to address these pressing concerns and to contribute to the quite recent but now growing literature on peacemaking. Though the editors (a Roman Catholic and a member of The United Church of Canada) and most of our authors (with one exception) do not stand within the tradition of Christian pacifism found in the historic "peace churches," we honor that tradition and recommend the accumulating wisdom and experience of the practice of nonviolence as it has found expression in numerous recent publications.

This book has been designed to record and reflect upon actual efforts and achievements by Christian churches, organizations, and individuals toward reconciliation in many different circumstances of ethnic, cultural, or religious conflict. We do not imply that only Christians have a responsibility for reconciliation or that only Christians have contributed to peacemaking efforts around the world. On the contrary, we believe Christians must repent of their enormous failure in this respect. But, as Christians, we feel that our particular faith tradition offers resources for reconciliation that need to be emphasized and made explicit. We have attempted, by gathering together a number of stories and reflections, to contribute to a growing wisdom, so that people in far-flung parts of the world may learn from one another how peace may be achieved, or at least how steps toward reconciliation may be taken. We have tried to avoid uncritical accolades or glowing success stories, for we are aware of the limitations and ambiguity of nearly all such efforts.

The research done by Ralph Premdas, one of our authors, on the churches' reaction to ethnic conflicts in the Third World has led him to make the following recommendation:

> The leaders of the churches will have to take the issue of ethnic conflict more seriously. Of utmost importance is a better understanding of the social, political and theological factors involved. The churches will have to appoint committees that investigate the historical origin of the conflict, examine the social scientific literature on ethnic conflicts, study the theory and practice of conflict resolution, and devise instruments of popular education that raise people's awareness of the issues at stake and communicate the biblical message of reconciliation.[1]

In this brief preface we shall not attempt to analyze in any depth the complex roots of what appears to be a worldwide escalation of hostility among peoples. However, a few highly visible factors may be mentioned. The collapse of communism in the Soviet Union and eastern Europe in 1989 has created a very different world order, one in which old and seething national, ethnic, or religious hatred has erupted to the surface in many places. At the same time, the increasing power of multinational capital and the accompanying decline in the significance of nation states and their governments appear, ironically, to release new passions for cultural, ethnic, and religious identity. Moreover, dreadful economic strain and suffering in some parts of the Third World, especially in Africa, due to the tightening squeeze of the capitalist world system and its "structural adjustment" strategies help to break down the authority of governments. All of this fuels the despair and restlessness of peoples, who become more vulnerable than ever to disorder and violence.

The scene is not wholly negative, however. The new self-affirmation of peoples long oppressed or disadvantaged must be seen in a positive light. Indigenous peoples, long ago invaded, enslaved, or suppressed by colonizing powers, robbed of land, exploited for their labor, have now found the courage and resources to assert their cultural and religious identities. A recurring theme of this book is that true reconciliation cannot be achieved at the cost of injustice and continuing oppression. The surfacing of conflict, therefore, can be a positive event. The spectacular breakthrough against apartheid in South Africa after long and costly resistance to injustice, and the new era of reconstruction that has begun there, seemed to warrant two articles, one reflecting on the process that led to the end of apartheid, the other focusing on the need for reconciliation in the new situation.

Many other indigenous peoples around the world continue to be deprived and disadvantaged. Native public protest and potentially violent conflict have flared up in many places in Canada. In Quebec also, the francophone majority, living as a minority within the Canadian state, has forcefully asserted its linguistic, cultural, and national identity. The disadvantages and discontent of Quebec francophones are not comparable to the oppression experienced by South African blacks, or Canadian Natives. However, their concerns can be seen as representative of other minority peoples who have found themselves stranded on the losing side of old colonial battles or imperial wars. Their grievances and aspirations call for a sensitive hearing.

Accounts here of the two genocidal events that first prompted this book— Rwanda and Bosnia—are mainly stories of failure, which move us to reflect on our human and Christian responsibility to speak out and to resist atrocities. Yet even in the face of such vast wickedness, wisdom, compassion, courage, and martyrdom were not absent from the scene.

Again, peoples divided (the Irish, the Koreans), peoples persecuted internally by their own ruling elite (Chileans, Fijians), peoples tragically deprived of land and home (Palestinians), and peoples torn apart by war (the Germans, the Polish) all have something to teach us about positive efforts to achieve reconciliation.

We have been delighted by the caliber of the authors who have agreed to contribute to this volume and the quality of the material they have provided. As editors, we have offered, respectively, an opening article and a closing Afterword that are explicitly theological. Yet each of our authors has, in the context of his or her story, gifted us with important theological insight. We warmly thank them for their rich stories and reflections, and we honor the contribution that some of them have themselves made to the struggle for human reconciliation.

Note

[1] Ralph Premdas, "The Church and Ethnic Conflicts in the Third Word," *The Ecumenist* (May/June 1994), p. 56.

1

Theology for Reconciliation

Biblical Perspectives on Forgiveness and Grace

HAROLD WELLS

The gospel of Christ calls us to a ministry of reconciliation and to be peace-makers. In this book several authors tell their stories about the efforts of Christians to achieve reconciliation in various situations of human conflict, most of them in circumstances of gross injustice and grave offense. Readers will find theological insight in each of the articles included here, and my co-editor, Gregory Baum, gathering up many of these insights, offers further theological reflection in his Afterword. This article deals explicitly with the *theology* of reconciliation, exploring the concepts that are at work in the other articles (though I do not assume that all the authors agree with the ideas expressed here).

Theological ideas are powerful. Anyone who doubts this may consider the importance of the "religious right" in American politics or the influence of the theological ideas of the "religious left" over the last several decades in North America in such matters as social security, racial equality and civil rights, the status of women, capital punishment, and homosexuality. But theo-logical concepts are often operative at a more subtle level. Not only explicit social and moral ideas but doctrinal formulations also have to be investigated regarding their practical, ethical, and political repercussions.[1]

I do not propose a theological method which proceeds by asking, "What do people need to believe in order that human relations may improve?" The-ology is a listening and obedient discipline of thought, attending to God's revelation in Jesus Christ, and it cannot be calculated according to our con-ceptions of what is socially necessary. Nevertheless, particular doctrinal formulations *are* of human design, and one of the ways in which we should test our doctrines is to ask about their ethical and political implications. We begin with the premise that the Holy One of Israel, whom we have encoun-tered in Jesus Christ, is the God of justice, love, and peace. The content of these concepts is provided by the biblical narratives, especially Exodus—so formative for the whole Hebrew tradition—and the life and ministry of Jesus, his cross and resurrection. We must also hear the Hebrew prophetic hopes and visions of a world reconciled to God, and the teaching of Jesus, as these are found in scripture. In the Bible, justice, love, and peace have to do with slaves being set free from bondage, the care of widows and the fatherless, kindness to strangers and sojourners, compassion for the sick and disabled, fair wages to workers, economic security, the inclusion of the marginalized, liberation from oppression, and the end of war.

Yet it is tragically evident that the teaching of the churches can be insidiously destructive in its power to inspire injustice, hatred, and violence. First, a doctrine of scripture that equates the words of the Bible with the Word of God is dangerous indeed. The Bible must be read cautiously when it appears to condone the conquest and annihilation of enemies (in Joshua and Judges), contempt for other peoples and their religions (Dt 7), exclusion of the disabled (Lv 21), the institution of slavery and the subordination of women (Eph 5), or passivity toward the state (Rom 13). The Bible, as the indispensable and incomparable source of the gospel, rightly functions as holy scripture in the church, and therein lies its power. Nevertheless, Christians will naturally read the Bible critically in light of the divine self-disclosure in Jesus. When scripture is not read and understood within the Spirit of Christ, it is apt to be coopted for hateful and destructive purposes, and such misuse has been endemic in recent history. Examples of this are well known: the distortion of evangelical mission in the infliction of slavery and exploitation by Christian imperialism upon indigenous peoples; the Nazi cooptation of biblical and theological antisemitism for the fuelling of genocide; the South African legitimization of apartheid through the interpretation of biblical texts; the subtle functioning of creation texts to bless the rape of the natural world; the identification of Christianity with the "American way of life," which blesses capitalist individualism and consumerism.

All of this is not to encourage the self-importance of theologians. We must not flatter ourselves that Christian theology is responsible for all the evils of the world! Obviously other factors are at work. Nevertheless, it is true that bad theology makes bad politics.

On the other hand, many salutary developments for social equality and peace have also been generated in the twentieth century by the Social Gospel, by Neo-Orthodox theologies, and more recently by black, liberation, feminist, and ecological theologies. It is these latter that have made us aware of the need to be intentional about the social and political "fall out" of scriptural interpretations and church doctrines. Since Christianity is alive and influential in various degrees in every part of the world, what we teach about sin, forgiveness, and grace will send its ripples, or tidal waves, deep into the hearts and minds of human beings and deep into the relationships of races and peoples. Thus we need a theology *for* reconciliation.

The Hebrew Vision of a Reconciled World

It is fundamental to the biblical story that human beings exist in enmity, are alienated from God and from one another, and that Yahweh, the God of Israel, wills to overcome this enmity. The Holy One who spoke to Moses, undermined the false authority of the deified pharaoh, and so led Israel out of Egypt, is the One who sides with victims against oppression and injustice. The covenant of Yahweh with Israel, founded upon the deliverance out of Egypt, has to do with relationships of justice and peace. Yahweh is wrathful in the face of the people's lovelessness, threatens and executes judgment upon them, weeps over them, pleads with them to repent, and continually forgives and restores. These themes are prominent, for example, in Hosea, Jeremiah, and Jonah. While the term *reconciliation* is not used in the Hebrew scriptures, the overcoming of hatred and enmity and the achievement of peace and love between God and human beings, and among all people, are plainly the purpose and will of God: "Hear O Israel: the Lord is our God, the Lord alone. You shall love the Lord your God with all your heart, and with all your soul, and with all your might" (Dt 6:4-5).[2] Also: "You shall not take vengeance or bear a grudge against any of your people, but you shall love your neighbor as yourself. I am the Lord" (Lv 19:18). The God of liberation, the God of Exodus alone is Lord. That is why in this Leviticus text (later placed together by Jesus with the Deuteronomy text) vengeance is forbidden.

Another voice sounds in the scripture that must not be overlooked. It is the voice of cursing, a beatitude in reverse, in the face of the enslavement and massacre even of little children: "O daughter Babylon, you devastator! Happy shall they be who pay you back what you have done to us! Happy shall they be who take your little ones and dash them against the rock!" (Ps 137:9). Righteous human outrage and divine wrath find their expression here. The atrocities that human beings inflict upon one another cannot be covered over with facades of false peace.

It is a cliché, but a necessary one, that peace cannot be achieved without justice, and this is always understood and assumed in the Bible. "Righteousness and peace shall kiss each other," says the psalmist (Ps 85:10). Righteousness (right relations with God and with one another) and justice are essentially synonyms in Hebrew usage, and when righteousness flourishes and peace abounds we are reconciled even with the natural order:

> . . . until a spirit from on high is poured out on us
>   and the wilderness becomes a fruitful field,
>   and the fruitful field is deemed a forest.
> Then justice will dwell in the wilderness,
>   and righteousness abide in the fruitful field.
> The effect of righteousness will be peace,

and the result of righteousness quietness and trust
forever
—Isaiah 32:15-17

Reconciliation does not replace justice. Reconciliation is the result of justice.[3] Living as I did for several years in southern Africa during the apartheid era, I often heard on the radio the white South African heads of state appealing to the people for reconciliation: "Why must we always live with conflict and unrest? Why can we not live peacefully together in this beautiful land? Let us all work together for national reconciliation!" (or some such words). The admonitions were spoken with a certain tragic, blind sincerity. Black people greeted such exhortations with a mixture of fury and hilarity.

They have treated the wound of my people carelessly,
saying "Peace, peace,
when there is no peace!"
They acted shamefully, they committed abomination;
yet . . . they did not know how to blush.
—Jeremiah 6:14-15

Justice is always the prerequisite of true peace, whether among races and religions, workers and owners, women and men, peoples and nations. When grave offenses have occurred, reconciliation is costly. Christians engaged in the work of reconciliation, when they take the Hebrew scriptures seriously, will not indulge in cheap admonitions to victims to forgive and forget.

The prophets of Israel, speaking out of deep communion with Yahweh and out of the Exodus tradition, not only denounced idolatry and injustice but envisaged a time when oppression and war would cease and peace would reign in the whole world. Human beings, it is understood, cannot achieve this of themselves. It will be by the work of God's Spirit that justice and peace will reign. The following passage is one of the most magnificent biblical expressions of this prophetic, messianic hope, which may be described as an eschatological vision of a "reconciled" world. We should note that judgment is not missing from this vision:

The spirit of the LORD shall rest on him . . .
He shall not judge by what his eyes see,
or decide by what his ears hear;
but with righteousness he shall judge the poor
and decide with equity for the meek of the earth;
he shall strike the earth with the rod of his mouth,
and with the breath of his lips he shall slay the wicked.
Righteousness shall be the belt around his waist,
and faithfulness the belt around his loins.

> The wolf shall live with the lamb,
> 　the leopard shall lie down with the kid,
> the calf and the lion and the fatling together,
> 　and a little child shall lead them.
> The cow and the bear shall graze,
> 　their young shall lie down together;
> 　and the lion shall eat straw like the ox.
> The nursing child shall play over the hole of the asp,
> 　and the weaned child shall put its hand on the adder's den.
> They shall not hurt or destroy
> 　on all my holy mountain;
> for the earth will be full of the knowledge of the LORD
> 　as the waters cover the sea.
> 　　　　　　　　　　　　　　　—Isaiah 11:2-9

This utopian vision of a reconciled world, from Exodus to the prophets, has been and continues to be a rich source of inspiration for social hope and transformation. It clearly ties peace together with justice and looks forward with hope to a world transformed through the power of God's Spirit.

The Teaching and Deeds of Jesus

I said above that Christians must read scripture within the Spirit of Christ. This cannot be done without listening carefully to Jesus, as he is presented in the New Testament.

The deeds and teaching of Jesus have often been downplayed by Christian theology. They are even totally absent from the classical creeds, which pass immediately from his birth of the Virgin to his death under Pontius Pilate. In the gospels it is abundantly evident that Jesus is a child of this Hebrew tradition. The gospel writers proclaim that he is the messianic bearer of the Spirit, announcing and embodying God's reign of justice and peace. Of particular interest to us here is Jesus' teaching about reconciliation and his actual conflict with the forces of injustice.[4] Where reconciliation is concerned, the biblical material about Jesus does not present us with a simple or unambiguous picture. Jesus' life and teaching are characterized by a certain dialectic, for he holds together, on the one hand, a radical love of the enemy, and, on the other, forthright confrontation with the perpetrators of injustice. We distort the wisdom of his teaching if we neglect either of these.

The call to a radical love in the teaching of Jesus is extraordinary. When he is asked, "'If your brother sins against you, how often should I forgive? As many as seven times?' Jesus said to him, 'Not seven times, but, I tell you, seventy times seven'" (Mt 18:21-22). For Jesus, reconciliation is more important than ritual, and here he stands in the prophetic tradition.

"If you are offering your gift at the altar, and there remember that your brother has something against you, leave your gift before the altar and go; first be reconciled to your brother, and then come and offer your gift." (Mt 5:23)

Followers of Jesus cannot evade the command about the love of enemies: "I say unto you, Love your enemies, and pray for those who persecute you" (Mt 5:44). Jesus illustrates the love of enemies in his parable of the Good Samaritan, where an ethnic and religious "enemy" is the hero of the story (Lk 10:29-37). Jesus also praises a Roman centurion (Mt 8:5-10) and the Samaritan leper, "this foreigner," who alone returned to give thanks (Lk 17:17). He offends the people of Nazareth when he suggests that God's blessing rests upon such foreigners as the widow of Zarephath in Sidon and Naaman the Syrian (Lk 4:26-27). In all of this, Jesus' teaching stands as a sharp rebuke to all who call themselves Christian, attend worship, receive the sacraments, yet nurture in their hearts a hateful ethnicism, racism, or a feeling of religious superiority. It is sad that this attitude of Jesus about "others" has been so neglected in the teaching of the churches that Christians can engage in ethnic hatred, torture, and even genocide without realizing that they directly disobey their Lord.

Jesus spells out what love of enemies might entail when he says: "You have heard that it was said, 'An eye for an eye and a tooth for a tooth.' But I say unto you, Do not resist an evildoer. But if anyone strikes you on the right cheek, turn the other also" (Mt 5:39). I cannot deal adequately here with the complex debate about violent and nonviolent methods of overcoming aggression and oppression. Surely nonviolent action is far preferable. The long tradition of Christian pacifism, still very much alive in the historic peace churches and other creative movements for nonviolence,[5] is important and deserves respect. Christianity generally has so neglected Jesus' teaching about nonviolence that it is seldom tried very seriously; we rush to violent solutions. Still, many of us are not convinced that the teaching of Jesus requires that we must *always* be nonviolent in all circumstances. The distinction between "violent" and "nonviolent" coercive strategies, in any case, is not absolute, since nonviolent strategies are also often injurious to the neighbor.[6] Jesus did not give us binding, inflexible moral regulations. To love God and to love the neighbor as oneself is "the whole of the law and the prophets" (Mt 22:40), and this cannot be formulated into rigid principles. Those engaged in tragic and desperate struggles generally know that there are no simple rules or formulae for loving neighbors, or for achieving justice or reconciliation. Sometimes love of the enemy requires precisely that the enemy be effectively resisted. Sometimes, I believe, the armed and "violent" activities of defenders, peacekeepers, police, or revolutionaries have to be supported.[7]

What must be seen together with Jesus' radical teaching about forgiveness and the love of enemies is that he does not flee from confrontation or gloss over painful conflict. He is severe indeed in his verbal attacks upon some religious leaders and teachers, whom he accuses in the most vivid terms of self-righteousness, hypocrisy, and injustice. He wields a whip of cords to cleanse the temple, which had become a "den of thieves" (Lk 19:46). He declared, "Do not think that I have come to bring peace on the earth. I have come not to bring peace, but a sword" (Mt 10:34). These are the words and deeds of one who aggressively confronts what he sees as evil. According to Luke, Jesus at one time instructed his disciples, "The one who has no sword must sell his cloak and buy one" (Lk 22:36). He is aware of the reality of conflict and struggle and of the necessity to resist evil actively.

Unfortunately, very often the attitude of Jesus about forgiveness and his own unresisting way to the cross are emphasized to the exclusion of this other sharply confrontative dimension. To many of those engaged in fierce struggle Jesus seems to be merely soft and passive, irrelevant to the urgency of the fight that must be fought. At the same time, his call to radical love and forgiveness has been simply ignored by Christians who engage in hateful and spiteful practices of revenge. Jesus was considered dangerous enough to be gotten rid of by the authorities. His enemies were never reconciled with him. He sought no false peace with those who oppressed the people. Yet he was able to love them even as they tortured and executed him: "Father forgive them, for they do not know what they are doing" (Lk 23:34). These words are precious to us, for they have become an assurance of the breadth and depth of the divine mercy. Jesus' teaching and courageous example make us poignantly aware of our universal failure, indeed our own powerlessness to love as we should, and to forgive as we should.

The Universality of Sin

The doctrine that "we are all sinners," that "all have sinned and fall short of the glory of God" (Rom 3:23) is undisputed. The apostle Paul carries forward the Hebrew tradition about the universality of sin, quoting Psalm 14: "None is righteous, no, not one, together they have gone wrong; no one does good, not even one" (Rom 3:10-12). The Hebrew scriptures are replete with narratives of sin—of individuals, of the nation, and of humanity as a whole. Cain murders Abel. Jacob cheats Esau of his birthright. David, out of lustful desire for Bathsheba, arranges the death of her husband. The prophets rage against the rich and powerful, and sometimes against the whole nation that has turned away from the true God and turned to idols and to injustice and oppression. Genesis 3 depicts humanity (Adam) as proudly rebellious, seeking to know good and evil and so seeking to "be as God." Jesus knew that morally respectable people also sin "in their hearts" (Mt 5:28). The way in which the doctrine of the universality of sin is construed is significant for the practice of reconciliation. It can be a reconciling doctrine or a misleading and unhelpful one.

That we are all sinners has traditionally been understood in terms of the doctrine of original sin: We do not decide to become sinners; we discover our

own alienation as a given that we have not consciously chosen, and it is pre-
dictable of every child even before birth that he or she will be a sinner. We are
all implicated in the "fallenness" of a broken world, and this has sometimes
been understood as a kind of biological inheritance. Human beings have a
sense of being under the power of sin, or of an evil spirit (Satan), or of sin
itself dwelling within them and a feeling that they are helpless in the face of it
(see, for example, Rom 7:19). In this century theologians have spoken not so
much of inherited sin, but of "structural" or "systemic" sin. This means that
sin cannot be understood adequately in personal and individual terms, that
our personal sinfulness both contributes to and is a result of the sinfulness of
our social structures and of a long history and world system of greed and
violence. We are all implicated in the systemic injustice that leaves so many
helpless, hungry, and poor, all participants more or less willingly in economic
and societal systems that benefit some at the expense of others.

The recognition of sin as structural and systemic is important if we are to
pass beyond the popular view of sin as having to do mainly with sexual mis-
demeanors, personal lying, stealing, and cheating. Such a superficial concept
enables us to pass over gross class or racial inequities as though they have
nothing to do with sin at all. If sin is systemic, preachers and theologians
cannot neglect politics and economics. To suppose, then, that reconciliation
can be achieved by moralizing on a personal level is naive and dangerous.

The universality of sin and the recognition of its systemic character also
militate against self-righteousness and mutual condemnation. "Let the one
who is without sin among you be the first to throw a stone at her," Jesus said
in defense of an adulterous woman (Jn 8:7). Many ongoing feuds among religious and ethnic groups are fuelled precisely by colossal group self-
righteousness and blind mutual blaming. Here the saying of Jesus is worth
hearing: "Judge not, that you be not judged" (Mt 7:1). Even in circumstances
of clear oppression and victimization, victims are not without sin. In other
circumstances and other relationships, victims can be oppressors too. This
means that no absolute distinctions can be drawn between victims and oppressors, or between the sinners and the sinned against.

But there is another side to this. The concept of the universality of sin can
be misused to gloss over the real differences between victim and perpetrator.
We say complacently, "We all have our faults; we're all sinners, after all."
This can become an alibi for refusing to defend the victimized against those
who attack them. Our language of collective sin can be so general as to dull
the edge of the indignation and outrage that is sometimes called for. Nor can
personal responsibility for actual sins of omission or commission be set aside.
The universality of sin and the absolute need of every person for forgiveness
and grace should not be confused with an equality of objective guilt. It is
fatuous to treat the rapist and his victim as equally guilty. It is scandalous to
suggest that those who courageously resist the evil of genocide, at great cost
to themselves, and those who passively cooperate in it, are equally guilty.

Jürgen Moltmann seems to have the Nazi mass murder of the Jews in mind when he writes:

> Some of the people involved also hide their individual guilt in collective guilt, maintaining that "we are all more or less guilty and supported the totalitarian regime." Other people are glad to lose themselves in obscure and cloudy speculations about allegedly "tragic combinations of circumstances" to which we all succumbed—to a greater or lesser degree of course. These attempts to exonerate oneself personally through collective accusations founder in the face of the people who resisted, and did not become guilty and were imprisoned or murdered as a result. These people force us to confess personally where we failed, and when, and to find out why.[8]

Whether we speak of universal sin or of personal responsibility and guilt, we are faced with an apparently hopeless human situation of overwhelming guilt and spiritual weakness. Where profound oppression has occurred over a long period of time, what power can move the oppressor to true repentance and the oppressed to genuine forgiveness?

Atonement: The Divine Solidarity

The New Testament persistently proclaims (in Paul, in the synoptic gospels, in John, Hebrews, etc.) that "Jesus died for us," that through his broken body and his blood poured out we are reconciled to God. By his life, death, and resurrection, Jesus brings atonement ("at-one-ment," harmony, peace) between God and humanity. In the light of the resurrection of Jesus, and drawing upon the Hebrew priestly and prophetic traditions, the first Christians interpreted his death as a divine event of redemption and reconciliation: "God was in Christ reconciling the world to himself, not counting their trespasses against them, and entrusting the message of reconciliation to us" (2 Cor 5:19). Even more explicitly, "in him all the fullness of God was pleased to dwell, and through him God was pleased to reconcile to himself all things, whether on earth or in heaven, by making peace through the blood of his cross" (Col 1:19-20). Jesus is seen as "a ransom for many" (Mk 10:45), "the lamb of God who takes away the sin of the world" (Jn 1:29), a high priest who sacrificed himself "once and for all" (Heb 7:27).

Today the theology of atonement has become extremely controversial. Many find these concepts unintelligible. Others argue that this is an immoral doctrine, encouraging us to think of God as an omnipotent child abuser who demanded the tortured death of his own Son to "satisfy" his sense of offended honor, as though God had to be "paid off" as the price of forgiveness. This is an incomplete and inaccurate rendition of the teaching of the medieval theologian Anselm[9] (to whom it is often attributed), yet something like this is preached daily on our television screens. Such explanations of the sacrifice of the cross are subtly destructive, legitimizing a cruel patriarchalism.[10] Is it possible to love and worship a deity who demands the blood sacrifice of an innocent person as a prerequisite to forgiveness? Such "divine" behavior does nothing to inspire human beings to generous forgiveness or love of enemies. Surely this doctrine needs to be construed very differently. As we so often hear it, it is incongruent with Jesus' teaching about the passionate love of God that reaches out to embrace us.

Jesus' teaching about forgiveness and the love of enemies is founded in the undiscriminating graciousness of his *Abba*. We should love our enemies, Jesus taught, in order "that you may be children of your Father in heaven; for he makes his sun rise on the evil and on the good, and sends rain on the righteous and on the unrighteous" (Mt 5:45). His parable of the Prodigal Son (Lk 15:11-32) depicts a passionately loving father who anxiously watches for the return of his delinquent son and rushes out to welcome him. In other parables God is a shepherd seeking for one lost sheep, a woman sweeping her house for a lost coin. Jesus preached the coming of the reign of the same God of Israel, Lord of the Exodus, who now, through the prophetic message of Jesus, offers reconciliation. Any doctrine of atonement that negates the graciousness of the Father is contrary to all that we learn from Jesus.

It would be easy to discard or trivialize the doctrine of atonement as religiously and culturally antiquated. Yet its presence everywhere in the New Testament gives us pause. Are we not being told something profoundly important that we cannot tell ourselves, something deeper than our modern consciousness finds palatable? The doctrine of atonement through the sacrifice of Christ speaks to a persistent human need. Many ancient religious traditions, including African and European, practiced some form of blood sacrifice—animals, birds, and sometimes human sacrifice—in a quest for atonement or harmony with the gods. Israel too sacrificed the "scapegoat," transferring sins to the goat, who carried the people's sins out into the desert (Lv 16: 20-22). The temple of Jerusalem was the scene of animal sacrifices for the purpose of atonement.

The truth in all such means of atonement is the recognition that our evil deeds cannot be taken lightly. Reconciliation is costly. God does not wink at our cruelty and injustice. Neither our petty failures and selfishness nor the gross social injustices in which we are implicated can be eliminated with an indulgent smile. The Holy One whom we meet in Jesus takes us seriously and takes our choices seriously. Moreover, many of those who know themselves guilty of grave offenses cannot easily forgive themselves. Nor can any human being grant forgiveness to murderers in the name of their victims.[11] Atonement is necessary, but there is nothing that we, or they, can do to undo the past or make it good. It is precisely the long Christian tradition of the all-sufficient sacrifice of Christ that has made animal sacrifices unnecessary and meaningless for us.

As we know from our own experience of human relationships, when deep hurt has occurred, reconciliation is costly. When we forgive, we do, in a manner of speaking, "bear" the guilt of the one forgiven. The cross shows us that reconciliation is also costly to God. It is not that God demands that someone else pay. On the contrary, it is God who, in Christ, offers reconciliation and bears the cost of our refusal. Moreover, Christ does not go as an unwilling victim to the cross, but, in profound unity with his Father, offers himself utterly for the sake of a reconciled world. Moltmann writes of this:

> God . . . is the one who suffers vicariously "for us" and "for many" as our representative. . . . How does this happen? It happens because by "carrying," or "bearing" human guilt, God transforms it into [God's] own suffering. According to the New Testament, Christ does not only become the Brother of the victims. He becomes the one who atones for the guilty too.[12]

We can only begin to fathom this if we acknowledge the oneness of Jesus Christ with God.[13] It is only because "God was in Christ" that his death can have atoning significance. The incarnation of God in Christ was, in the words of Elsa Tamez, "the greatest possible solidarity of God with humankind, to the point of taking on their humanity and even more specifically the humanity of the poor. . . . In the Son, God entered into the perverse and deadly logic of sin in order to condemn it."[14] Indeed, we can say that in his abandonment to torture and death, Christ took on not only our humanity but also our condemnation and damnation. As the creed says, "He descended into hell."

Not only his death, but his whole life of love and service, and his resurrection too, have salvific meaning. Jesus died because of the way he lived, in faithfulness to his *Abba*. The cross is not some arbitrary design of God but the inevitable political outcome of his faithful life. The resurrection too is an essential moment in the work of the atoning God. God also judged and pronounced sentence in the resurrection, which was the vindication of the victim, the triumph of all the persecuted of history and the judgment of the victimizers. Moltmann writes: "The dead return, those who have gone rise again, and the nameless are called by their names. That is the judgment. Ultimately the murders will not triumph over their victims and the torturers will be called to account."[15]

The doctrine of atonement, then, so potentially dangerous to the human spirit when misunderstood, can be a profound source of reconciliation among the perpetrators of crimes and their victims. Victims and perpetrators stand together before the cross, all in need of atonement. Yet injustice and oppression are taken with absolute seriousness. They cannot be lightly shrugged away. God, in Jesus Christ, is the brother of all tortured victims, and the risen, vindicated Judge of their tormentors. God is in total solidarity with the suffering victim. God is not, then, the bloodthirsty patriarch demanding "payment." Rather, God is the vulnerable One, the self-giving One, who moves us not to revenge but to forgiveness. The guilty too are offered hope, for God, in Christ, has "descended into hell" for them too. Here are deep wells of grace and hope, and powerful grounds for repentance and reconciliation.

Justification: A Reconciling Doctrine

The doctrine of justification and the way in which it is articulated also have enormous implications for practical reconciliation. As we have seen, Christians ground their life and hope in the firm rock of God's sovereign reconciliation of the world in Christ. God has embraced the whole cosmos irrevocably in the life, death, and resurrection of Jesus. We are called to respond. We are entrusted with the ministry of reconciliation, and as "ambassadors for Christ" are called to "be reconciled to God" (2 Cor 5:20). The Pauline literature speaks of this reality in the language of justification. To be "justified" is to be acquitted as innocent, put straight, set in right relation to God. Paul is emphatic that justification is not earned by doing the works of the law. It is a free gift of God's grace, received through faith, through humbly believing and accepting the love of God poured out for us in Jesus Christ. "By grace you have been saved through faith, and this is not your own doing, it is the gift of God, not because of works lest anyone should boast" (Eph 2: 8-9). But this doctrine is not exclusively Pauline. We also find Jesus in the gospels calling people to respond to God's freely offered love, discounting the "righteousness" of those who think they are already right with God. "I have come not to call the righteous but sinners" (Mt 9:13). The "righteous" man who stands in the Temple thanking God that he is not a sinner like others is compared unfavorably to a disreputable tax collector, who can pray only "God be merciful to me a sinner." Jesus declares, "I tell you, this man went down to his home justified rather than the other" (Lk 18: 10-14).

The theology of justification has power to undermine the moral smugness and superiority that feed so much human hatred and conflict. But every good thing can be distorted and abused. The doctrine of justification by faith has all too often become the basis for a do-nothing complacency, and even a license for cruelty and injustice. The doctrine is used to reinforce the idea of sin as a purely individual thing, ignoring the reality of structural sin. It is used to imply that the vertical relation to God is all that matters where "salvation" is concerned, and that one can be "right with God" while continuing to hate and despise one's neighbor. In Wesleyan terms, this is the fatal error of separating justification from sanctification, that is, the actual transformation of life. To insist that reconciliation with the neighbor is implied in reconciliation with God is not a form of pelagianism, whereby we are "saved" in part by our good works. Elsa Tamez, Latin American feminist theologian (a Methodist), is clear about this: "God does justify and pardon the ungodly, reconciles all humanity in Jesus Christ, and does so by pure grace, without human collaboration."[16]

This insistence on the character of grace as an absolutely free gift is essential to the liberative and reconciling character of the doctrine.

However, she goes on,

> justification viewed from an abstract, individual and generic plane is good news more for the oppressors than for the poor. By beginning with the event of justification, the former can feel relieved of guilt—pardoned of their sins—by grace without confronting the "wrath of God" or judgment, or the justice of God, and without any need for any conversion or change of practice.[17]

The poor are generally all too aware that they are sinners. It is the powerful, experiencing so much success in life, who are allowed to imagine that they are "right with God" through grace. Tamez insists that we must reject every theological approach that favors the rich to the detriment of the poor. The trivialization of the doctrine comes clear when she asks: "How can one say to the mothers of the Plaza de Mayo in Argentina that they should forgive the soldiers, the torturers and assassins of their children? No one with a minimum of integrity has the authority to do so."[18] We must avoid, then, the "cheap grace" of justification without repentance—without faith and love—as though the gospel contained no warnings of "weeping and gnashing of teeth" (Mt 25:30).

Yet the doctrine of justification is a reconciling doctrine if both victims and perpetrators cease to claim a righteousness of their own and acknowledge their own need for forgiveness and grace.

The Dynamic of Grace: A Spirituality

It is truly awe inspiring when forgiveness and reconciliation actually happen. It is a work of the Holy Spirit.

I am thinking of Elias Chacour, the Palestinian Christian pastor, whose family was driven from its Galilean village when he was a child, who spent much of his childhood in a refugee camp, and who, though his people remain oppressed, harbors no bitterness and has devoted his life to reconciliation between Palestinians and Jews.[19]

I am thinking of a Nicaraguan Sandinista politician, Tomas Borge, who had been imprisoned and brutally tortured, and whose wife had been raped, tortured, and murdered. When the Sandinistas came to power he was part of the decision against capital punishment of Somoza's murderous supporters. Because of his Christian faith, he said, he was even able to find the murderer of his wife and to go to him and to forgive him.[20]

We find in the New Testament a dynamic of grace that goes deeper than moral exhortations. *Grace* means an empowerment that comes to us from beyond ourselves, a power of unmerited love and acceptance—not a cheap, but a costly love, as costly as the agony of Christ's death on the cross. We find it already in the teaching and deeds of Jesus. Zacchaeus, the chief tax collector who was rich through cheating and extortion, is moved by the friendship of Jesus to turn his life around and to pay back fourfold what he had stolen from his victims. Jesus announces, "Today salvation has come to this house" (Lk 19:9). Again, we hear of a "sinner" woman, befriended by Jesus, who was so moved by his graciousness toward her that she came to anoint his feet in the presence of his enemies. In reply to those who condemn her, he declares, "Her sins, which are many, are forgiven, for she loved much; but he who is forgiven little loves little" (Lk 7:47). It is in keeping with this teaching of Jesus that Robert Schreiter speaks of the grace that leads to repentance:

> We discover and experience God's forgiveness of our trespasses and this prompts us to repentance. In the reconciliation process, then, because the victim has been brought by God's reconciling grace to forgive the tormentor, the tormentor is prompted to repent of evildoing and engage in rebuilding his or her humanity.[21]

Of course this does not always happen, and it is rarely a swift or simple process. Sometimes "peaceful" coexistence is all that can be achieved. Authentic reconciliation may take a very long time. As Schreiter insists, it is "not a managed process." People cannot be merely exhorted or manipulated into a truly heart-felt reconciliation. It most often has to be initiated from the side of the victim, since the perpetrators are often unable to forgive themselves or even to recognize honestly the enormity of what they have done. "It comes upon us like a healing," for "reconciliation is something that comes upon the victim, something that the victim discovers, rather than a well-managed therapy or process. It is more a spirituality than a strategy."[22]

•

Reconciliation is part of the ongoing mission of Jesus Christ in the power of the Holy Spirit. It is therefore part of the church's mission and of the ministry of every Christian. In a time such as ours, when racial and ethnic tensions are more visible than ever before, we are all called to the ministry of reconciliation, in large or small ways, wherever we are. As the articles in this volume demonstrate, it is a task that requires far more than moral preaching. It is one that can be undertaken only as a channel of the power of God's grace.

Notes

[1] This theme is developed by Ellen T. Charry in her article "Is Christianity Good for Us?" in *Reclaiming Faith: Essays on Orthodoxy in the Episcopal Church and the Baltimore Declaration*, ed. E. Radner and G. R. Sumner (Grand Rapids, Mich.: Eerdmans, 1993).

² Biblical quotations are taken from the New Revised Standard Version (1990).

³ Cf. J. M. Lochman, *Reconciliation and Liberation* (Philadelphia: Fortress Press, 1980).

⁴ The question of what exactly constitutes the teaching and deeds of Jesus is, of course, a matter of enormous debate. Remaining cognizant of this problem, I shall deal with the biblical material as it stands, since this is what the people encounter in the regular reading of scripture in the church.

⁵ See Graeme MacQueen, ed., *Unarmed Forces: Nonviolent Action in Central America and the Middle East* (Toronto: Samuel Stevens and Co., University of Toronto Press, 1992).

⁶ See Harold Wells, "Raising Power against the Power Structures," *Journal of Theology for Southern Africa* 30 (March 1980), pp. 63-68.

⁷ See the eloquent testimonies of the Amanecida Collective in *Revolutionary Forgiveness: Feminist Reflections on Nicaragua* (Maryknoll, N.Y.: Orbis Books, 1987); see also the many fine articles in *Theology and Violence: The South African Debate*, ed. Charles Villa-Vicencio (Johannesburg: Scotaville Publishers, 1987).

⁸ Jürgen Moltmann, *The Spirit of Life: A Universal Affirmation*, trans. M. Kohl (Minneapolis: Fortress Press, 1992), p. 126.

⁹ Cf. Anne Carr, *Transforming Grace: The Christian Tradition and Women's Experience* (San Francisco: Harper & Row, 1988), pp. 183, 185.

¹⁰ Mary Grey, *Feminism, Redemption and the Christian Tradition* (Mystic, Conn.: Twenty-Third Publications, 1990), p. 182.

¹¹ See discussion of this theme by Jürgen Moltmann, *Jesus Christ for Today's World* (Minneapolis: Fortress Press, 1994), p. 40.

¹² Ibid., p. 41.

¹³ Julio de Santa Ana writes of this: "It is Godself, incarnate in Jesus Christ, who is sacrificed. God does not require that others be sacrificed. . . . Jesus definitively abolishes sacrifices." He reasons from this that sacrifice of the innocent poor to the great idol Capital must be rejected, for God does not require "new expiations, new holocausts, new immolations" (quoted by Elsa Tamez, *Amnesty of Grace: Justification by Faith from a Latin American Perspective* [Nashville: Abingdon, 1993], p. 159).

¹⁴ Tamez, p. 114.

¹⁵ Moltmann, *Jesus Christ for Today's World*, p. 67.

¹⁶ Tamez, p. 20.

¹⁷ Ibid., p. 21.

¹⁸ Ibid., p. 22.

¹⁹ Elias Chacour, *Blood Brothers* (New York: Chosen Books, 1984).

²⁰ Andrew Reding, ed., *Christianity and Revolution: Tomas Borge's Theology of Life* (Maryknoll, N.Y.: Orbis Books, 1987).

²¹ Robert J. Schreiter, *Reconciliation: Mission and Ministry in a Changing Social Order* (Maryknoll, N.Y.: Orbis Books, 1992), p. 45.

²² Ibid., pp. 70-71.

2

The Dialectic of Reconciliation

Church and the Transition to Democracy in South Africa

JOHN W. DE GRUCHY

The achievement of a negotiated revolution in South Africa, which reached its symbolic climax in the inauguration of Nelson Mandela as president on 11 May 1994, has rightly been hailed a modern miracle. Outside observers can be forgiven for having anticipated that South Africa would turn into the nightmare of a Beirut, Bosnia, or worse, given the long history of colonial oppression and the forty or more years of bitter apartheid repression. All the signs of such a descent into hell were apparent. As the armed struggle intensified, international economic and political sanctions increased and resistance inside the country became more militant, so the government embarked on its strategy of destroying all agents of what it perceived to be the "total onslaught" of communism. Details of the horrific lengths to which its agents were prepared to go in countering the revolution are only now coming to light, but no one engaged in the struggle had any doubts about them at the time.

The miracle is that within the short space of four years the spiral of violence which threatened to trash the country was countered. Violence, it is true, escalated even during the negotiations and hope see-sawed with despair with unnerving regularity as South Africa staggered from one brink of disaster to another in the quest for freedom. Nonetheless the spiral downward into racial war was halted as politicians and parties clawed their way out of the morass and up the ladder of tough negotiations toward national reconciliation. Even hardened cynics could only marvel when the new South Africa was born amid global applause.

The honeymoon period is now nearing its end, and the enormity of the task of democratic transformation becomes more apparent by the day. Critical assessment of what has been achieved, how it was achieved, and what is now happening in the country has become necessary. Indeed, the high expectations of many have not been realized, and frustration with the government's apparent inability to deliver on its promises is already evident among those who had anticipated tasting the fruits of utopia in the short term. In certain areas, notably KwaZulu-Natal, violence continues to hamper democratic transformation. To negotiate a revolution takes enormous effort and considerable time, and the task of social transformation is a process that cannot be achieved over night. Yet nothing can gainsay the miracle of reconciliation that we have witnessed and its potential for growth to maturity. Our task in this chapter is to reflect theologically on the process of reconciliation as we have experienced it and to consider the role of the church in helping it to become a reality and ensuring that it remains so.

Reconciliation as an Instrument of Struggle

It is difficult to remember that it was only ten years ago, amid the scenario of growing resistance and repression, that the celebrated *Kairos Document* was published. Central to its critique was an attack on what it named "church theology" with its espousal of "cheap reconciliation":

> In our situation in South Africa today it would be totally unChristian to plead for reconciliation and peace before the present injustices have been removed. Any such plea plays into the hands of the oppressor by trying to persuade those of us who are oppressed to accept our oppression and to become reconciled to the intolerable crimes that are committed against us. That is not Christian reconciliation, it is sin. It is asking us to become accomplices in our own oppression, to become servants of the devil. No reconciliation is possible in South Africa without justice.[1]

Those words were drafted in 1985. During the next four years South Africa plunged ever deeper into crisis. Then, in February 1990, F. W. de Klerk announced the unbanning of the liberation movements and the release of Nelson Mandela from twenty-seven years in prison.

There had been intimations that something was afoot for some time before that. We now know that tentative secret talks between Mandela and the government were under way at the very time the *Kairos Document* was being written.[2] Those who were engaged in the liberation struggle, and who came to know of these talks, were at first concerned that Mandela had sold out and become engaged in an exercise of cheap reconciliation, the very temptation against which the *Kairos Document* warned. But that was not what Mandela was doing. He had not served such a long time in prison for the sake of selling out the birthright of the oppressed. As far as he was concerned there could be no negotiated settlement unless the government was prepared to accept the goal of a nonracial democratic society. There could be no reconciliation without liberation and justice. Until that was accepted in principle, he would stay in prison, the armed struggle would continue, and sanctions would remain in place.

The fact that Nelson Mandela initiated the secret talks, and the way in which he entered into them, indicate that while he was unprepared to dilute the demands of the liberation movement, he was, nevertheless, committed to pursuing the path of reconciliation as an integral part of the process of achieving its ultimate goal. It had become abundantly clear to him that there was no alternative. Neither the state nor the liberation movement had the capacity to achieve a decisive victory, and the prolonging of the vicious stalemate could only spell disaster for the country as a whole. Seeking reconciliation was, paradoxically, an instrument of the struggle to end apartheid and establish a just social order. The path of reconciliation was not only the goal of liberation but a means to achieve that end. It was an instrument in which the revolutionary struggle, political realism, and moral integrity combined to produce an almost irresistible force. As it happened, the choice of such a path was neither cheap nor easy. Many died as a result of state terror and "third force" violence, which wracked certain parts of the country right to the end. Miracles of reconciliation such as we have witnessed do not come without pain and suffering.

All the evidence indicates, then, that although Mandela chose the reconciliation route and pursued it with conviction, he refused to demean either himself or his cause through compromises which would have undermined the cause of justice. If we are to speak of compromise at all, then we must speak of principled compromise, the willingness to give ground on what is not essential for the sake of the greater good. Mandela recognized the need to allow those in power to discover space in which to maneuver within their own constituency without loss of face. He helped them to catch his vision of a new and just South Africa with its promise not only of the liberation of the oppressed but also of the restoration of their own humanity. Mandela may have been a prisoner of the state, but he had the moral upper hand; mass support and history were undoubtedly on his side. Yet it was his choice of the path of reconciliation that qualitatively heightened his moral and political stature so that even former enemies recognized that he was the key to the future, the undisputed candidate for the presidency of the new South Africa.

Fortunately there were those in government who were willing to risk responding positively to Mandela's overtures. Their role in the process must not be underestimated. We must also acknowledge that Nelson Mandela was not the only leader within the liberation movement, and that he could never have achieved what he did without the massive involvement of others both over the long haul of the struggle as well as in the final years and agonizing moments of achieving the goal of democratic transition.[3] The full story of the struggle in all its phases and dimensions is yet to be told in detail, but the evidence already gathered is of epic proportions.[4] Exiles, political prisoners, students and academics, professionals, workers, politicians, priests and ministers, women and men joined forces in seeking to topple a dehumanizing system labeled a "crime against humanity" by the United Nations. Yet it was Mandela who became the mediator and embodiment of the just reconciliation that many hoped for but few thought possible.

Just as we must avoid crediting President Mandela alone for what has been achieved, so we must avoid romanticizing what happened on 11 May 1994. This was not only preceded by years of struggle in which many from all segments of society and from all classes and ethnic communities were involved, but it was also the result of political skill, insight, and hard work on the part of the negotiators. Providential moments in history such as we have experienced are always the product of a synergy between the unexpected surprises of grace and the practical reason, guts, and determination of human nature. Those engaged in the liberation struggle and those in government recognized their responsibility to pursue the art of the possible in weighing up the options. Behind the media images of presidential handshakes with former enemies lay the hard bargaining of the negotiators. We cannot but think here of the role played by the late Joe Slovo, former secretary general of the South African Communist Party and cabinet minister in the new government, whose integrity and spirit as well as his timely proposal of the "sunset clause" made the Government of National Unity (GNU) a possibility. But he, too, was only one of several on both sides of the political divide whose efforts were crucial in ensuring that the process would succeed and that the goal of national unity, reconciliation, and reconstruction would become the paramount interest of all participants in the process. In the end they chose the common good rather than group interest, though in doing so they discovered that group interest was best served by pursuing the good of the country as a whole.

So it was that the Interim Constitution approved late in 1993 as the basis for the election of a new government had a final clause on national unity and reconciliation:

> This Constitution provides a historic bridge between the past of a deeply divided society characterized by strife, conflict, untold suffering and injustice, and a future founded on the recognition of human rights, democracy and peaceful co-existence and development opportunities for all South Africans irrespective of color, race, class, belief or sex.

The pursuit of national unity, the well-being of all South African citizens, and peace require reconciliation between the people of South Africa and the reconstruction of society.

The adoption of this constitution lays a secure foundation for the people of South Africa to transcend the divisions and strife of the past, which generated gross violations of human rights; the transgression of humanitarian principles in violent conflicts; and a legacy of hatred, fear, guilt, and revenge.

These can now be addressed on the basis that there is a need for under-standing but not revenge, a need for reparation but not for retaliation, a need for *ubuntu*[5] but not for victimization.

The constitution concluded with a paragraph on the need for amnesty for those who had been engaged in certain political crimes as a necessary precon-dition for reconciliation and reconstruction, a subject to which we will return. But for the moment we may justly refer to the words we have quoted as ex-pressing a remarkable human and political achievement. But what of the churches in achieving this goal? To answer that question we need to reflect back on the process as it began to develop during the decade within which Mandela's overtures to the government began.

The Churches, the Struggle, and Reconciliation

The role of the churches within the liberation struggle was complex and be-yond the scope of this essay to describe in detail.[6] A brief historical overview and some comment on the final phase must suffice. We may date this phase from the student uprising in Soweto in 1976, which resulted in the banning in 1977 of the Black Consciousness Movement led by Steve Biko. These events also led to the banning of the Christian Institute and its prophetic leader, Beyers Naudé, previously in the forefront of Christian resistance to apartheid.[7] As a result, ecumenical leadership in the struggle was increasingly located within the South African Council of Churches (SACC), especially after Bishop Desmond Tutu became its general secretary in 1978. The Roman Catholic Church, an observer member of the SACC, and the South African Catholic Bishops' Conference (SACBC), cooperated closely with the SACC through-out this period.[8] The SACC's major concern was to spearhead the struggle against apartheid and, at the same time, to care for and assist the victims of apartheid. Without that solidarity, and the international ecumenical support which made it possible, it is highly unlikely that the resilience and hope of those who suffered so greatly in prison, under house arrest, and in many other ways, could have been sustained.

After the Soweto uprising, internal resistance and dissent were kept in check by an increasingly powerful national state-security system. At the same time, the war in Namibia and the intensification of the liberation struggle both ex-ternally and internally forced the South African government to introduce some changes in order to gain international legitimacy and prevent a full-scale revo-lution. However, P. W. Botha's attempt to broaden democracy through the introduction of the tricameral parliamentary system simply meant the per-petuation of white power and set off a new wave of resistance to apartheid under the leadership of the United Democratic Front (UDF), launched in 1982. A broad coalition of anti-apartheid organizations, the UDF was in effect the internal wing of the African National Congress and had the support of many Christian activists around the country.

In response to growing resistance, Botha intensified efforts to destroy the liberation movement internally as well as externally. Rejecting appeals by the world community to negotiate, he opted for a state-security solution to his dilemma with the declaration of a general State of Emergency in 1986, a situation which was to last until 1990. Part of Botha's strategy was to coopt whatever church groups he could and to try to discredit and destroy the witness of those he could not. Direct security police action against Christian activists was supported by a continuous propaganda attack on "radical Christians" and "liberation theology" by the state-controlled media and right-wing fundamentalist groups financed by the state.[9]

One response to the deepening crisis in South Africa was the National Initiative of Reconciliation (NIR), which was launched in Pietermaritzburg in 1985. Sponsored by Africa Enterprise, an evangelical para-church organization, the NIR managed to gather together a wide range of Christian leaders, including white Dutch Reformed church leaders and SACC representatives. In a display of unity on political issues remarkable for that period, the NIR issued a statement that called for the release of all political prisoners, the return of exiles, and talks between the government and the "authentic leadership of the various population groups with a view toward equitable power sharing in South Africa."[10]

A more radical response was that expressed in the *Kairos Document* a few weeks later. While the NIR recognized the connection between justice and reconciliation, and called for an end to apartheid, the Kairos theologians, as we have already noted, argued that the notion of reconciliation was being widely abused in the church as a means to obviate the need for fundamental change. Recognizing that the basic differences among Christians in South Africa were not primarily denominational or confessional but political and economic, the *Kairos Document* perceived that the church itself was a site of the struggle against apartheid.

There were several key issues at stake. The obvious one was the struggle against "state theology" or the theological legitimation of apartheid.[11] A more subtle issue was that of cheap reconciliation. For, after all, no one could deny that the message of reconciliation was fundamental to the gospel. And yet, as the *Kairos Document* perceived, the perversion of this doctrine was at the heart of "church theology," a theology which wanted peace even at the expense of justice. Recognizing a moment of judgment as well as opportunity, the *Kairos Document* called for direct Christian participation in the struggle, including acts of civil disobedience in resistance to government tyranny.

Heated controversy ensued within the churches, and state repression against Christian activists intensified. Much of this had to do with the advocacy of civil disobedience. But the debate about reconciliation was equally intense,[12] reminding one of the responses to Dietrich Bonhoeffer's attack on the way in which the Lutheran *sola gratia* had been reduced to cheap grace within the German Evangelical Church during the Third Reich.[13] The fundamental problem was the prevailing notion among many Christians and church leaders that they could be neutral, acting as agents of reconciliation without being engaged in the struggle for justice as its prerequisite.[14] But even churches and church leaders who had rejected apartheid and who were leaders in the struggle to end it, such as Archbishop Tutu, were unhappy about the way in which "church theology" and reconciliation were, in their terms, caricatured and criticized. Clearly there was hesitation about the ideological abuse of such a key doctrine of Christian faith, whether by those who used it in defense of their supposed neutrality or those who rejected it as counterproductive to the struggle.

Nonetheless, the *Kairos Document* provided the theological tools for prophetic Christian witness amid increasing repression. It also had an important influence on "The Harare Declaration" adopted by a conference of ecumenical church leaders from around the world which met in the Zimbabwean capital in December 1985.[15] Among its recommendations, the Declaration called on the ecumenical church to give its support to the liberation movements and on the international community to apply comprehensive sanctions against South Africa immediately. This was precisely the time, as we have previously seen, that the imprisoned Nelson Mandela began to explore the possibility of negotiations and set off down the path of reconciliation, thereby opening up a new and necessary front in the struggle. The result was a two-pronged attack on the apartheid regime which may be described, in hindsight, in terms of a dialectical understanding of reconciliation.

The Kairos theologians were right to criticize cheap reconciliation, for reconciliation cannot be achieved without justice being done to the oppressed. Yet those church leaders who were engaged in the struggle for justice were equally right in being uneasy about the way in which the *Kairos Document* handled the subject. They were also critical about cheap reconciliation, but their concern was that the critique should not undermine the potential of reconciliation as an instrument for achieving justice. The dialectic between reconciliation as a path leading to justice and the result of achieving justice was in danger of being lost. In the end, the dialectic was maintained and the goal achieved. This set the pattern for the path that both politicians and the church soon would be called upon to pursue in the democratic reconstruction of South Africa.

Between February 1990 and the decision by Parliament in September 1993 to establish a transitional executive council (TEC) that would share in the government of the country in preparation for the first truly democratic election, the country was plunged into a new cycle of escalating violence which threatened to tear it apart. It was within this context that the churches once again became directly involved in the political arena, seeking ways to end the violence and to monitor events that could result in it erupting.

The role of the churches as mediators between conflicting parties became crucial to both the negotiating process and the attempt to deal with the violence. Attempts by church leaders to bring various groups together, notably the ANC, Pan Africanist Congress (PAC), and Inkhata, brought positive results in some places, though not all, and enabled greater communication and understanding of the problems and difficulties that have kept such groups apart. In situations of great conflict and even greater potential for conflict, such lines of communication are essential if the process toward democracy is to take place and succeed. But it also requires mediators who can be trusted by all the parties concerned. This was one reason why the bishops of the Church of the Province (Anglican) decreed in 1990 that no priest should belong to any political party or organization.

Some churches and Christian activists also played an indispensable role in the various national and regional peace structures, assisted by international ecumenical monitors. There can be little doubt that the ecumenical peace-monitoring task force established by the SACC with the help of overseas ecumenical partners was of considerable importance as part of the wider monitoring task force provided by the United Nations and by the National Peace Committee. As a church-based project it had its own unique and specific contribution to make because of its direct connection to grassroots communities and their leadership. By also assisting in the enormous task of voter registration and education, the churches played a vital role in helping to prepare the way for free and fair elections with the maximum of participation.[16] Mediating and monitoring are, however, ad hoc tasks made necessary by circumstances. What is ultimately more important is the need to create a democratic culture and socio-economic situation within the country that will deal with the causes of violence and provide the means to pursue the task of social transformation.

The Churches and Democratic Transformation[17]

In an address in December 1992, Mandela acknowledged the role some churches had played in the struggle against apartheid. He then went on to challenge the church "to join other agents of change and transformation in the difficult task of acting as a midwife to the birth of our democracy and acting as one of the institutions that will nurture and entrench it in our society."[18] In responding to this challenge, the question may be raised as to whether the analysis and prophetic prognosis of the *Kairos Document* remains pertinent.

At one level the answer is clearly no. After all, central to the *Kairos Document* was its reading of the times, its social analysis. It is obvious that our present historical moment is fundamentally different from that which pertained in the mid-1980s. What is required now is, as the Interim Constitution declares, reconstruction not revolution, reconciliation not conflict. Yet, at another level, the task of reconciliation and reconstruction still requires pursuing justice, or, as the constitution puts it, there is the urgent need for reparation. Unless fundamental injustices of the past, such as the distribution of wealth, land, and other resources are redressed, and unless the conditions of poverty, unemployment, and violence are overcome, reconciliation will have meaning only for the privileged in society. The danger that this might happen is already apparent, and a failure to tackle it head on will sow seeds of class conflict in the years to come. The real threat to the ANC-led government does not come from white right-wingers but from the millions whose expectations for a better quality of life have not yet been met. In order for miracles to be believed, they have to deliver more than the euphoria of the moment in which they occur.

Thus the prophetic theology and witness of the *Kairos Document* remains pertinent even though it has to be recast in the light of the current *kairos* of democratic transformation. What is now at stake is the kind of democratic society that should replace apartheid, and how this should be achieved. But as is the case in any kairotic moment, the urgency with which this has to be addressed in real terms is crucial. This raises important questions about the role of the church and presents a critical challenge to theological reflection as it moves from the mode of opposition to apartheid to that of national reconstruction.[19]

The need for the church to remain true and faithful to its prophetic vocation is fundamental. One way of describing this now is in terms of *critical solidarity*. Being in critical *solidarity* means giving support to those initiatives which may lead to the establishment not only of a new but a just social order. It means that the church remains prophetic in its stance toward the emergent nation, but now on the basis of a shared commitment to the realization of that new nation. Being in *critical* solidarity means continued resistance to what is unjust and false, and continued protest on behalf of what is just and true. The prophetic struggle against injustice must continue; standing for the truth never comes to an end. One of the major problems facing the church is how to help build a new nation without being party to an uncritical and destructive nationalism or being silent in the face of any form of discrimination, corruption, or tyranny. Moreover, given the economic and other strengths of South Africa in the region, the church also has to prevent the growth of a South African nationalism which might become a threat to the wider region in the years ahead. One cannot be concerned about just democracy in South Africa and unconcerned about justice in relations with other nations.

There are three touchstones for determining the concrete meaning of critical solidarity. First, it means taking sides with all who remain oppressed in one form or another in a new democratic society and participating with them in their never-ending struggle for justice, human dignity, and liberation. In particular, the church has to warn against the "danger of superficial changes that may leave power and privilege in the hands of whites and a sprinkling of affluent blacks."[20] The churches need to be engaged in helping bring about a new economic order that is able to redress the unjust economic legacy of apartheid. Democracy cannot survive in South Africa without bridging the vast disparity in wealth between the affluent and the poor.

The second touchstone of critical solidarity is defense of the human rights of all people, especially minority cultural and religious groups. Even though "radical Christians" will oppose "reactionary Christians" both in the church and society, they have the right to exist, to organize, and to express their views in a democratic society unless their actions are illegal and socially destructive. In the days of the struggle, confronting heresy almost invariably led to intolerance of those whose views were regarded as counterrevolutionary and reactionary. As Bonhoeffer recognized in the struggle against Nazism, even those involved in the resistance became tainted. Hence his poignant question to his fellow conspirators: "Are we still of any use?"

> We have been silent witnesses of evil deeds; we have been drenched by many storms; we have learned the arts of equivocation and pretense; experience has made us suspicious of others and kept us from being truth and open; intolerable conflicts have worn us down and even made us cynical.[21]

Apartheid led to the subversion of fundamental human values, so crucial for the flourishing of democracy. It has led to a disrespect for law and authority, the cheapening of life, the destruction of the family, the subversion of the truth with lies, the manipulation of natural cultural differences, the abuse of human rights, and the strengthening of the rich through corruption at the expense of the poor. There can be little doubt that violence has destroyed not only lives but also respect for democratic principles and respect for the views of others. Hence the urgent need to create a democratic culture in which the transition to democracy can take place and democratic transformation be pursued.

The third touchstone for determining the church's prophetic witness of critical solidarity is its own self-critique. The message of the prophets must always be addressed first of all to their own community of faith if it is to have any integrity. Judgment begins with the church. And there can be no gainsaying that the church in South Africa has in large measure failed to overcome its own racial, gender, and cultural divisions. It is also painfully apparent that even some churches and leaders who were ecumenically engaged in the struggle against apartheid have now retreated into their denominational ghettos, returning to "business as usual" in the pursuit of piety.

Nonetheless, there are many signs of genuine community within the church in South Africa, not least within ecumenical organizations, women's organizations, youth movements, para-church organizations, and grassroots Christian communities, where a tradition of participation and accountability has developed in the struggle against apartheid. The jointly sponsored World Council of Churches/South African Council of Churches Consultation in March 1995 suggested that a new phase in ecumenical commitment to democratic transformation is in the process of gestation. Central to this commitment is a recognition of the dialectic of reconciliation in which the goal of transformation is pursued not only through confrontation but through the building of a united nation.

Paradoxically, partly because the church does represent a diversity of culture and ideology, it also embodies the potential of enabling conflicting groups to enter into a nonviolent and creative dialogue with each other. It can, in fact, be both a model of a new society as well as the laboratory within which such a society is created. The church has the potential for creating a common culture precisely because of its cultural and political diversity and its witness to the reconciling power of the gospel, which can transform conflicting cultures and create new possibilities. Insofar as the church provides a living context within which people from very different backgrounds can share their stories, their deep concerns, their pain and suffering, then a new, enriched common history and tradition in which all can share could be achieved through the instrumentality of the church and other religious communities. Of critical importance in achieving this goal, however, is the need to deal with the past and to make reparation for the gross violations of human rights which were perpetrated in the name of apartheid. It has become increasingly apparent that reconciliation without acknowledgment of the truth of what happened, as well as dealing with the past in a way which heals the nation, will not endure.

Reconciliation as Overcoming the Past

Clearly it would be impossible to make adequate reparation for all the injustice and hurt caused by apartheid and the centuries of colonialism that preceded it. Nonetheless, it is essential that as much is done as possible to overcome the legacy of apartheid and redress historic wrongs. This is the major concern of the government's Reconstruction and Development Programme (RDP), which is now coming into effect, even though hampered by financial constraints and a civil service that is not always cooperative. Central to the RDP is the redistribution of land; fundamental change in education, health, and housing policies; and far-reaching affirmative action programs in the public as well as the private spheres. The problems are enormous, and they have to be tackled urgently. This does not mean that all the injustices of past oppression and racism will be overcome, but it is the least that must be done.

There is, however, another related issue that is more controversial and problematic. The RDP is geared to redress the wrongs of apartheid in a broad sense, but what about those horrendous crimes committed by death squads? What about the torturers and murderers who were paid to silence apartheid's opponents? What about gross violations of human rights which were even illegal in the apartheid era, but which were condoned and perpetrated by its defenders? In response to this question the South African Parliament, on 21 October 1994, approved a bill establishing a Commission of Truth and Reconciliation. The commission's mandate is to provide a record of gross human rights violations committed between 1 March 1960 (when the liberation movements were banned) and 6 December 1993, by both the upholders of apartheid and the liberation movements; to identify the victims and their fate; to recommend possible measures of reparation; to process applications for amnesty and indemnity; and to make recommendations with regard to measures necessary to prevent future gross human rights violations.

While the commission will have investigative powers and follow due process, it will not perform judicial functions. Certain cases may be handed to the attorney general for investigation and possible prosecution, however, though exactly how this relates to amnesty is not presently clear. It is clear that those seeking amnesty or indemnity will have to make a full disclosure of the crimes they committed, and they will have to do so by a fixed date. The emphasis in the bill is, however, not so much on the perpetrators of crimes as it is on their victims. After all, many people have already been given amnesty or indemnity.

The major objection made by opponents of the commission is that it will undermine reconciliation and even destroy the government of national unity that President Nelson Mandela has managed to construct. This has worked remarkably well since the April 1994 elections, and Mandela has gone out of his way to ensure that national reconciliation be pursued with vigor. There is some indication that he was at first wary of the establishment of the commission, fearing that it might prove counterproductive to the task of nation building.

No one denies the immense difficulties facing the commission or the dangers of raking up the past. It may lead to destructive acts of vengeance and reactivate the reactionary "third force," which was responsible for much of the violence before the election. So there is a point to the argument that the need to protect the infant democracy is more important in the long term than dealing with the past if in doing so there should be any retrogression. Yet, it is also true that unless the past is dealt with properly and expeditiously it could return to haunt the future. For if a culture of human rights is to be nurtured and respect for the law established, then the crimes of the past must not be swept under the carpet. This is also necessary to prevent the past from repeating itself and, most important of all, to help rebuild the lives of the victims.

Victims generally do not express any desire for vengeance—they want the truth to come out so that they can meaningfully forgive and, where possible, receive their rightful due. So remembering the past may be costly, but it may be more costly not to remember it in a way that can contribute to healing and genuine reconciliation. The establishment of the commission indicates, in Omar's words, "a commitment to break from the past, to heal the wounds of the past, to forgive but not to forget and to build a future based on respect for human rights."

The Christian understanding of repentance, forgiveness, and reparation is of fundamental importance in helping to shape the national consciousness of what is required for healing the land, genuine reconciliation, and building a moral and democratic culture. The debate in and outside Parliament about the work of the commission has often sounded much more theological than it has political or judicial. Moreover, the churches, together with other religious communities, have an indispensable pastoral role to fulfill which could go a long way to ensuring that the work of the commission achieves its goal of healing the nation. They have a ministry to the perpetrators of crimes: enabling them to come clean and helping them to become morally responsible citizens. And they have a special responsibility to help the victims tell their stories and, in doing so, deal with their deep hurts and anger. The healing of shame and memories, both personal and corporate, is a long and difficult task, but it is fundamental to the moral reconstruction of South Africa and central to the message of the gospel. In the words of the South African Council of Churches:

> The Commission for Truth and Reconciliation is not another Nuremberg. It turns its back on any desire for revenge. It represents an extraordinary act of generosity by a people who only insist that the truth, the whole truth and nothing but the truth be told. The space is thereby created where the deeper processes of forgiveness, confession, repentance, reparation and reconciliation can take place.[22]

Nothing better expresses the ongoing process we have labeled the dialectic of reconciliation, and nothing indicates more clearly the indispensable ministry of social and personal healing the churches are called upon to exercise in the building of the new South Africa.

Notes

[1] *The Kairos Document: Challenge to the Church*, rev. 2d ed. (Johannesburg: ICT, 1986), art. 3.1, p. 9.

[2] The remarkable story of these talks is told in Nelson Mandela, *Long Walk to Freedom* (Randburg: Macdonal Purnell, 1994); Alister Sparks, *Tomorrow Is Another Country: The Inside Story of South Africa's Negotiated Revolution* (Cape Town: Struik, 1994).

[3] A comprehensive survey of the various components of the liberation movement and the roles which they played can be found in Ian Liebenberg, Fiona Lortan, Bobby Nel, and Gert van der Westhuizen, eds., *The Long March: The Story of the Struggle for Liberation in South Africa* (Pretoria: HAUM, 1994).

[4] The Mayibue Centre at the University of the Western Cape is the main archive of the liberation movement in South Africa and has extensive documentation on the subject in all its dimensions.

[5] *Ubuntu* is a Xhosa word meaning "human solidarity."

[6] John W. de Gruchy, *The Church Struggle in South Africa*, 2d ed. (Grand Rapids: Eerdmans, 1986); Charles Villa-Vicencio, *Trapped in Apartheid* (Maryknoll, N.Y.: Orbis Books, 1988).

[7] Peter Walshe, *Church Versus State in South Africa: The Case of the Christian Institute* (Maryknoll, N.Y.: Orbis Books, 1983); Charles Villa-Vicencio and John W. de Gruchy eds., *Resistance and Hope: South African Essays in Honour of Beyers Naudé* (Cape Town: David Philip, 1985), pp. 3ff.

[8] Peter Walshe, "South Africa: Prophetic Christianity and the Liberation Movement," *The Journal of Modern African Studies*, vol. 29, no. 1 (1991), pp. 45f.

[9] On "right-wing" Christian movements in South Africa, see the *Journal of Theology for Southern Africa* 69 (December 1989).

[10] "NIR Statement of Affirmation," *Journal of Theology for Southern Africa* 54 (March 1986).

[11] See John W. de Gruchy and Charles Villa-Vicencio, eds., *Apartheid Is a Heresy* (Grand Rapids: Eerdmans, 1983).

[12] See *Journal of Theology for Southern Africa* 58 (March 1987); John W. de Gruchy, "The Struggle for Justice and the Ministry of Reconciliation," *Journal of Theology for Southern Africa* 62 (March 1988).

[13] Dietrich Bonhoeffer, *The Cost of Discipleship* (London: SCM, 1984), pp. 35ff.

[14] Tony Balcomb, *Third Way Theology* (Pietermaritzburg: Cluster Publications, 1993).

[15] "The Implications of Harare," *ICT News* (March 1986), pp. 3ff.

[16] Sheena Duncan, "The Church's Role in Preparing for Free and Fair Elections," *Diakonia* [Durban] (1992). Among the many documents being prepared by the churches for use in educating voters, see "Democracy and Voting in South Africa," An Information Manual, no. 2, published by the SACC as part of its Education for Democracy Programme.

[17] For a more detailed discussion of the issues, see John W. de Gruchy, *Christianity and Democracy: A Theology for a Just World Order* (Cambridge: Cambridge University Press, 1995).

[18] Speech delivered by Nelson R. Mandela, President of the ANC, to the Free Ethiopian Church of Southern Africa, Potchefstroom, 14 December 1992.

[19] Charles Villa-Vicencio, *A Theology of Reconstruction: Nation-building and Human Rights* (Cambridge: Cambridge University Press, 1992).

[20] Mandela, speech to the Free Ethiopian Church, 14 December 1992.

[21] Dietrich Bonhoeffer, *Letters and Papers from Prison* (London: SCM, 1971), p. 16.

[22] *The Truth Will Set You Free*, SACC Brochure (1995), p. 24.

3

Telling One Another Stories

Toward a Theology of Reconciliation

CHARLES VILLA-VICENCIO

*Non-racialism has always stood as a kind of beacon for the struggle.
. . . Now it has joined the ranks of motherhood and pap—an institution,
casually sanctified, something only a crazed cynic will dare ridicule in
public. But privately, honestly, we recognize in it the smell of failure.*[1]

Difference has been exploited by apartheid to impose separation on people of
different cultures, ethnic identities, and races. South Africans hardly know
one another. Our lived experiences, stories, and understandings of reality and
truth are often so diverse that with the best will in the world we all too often
"speak past" one another. It is not merely that we cannot agree on certain
specific issues, it is rather that our most fundamental and cherished assumptions and understandings about life are different.

The divisions, conflicting presuppositions, and contradictory world views
that have separated the past continue to undermine the present. These differences have the capability of destroying the future. Yet difference—being who
we are, is not a national liability. Difference is reality. We *are* not all the same.
We have lived different histories. Our disparate memories are deeply rooted.
Our separate stories provide different controlling images of existence. Does
this mean we cannot coexist, even build a common nation grounded in diversity and difference?

"Many Cultures: One Nation," the theme of President Nelson Mandela's
inaugural ceremony, captures the challenge of our times. Nonracism,
nonsexism, and national unity are ideals that (despite appearances) unite all
progressive political groupings in South Africa. The *means* to that end often
divides the liberation struggle, while the ultimate *goal* of the struggle unites.
The ANC, Azapo, the PAC, and other political organizations that employ par-
ticularist strategies to this end, no less than feminist and womanist collectives,

ultimately all affirm a form of national unity that transcends racial, ethnic, and gender discrimination.[2]

James Cone, the American black theologian, suggests it is perhaps only by sharing our stories with one another that we can hope to transcend the boundaries of our past and reach toward a shared future:

> Every people has a story to tell, something to say to themselves, their children, and to the world about how they think and live, as they determine their reason for being. . . . When people can no longer listen to the other people's stories, they become enclosed within their own social context. . . . And then they feel they must destroy other people's stories.[3]

We need to tell one another stories. It is perhaps the only basis for recognizing and yet transcending our differences. It is perhaps the only basis for gaining an understanding of both ourselves and the hopes and fears of others. It is the only basis on which different stories, different memories, and different histories can emerge as the basis for an inclusive nation-building exercise. H. Richard Niebuhr has reminded us that

> where common memory is lacking, where men [sic] do not share in the same past there can be no real community, and where community is to be formed common memory must be created. . . . The measure of our distance from each other in our nations and our groups can be taken by noting the divergence, the separateness and the lack of sympathy in our social memories. Conversely, the measure of our unity is the extent of our common memory.[4]

South Africa still awaits a unifying memory that incorporates provincial memories and partial pasts. This struggle, for symbols that unite and stories that bind, has only just begun. These are stories and symbols encapsulated in song, dance, poetry, and art. They are spoken and unspoken. They are written and oral. They are pre-oral and some are so deep within the human psyche that they cannot be adequately articulated—at least not yet, while the pain is still so acute. A new genre of theology is waiting to be born. Academic theologians would do well, however, to be beware of the pitfalls. Where seers, prophets, priests of the people, and poets have scarcely succeeded in uncovering the mysteries of the people's past, academics should tread warily! They should remove the shoes from their feet. They are on holy ground.

Difference

Difference is celebrated as a virtue in many situations around the world today. Martin Marty's essay "From the Centripetal to the Centrifugal in Culture and

Religion" says it all.[5] "The shift is from the 'global village,' 'the spaceship earth,' 'homogenization' and 'planetization' to 'particularism' and 'difference.'"

The problem is that the world has not coped very well with difference. The disintegration of former communist bloc countries, wars of ethnic cleansing, and the clash of nationalisms around the world are there to be seen. South African politics is no exception. We have never coped well with difference. It has either been exploited as a basis for deciding who can participate in the political and economic arena or promoted as a basis for separatism. In the period of colonialism, it was the former; in the apartheid era, the latter.

Colonialism opened the door (at least partially) to those who were prepared to be culturally assimilated. In so doing, colonialism established difference as the basis of discrimination. Missionized Africans who dressed in Western clothes and lived in square houses soon found themselves in a category above the "red people" who refused to be westernized. African chiefs who sent their children to Governor Grey's Kaffir College in Cape Town, designed to produce "black Englishmen," were regarded as the "good kaffirs," capable of assimilation.[6]

A similar process occurred regarding the political, socio-economic, and cultural fortunes of the South African Indians. The first immigration of Indians was that of indentured laborers, who came to the country in 1860 to work on the Natal sugarcane farms. Yasmin Sooka reminds us that "the Colonial Government [in India] was instructed to send no Brahmins . . . [and] requested medical officers to examine the hands of the immigrants to assess whether they were the hands of people accustomed to work."[7] The second wave of immigration was that of "free passage" Indians, consisting of traders and professionals who paid their own way. Many of them emerged as leaders in the South African Indian Congress (SAIC). Some called themselves "Arabs" in order to be differentiated from the "coolies" who worked as laborers on farms. When the colonial governments of India and South Africa entered into the Cape Town Agreement of 1927, the agreement was supported by the SAIC. The agreement allowed for the repatriation to India of those Indians who so chose, while an upliftment scheme was introduced for those who chose to remain in South Africa—*provided they assumed Western standards of living.*[8] Few Indians chose repatriation. Those able and willing to adapt to the demands of Western culture were gradually absorbed into mainstream society, at least until the imposition of apartheid in 1948. Those who clung to Indian culture were increasingly sidelined from mainstream society, while apartheid imposed further divisions in Indian society. The descendants of indentured laborers were separated not only from whites and merchant-class Indians but also from working-class Africans, whom the underclass Indians came to regard as their chief rivals for work, housing, and other material needs.

The colonial assimilationist mentality dies hard. It continues to raise its head as the only viable basis for incorporation into the dominant economic and social structures of society. Steve Biko's uncompromising attack on the vestiges of colonial assimilationism (which characterized white opposition politics in the 1970s) stands as a firm warning against any political model in the 1990s that simply invites blacks who have learned white ways to sit at the table prepared by whites.

> If by integration you understand a breakthrough into white society by blacks, an assimilation and acceptance into white society by blacks, an assimilation and acceptance of blacks into an already established set of norms and codes of behaviour set and maintained by whites, then YES I am against it.[9]

The rejection of assimilation makes difference a central category of South African politics. The affirmation of African identity is inevitable as the country seeks to turn away from a long history of dependency on Eurocentric values and colonial domination. The rejection of male domination by women, the affirmation of Muslim values, the place of Hindu identity, what it means to be an Afrikaner in a post-apartheid society, as well as the reemergence of colored identity in the Western Cape, are major factors to be dealt with in the decades ahead. Multicultural models of coexistence, although appealing to some minority groups in the United States and elsewhere, contain within them the danger of new and disguised forms of neo-apartheid in the South African context. Multiculturalism promises to provide African-Americans, Hispanics, Chicanos, and others in the United States with a living space apart from the dominant white American culture. This is acceptable to white America, provided it does not threaten the dominant center of "their" society. The challenge facing South Africa is precisely how to change the nation's center. It involves incorporating difference into the public, material, and cultural identity of South Africa.

The warning of Charles Long, an African American, is timely. He argues that African Americans have been driven into "an-other" (a counter-hegemonic) space by the politics of white American cultural hegemony.[10] It is this that motivates James Davison Hunter to speak of "cultural wars" as the characterizing mark of American politics.[11] An emerging South African democracy can scarcely afford to ignore Long's warning. If a rainbow is a unity of different colors, the notion of a rainbow people is not something that can be recognized readily in the American experiment.

Spirituality is the process through which a community creates itself and keeps itself in existence. Difference is yet to be tackled in South African politics. Talk of reconciliation is shallow and fruitless without a careful and thoroughgoing investigation of the difference that divides the nation. Again it is Niebuhr who assists our understanding. "Revelation," he tells us, "means that part of our inner history which illuminates the rest of it. . . . Revelation means that intelligible event which makes all other events intelligible."[12] Revelation is recorded in stories that encapsulate an event or events that give life its purpose and meaning.[13] Rosemary Radford Ruether speaks of a growing repertoire of such events that provide new insights into life. There are, she suggests, continually new liberating experiences in life that empower us "to write new stories, new parables, new *midrashim* on old stories."[14] These new (contemporary) stories, both oral and written from within the heat and passion of lived experience, function every bit as powerfully—if not more powerfully—than the stories of traditional religious texts in the shaping of our identity and self-understanding.

The parochial memory of a battle won, of a defeat suffered, of a celebration or a funeral, of an engaging event or bitter conflict often does more to unite and motivate a people than the most sacred events of established religion. At times these stories override the importance of established sacred symbols; at times they give established religious stories new vitality and contextual meaning. The memory of the Great Trek, Blood River, and the suffering of Boer women and children in concentration camps unites many Afrikaners. Sharpeville, the 1976 Soweto rebellion, *Umkhonto we Sizwe* (for some) and *Apla* (for others) unite blacks. These same stories, memories, symbols, and culture are at the root of the alienation that exists between most whites and most blacks. Nation-building of the inclusive kind that underpins the goals of the present era of South African politics requires that we transcend these memories. However, such memories will and must remain. They cannot simply be expunged from the collective memory.

The need is to fit these partisan memories into the greater story that unites. The exercise involves more than a careful analysis of what contributed to these different memories, although analysis is important. It involves sharing our recollections of the past. It involves telling our stories to one another and listening intently to the stories we are told—which involves reaching beyond the words and the "facts" to what lies behind the words. Herein lies the possibility of "cracking the code"—of gaining an understanding from the perspective of another's experience. It is a process that involves more than empathy. It involves hermeneutical relocation whereby we see, hear, and understand in a different way. The exercise involves more than the surrender of our own perception of truth. It involves what Gadamer called a fusion of horizons. His words deserve repeating:

> [The fusion of horizons] always involves the attainment of a higher universality that overcomes, not only our own particularity, but also that of the other. The concept of the "horizon" suggests itself because it expresses the wide, superior vision that the person who is seeking to understand must have. To acquire a horizon means that one learns to look beyond what is close at hand—not in order to look away from it, but to see it better within a larger whole and in truer proportion.[15]

Rational debate, ideological encounter, and the democratic rewriting of history are absolutely necessary. If we fail in the process to understand how and why another person perceived and perceives history in a certain way, we have failed to learn from the past as we pursue the Herculean task of creating a less divided future. We have failed to expand our horizon.

Karl Marx's dictum stands: "[People] make their history . . . not under circumstances chosen by themselves but under circumstances directly encountered, given and transmitted from the past. The tradition of all dead generations weighs like a nightmare on the brain of the living."[16] The different understandings and interpretations of the past, including those things that we would rather forget, do not simply disappear. They fester on. Perhaps the only cure is for "others" to concede our story, to at least recognize the deeper anguish, passion, and meaning for which our story is often a code. True stories, historic myths, epic poems, and national memories point to the things of the spirit by which a people lives. It is here that reconciliation must begin.

Truth

The inevitable question that follows every story concerns the nature of truth, recognizing that *truth* is a laden word. The Afrikaner poet Antjie Krog illustrates the point by telling of Nadine Gordimer, who asked a black writer: "Why do you always picture a white woman lounging next to a swimming pool? We are not all like that!" He replied: "Because we perceive you like that." Krog tells too of a young comrade arriving from Kroonstad who refused to speak Afrikaans to her. He called it a colonial language. "What is English then?" she asked. "English doesn't come from over the sea," he said. "English was born in Africa. It was brought here by *Umkhonto we Sizwe*."[17]

Krog's stories point to the importance of perception, the ambiguity of language, and different levels of truth. What we call "factual truth" (either English came from over the sea or it did not) is important. Equally important is the truth being conveyed by the young comrade. Krog relates her remarks to the proposed Truth and Reconciliation Commission, whose task is to discern truth but also to reconcile:

> If this commission is only trying to find the truth so that justice can be done in the form of amnesty, trials and compensation, then it has actually chosen not for truth, but for justice. If it sees truth as the widest possible compilation of people's perceptions, stories, myths and experiences, then it has chosen the road of healing, of restoring memory and humanity.[18]

Michel Foucault notes the integral relationship between truth and power: "The exercise of power perpetually creates knowledge, and conversely, knowledge constantly induces effects of power."[19] Rejecting any notion of "essential truth," Foucault argues that what is perceived as truth in a given situation is inevitably shaped by what he defines as the prevailing "regime of truth" in a particular society.[20] This involves more than merely being politically correct.

It suggests that each society is governed by a set of presuppositions in terms of which truth is assessed. There is at the same time a sense of "factual truth," which sobers us beyond postmodernist relativity. Either something occurred or it did not occur. Interpretation is governed by certain realities. It is, nevertheless, comparatively easy to conclude that a person was killed in comparison with unraveling the exact motive of the alleged assassin or murderer. This is where Foucault's insights are most valuable. Reaching beyond what is the dominant perception on such matters, shaped as it is by prevailing power relations, the quest must be for a broad understanding. It is this notion of truth that lies at the root of genuine reconciliation. Differently stated, we should not conclude too easily what is the exact and full nature of truth.

This is especially true when it comes to storytelling. What are the factors that determine what is remembered and what is forgotten? To what extent do we suppress memories that do not fit in with our perception of the truth as we perceive it? We may suppress into the depths of our unconsciousness what we choose not to remember, with human collectives (nations, groups, and political parties) being more apt at so doing than individuals—if the other Niebuhr (Reinhold Niebuhr) is to be believed.[21] The truth of the matter is, however, that we do not destroy the reality of the past.[22] The unremembered past endures. This is that part of the truth that each section of society is required to face. It can do so thoughtfully and carefully or risk the possibility that it will erupt in an uncontrollable manner. Suppressed and forgotten truth is part of the inclusive truth that must be uncovered if a polarized society is to be united in the healing process. More realistically, it is only as we pursue the *possibility* of uncovering the full truth that the *possibility* of healing is there.

In a daunting passage in *Nineteen Eighty-Four*, George Orwell speaks of the skillful capacity of modernity "to [both] know and not to know"—of its ability to be both honest and to tell "carefully constructed lies." This, he suggests, is the "ultimate subtlety" of the oppressive state. It enables one "consciously to induce unconsciousness, and then, once again, to become unconscious of the act of hypnosis you have just performed."[23] It is asking a great deal of any society to face its past and to transcend the "subtlety" of its own particular collective memory by opening itself to the stories of others. To fail to do so is to ignore the past. The problem is that the past does not disappear of its own accord. It is this that makes storytelling a worthwhile undertaking. It builds bridges of communication, even when forgiveness remains a long way off.

Telling Stories

Storytelling, in one form of another, is part of all traditions, cultures, and civilizations. "If you cannot understand my story, you do not accept me as your neighbor," Ellen Kuzwayo once told me. "I am an African woman. I've tried to share my soul, my way of seeing things, the way I understand life. I hope you understand." We continued to speak at some length. "Africa is a place of storytelling," she continued. "We need more stories, never mind how painful the exercise might be. This is how we will learn to love one another. Stories help us to understand, to forgive, and to see things through someone else's eyes."[24]

It takes time for true stories to be told. Stories that reveal the sacredness of life, that point to events that have hurt and healed, given life and death, are not easy stories to tell. Reconciliation cannot be forced. True stories are rarely told to strangers. "It was not easy for me to write my story. It was not easy to tell my story to people whom I did not know. Sometimes I do not fully understand it myself," Kuzwayo says. This is what makes the Truth and Reconciliation Commission's task of hearing stories of victims a strained albeit necessary exercise.[25] It is necessary to spring the trap that has prevented people from telling their stories and thus prevented them from being understood (Kuzwayo). Not telling our stories has, in turn, prevented us from broadening our national horizon (Gadamer). It has imposed an ideologically closed memory that has excluded and alienated the majority of South Africans. It is this partisan memory that needs to be reconstructed.

Archbishop Ndumiso Ngada, director of the Spiritual Churches Research and Theological Training Institution, draws on the orality of the African Independent Church (AIC) movement to help uncover this memory. He emphasizes the "unwritten and unsystematic nature theology of the majority church movement in South Africa (AIC), hidden in music, custom, ritual, dress and dance." "The institutional church theologians have not yet begun to discover these resources," he says. "There is, because of this failure, no ecumenical theology in South Africa. Not even the Kairos theologians, try as they did, were able to understand this richness of our identity as Africans and as Christians."[26] I asked him how this ecumenical encounter could happen. "Only with sensitivity and care," was his response.

> We have had enough missionaries and other well-meaning whites coming to tell us and others what we are supposed to believe. Maybe no Western theologian will ever fully understand the African soul and the oral mysteries of African Christianity. It will at least take a long time. An African is in no hurry to reveal the inner stories of her soul. But let us begin by telling one another stories. There is a wealth of memory and healing power in storytelling. Theologians must listen to these stories in order to discern their spiritual message. The church must become African if it is to grow on the African continent.[27]

"Scream as loud as you want; no one will hear you," torture victims in apartheid jails were often told by tormentors who were confident that knowledge of their crimes would never go beyond the cell walls. The defeat of the apartheid regime offers the opportunity for the suppressed anguish of these victims to be heard. "Now there is a chance for the whole world to hear the victims scream,"

Marlene Bosset of the Cape Town-based Trauma Centre for Victims of Violence and Torture told The South African Conference on Truth and Reconciliation organized by the Justice in Transition project.[28] People must be allowed to tell their stories. The nation is obliged to hear them. It is in the encounter of telling, hearing, and understanding that the reconciliation process can begin.

The Truth and Reconciliation Commission has clearly defined political objectives and legal parameters. Ultimately, however, the work of the commission is a deeply spiritual, theological, and moral endeavor. So much has been made of the Afrikaner poet Totius's reflection on the Afrikaner psyche in the wake of the Anglo-Boer War. In his poem "Forgive and Forget" he speaks of wounds that healed while the "scar grew greater."[29] But what about the blacks who suffered in that war?[30] White history, white memory, and popular literature are incomplete. The suffering of some has been so great that perhaps only God can ultimately forgive. Forgiveness is at the same time an ingredient of human existence that cannot be easily dismissed without significant personal and communal cost.

At the heart of traditional African society is the notion of *ubuntu*, which affirms an organic wholeness of humanity, a wholeness realized in and through other people. The notion is enshrined in the Xhosa proverb: *umuntu ngumuntu ngabantu* (a person is a person through persons), which gives expression to the universal understanding of humanity in all African traditions. Storytelling, as an idiom of what Martin Buber has called the I-Thou relationship, is central to this community.

While the complexity of African anthropology cannot be fully explored here, it is helpful to note the insights that Gabriel Setiloane offers into the African understanding of reality. He speaks of a "Force" or *Seriti* (Tswana) (*Isithunzi* in Xhosa), with its source in the divine, as present in all that is "human, animal, animate, inanimate and even spiritual." This dynamic, he says, is primarily present in the human person: "The great 'I' (calls) out the small 'thou' into relationship and communion."[31] Stanley Mogoba (standing within the Pedi tradition) relates African religion and Christianity in arguing: "The Gospel is about enabling people to realize their full humanity . . . and ubuntu is an African understanding of humanity that this country will do well to rediscover. It has to do with realizing one's full potential as a person."[32]

Given the presence of the divine, primarily within people, it is in relation to other people that the African person attains his or her full humanity. Taylor refers to a "centrifugal selfhood . . . interpermeating other selves in a relationship in which subject and object are no longer distinguishable. 'I think therefore I am' is replaced by 'I participate, therefore I am.'"[33] Returning to Setiloane: "The essence of being is 'participation' in which humans are always interlocked with each other—the human being is not only 'vital force,' but more: 'vital force in participation.'" This 'vital participation' is the "very soul of the community body [that] accounts for the miasma which attaches to the group, the clan, the tribe."[34] Life together is the quintessence of an African understanding of what it means to be human.

The African notion of an extended family has been widely debated. "Every person is related to another." These relationships—by blood, by marriage, or by mere association—are emotionally seated and cherished dearly.[35] Primarily the extended family involves kinship within one's own clan. Here, it has been suggested, we experience "social affinity" with people who share our values, customs and group identity even though they may be "personal strangers."[36] There is at the same time ample evidence in South African history of Africans drawing others (whether missionaries or white settlers—who later often turned against them) into kinship with themselves. An African sense of community includes rather than separates. Herein is a basis for building a common South Africanness—a basis for sharing stories that transcend the isolation of the past in the pursuit of reconciliation.

Identity and the contours of memory can never be reified. They are neither static nor inherently given. They emerge as part of a social construct, in dialogue and encounter with the identity, stories, and memories of others. Louise du Toit suggests that "what we call our 'selves' and our 'world' are effects or products of the particular, historical communities in which we find ourselves always already immersed." She argues that according to this theory "identity itself, previously regarded as the innermost essence of any particular person or thing, is seen as itself nothing more or less than a [social] construct. . . . It is not bestowed from above, but rather generated from the sides."[37] There is an African ring to such thinking.

The importance of the African understanding of community is so important that it requires the most vigorous critical analysis. Leopold Senghor, Gabriel Setiloane, and Leo Apostel, for example, stress the value and dignity of the individual in African society.[38] Olusola Ojo and Amadu Sesay, in their assessment of contemporary African culture as expressed in the African Charter on Human and Peoples' Rights, on the other hand, suggest that communal or peoples' rights are in practice often allowed to take precedence over individual rights in African society.[39] No tradition is static and no tradition can afford to be left unchallenged by the demands of each new age. This has resulted in many African women challenging the patriarchal bias of traditional African notions of *ubuntu*.[40]

Archie Mafeje speaks of the need for a "spirit of self-criticism" within which the conservative and progressive dimensions of African culture can be identified and analyzed. "For the social scientists, artists and philosophers," he observes, "the intellectual task of identifying, evaluating and synthesizing popular cultural notions, various progressive nationalist and socialist pre-conceptions and demands are Herculean but not impossible."[41] This challenge, of course, extends beyond Africa. All religions and traditions are obliged to do precisely this.

Christians in South Africa—whose identity is often still formed by privatized nineteenth century Eurocentric missionary Christianity—will do well to reread St. John and St. Paul, both of whom employ (although differently) the notion "in Christ" as emphasizing the place of sharing in the Christian life.

Located within the context of African notions of *ubuntu*, the New Testament image of being in Christ takes on new dimensions of community building (*koinonia*).[42] To be in Christ requires us to be in fellowship and community with one another (Acts 2:42f.). The early Christians experienced faith as the spiritual reality of empowerment by the Holy Spirit *and* as fellowship with one another. Their spirituality was inward and outward. Inward spirituality became manifest in the outward act of "sharing their belongings with one another" (Acts 2:44). C. F. D. Moule speaks of the "corporate Christ" as a neglected New Testament Christological model, within which Christians are organically united to one another as if they were a single, well-coordinated living body by virtue of being united with Christ.[43] In New Testament language, Christ is the Spirit that unites believers. In African parlance, to be human is to belong to a community. It is to share in the goodness as well as the suffering of all. An injury to one is indeed an injury to all. To be estranged from another is to be less than fully human. To belong is to be human. This is the challenge that underlies nation-building in South Africa. Storytelling is part of this exercise. Provided it shows sensitivity to the complexities of truth-telling, the Commission on Truth and Reconciliation can make a major contribution to this process. It can facilitate the process of building a common and inclusive memory and community. It can contribute to completing the partial, partisan, and limited stories of history that divide the nation.

An Unconcluding Postscript

This essay constitutes an attempt to underline the importance of the spiritual and psychological dimensions of reconciliation. No attention has been given to the urgent need for economic redistribution, political restructuring, and social rehabilitation.[44] Storytelling can never be a substitute for these concerns. In order to be authentic, it can only be carried out in relation to these material concerns. In so doing it can provide the political will and spiritual energy needed to ensure that reconstruction is adequately addressed. The Truth and Reconciliation Commission is part of the larger Reconstruction and Development Programme. Forgiveness, contrition, penance, repentance, restitution, and reconciliation are an integrated whole. There is no cheap grace.

Notes

[1] Hein Marais, "The New South African Identity Crisis," *Work in Progress* (November 1993), p. 11.

[2] See Robin Petersen, "Towards a South African Theology of Non-Racism," *Journal of Theology for Southern Africa* 77 (December 1991), pp. 18-26; Charles Villa-Vicencio, "The Quest for a National Identity," *JTSA* 86 (March 1994), pp. 26-27.

[3] James Cone, *God of the Oppressed* (New York: Seabury Press, 1975), pp. 102-3.

[4] H. Richard Niebuhr, *The Meaning of Revelation* (New York: Macmillan, 1967), p. 115. I am grateful to Dirkie Smit, who in his "Die Waarheid en Versoeningskommissie—

Tentatiewe Kerklike en Teologiese Perspektiewe" (an unpublished paper) has drawn on Niebuhr to stress the importance of storytelling in the South African context.

[5] Martin E. Marty, "From Centripetal to the Centrifugal in Culture and Religion: The Revolution within This Half Century," *Theology Today* 51:1 (April 1994), pp. 5-16.

[6] Janet Hodgson, "Zonnebloem College and Cape Town," *Studies in the History of Cape Town*, vol. 1/1984 (Centre for African Studies, University of Cape Town, 1984), pp. 125-52.

[7] Yasmin Sooka, "Hindu-Muslim Relations in a Reconciliatory South Africa," an unpublished paper.

[8] For "Cape Town Agreement, 1927," see Government of India, *Papers Relating to the Second Round Table Conference* (1932), Appendix 1, quoted in Sooka. See also Surendra Bhana and Bridglal Pachai, eds., *A Documentary History of Indian South Africans* (Cape Town: David Philip, 1984), pp. 150f.

[9] Steve Biko, *I Write What I Like* (London: Heinemann, 1987), p. 24.

[10] Charles Long, *Significations: Signs, Symbols and Images in the Interpretation of Religion* (Philadelphia: Fortress Press, 1986), p. 153.

[11] James Davison Hunter, *Culture Wars: The Struggle to Define America* (New York: Basic Books, 1991).

[12] Niebuhr, p. 93.

[13] Ibid., p. 109.

[14] Rosemary Radford Ruether, *Woman Guides: Readings toward a Feminist Theology* (Boston: Beacon Press, 1985), pp. xii, 247.

[15] Hans-Georg Gadamer, *Truth and Method* (New York: Crossroad, 1988), p. 272. I am grateful to Mieke Holkeboer, a graduate student, for her work on Hans-Georg Gadamer.

[16] K. Marx and F. Engels, *Selected Works: The Eighteenth Brumaire of Louis Bonaparte* (Moscow: Progress Press, 1968), p. 95.

[17] Antjie Krog, "Untold Damage of Anglo-Boer War," *Democracy in Action*, vol. 8, no. 5 (31 August 1994), p. 19.

[18] Ibid.

[19] Michel Foucault, *Power/Knowledge: Selected Interviews and Other Writings 1972-1977*, ed. Colin Gordon (New York: Pantheon Books, 1980), p. 52.

[20] Ibid., p. 70. Foucault similarly refers to the "general politics of truth."

[21] Reinhold Niebuhr, *Moral Man and Immoral Society* (New York: Charles Scribner's Sons, 1960).

[22] H. Richard Niebuhr, *The Meaning of Revelation*, p. 113.

[23] George Orwell, *Nineteen Eighty-Four* (Harmondsworth: Penguin Books, 1962).

[24] In personal conversation with Ellen Kuzwayo, at Kader Asmal's sixtieth birthday party, 16 October 1994. See also her book *Call Me Woman* (Cape Town: David Philip, 1985).

[25] The Truth and Reconciliation Commission makes provision for three separate but related committees: an amnesty committee, which considers the application for amnesty from perpetrators of gross human rights violations; a human rights committee, which hears the stories of victims of human rights violations; and a reparations committee, which seeks to provide reparation to victims where this is possible.

[26] In discussion with Archbishop Ngada, November 1994.

[27] The title of this essay is derived from this conversation.

[28] *Democracy in Action*, vol. 8, no. 5 (31 August 1994), p. 16.

[29] Totius (JD du Toit), "Forgive and Forget," in *The Penguin Book of South African Verse*, comp. and intro. Jack Cope and Uys Krige (Harmondsworth: Penguin Books, 1968), pp. 194-95.

[30] Bill Nasson, *Abraham Esau's War: A Black South African War in the Cape (1899-1902)* (Cambridge: Cambridge University Press, 1991).

[31] Gabriel Setiloane, *African Theology: An Introduction* (Johannesburg: Skotaville, 1986), pp. 13-16.

[32] Stanley Mogoba, in C. Villa-Vicencio, *The Spirit of Hope: Conversations on Politics, Religion and Values* (Johannesburg: Skotaville, 1993), pp. 194-95.

[33] J. V. Taylor, *The Primal Vision* (London: SCM, 1963), p. 41.

[34] Setiloane, p. 14.

[35] Ibid., p. 9.

[36] See the discussion on culture, ethnicity, and group identity in Gerhard Maré, *Ethnicity and Politics in South Africa* (London: Zed Books, 1993), p. 12.

[37] Louise du Toit, "A Narrative-Communicative Approach to Identity and Ethnicity," paper delivered at the Global Change and Social Transformation Conference, Centre of Social Development, November 1993. The word "social" has been substituted for "linguistic" in du Toit's text. The words are not synonymous but do not violate her essential argument.

[38] Leopold Senghor, *On African Socialism* (London: Pall Mall Press, 1964); Setiloane, *African Theology*; Leo Apostel, *African Philosophy: Myth or Reality* (Gent: E Story-Scientia, 1982). See discussion on this in Augustine Shutte, *Philosophy for Africa* (Cape Town: University of Cape Town Press, 1993), pp. 46-51.

[39] Olusola Ojo and Amadu Sesay, "The OAU and Human Rights: Prospects for the 1980s and Beyond," *Human Rights Quarterly* 8:1 (1966). For a discussion of the importance of African communalism as a corrective to Western individualism see Josiah A. M. Cobbah, "African Values and the Human Rights Debate: An African Perspective," *Human Rights Quarterly* 9:3 (1987).

[40] See the discussion in Denise Ackermann, "From Difference to Connectedness: A Feminist View on the Question of Difference," a paper read at the South African Academy of Religion, Pretoria (January 1994).

[41] Archie Mafeje, "African Philosophical Projections and Prospects for the Indigenisation of Political and Intellectual Discourse," *Seminar Paper Series No. 7* (Harare: Sapes Books, 1992), p. 27.

[42] For these different usages see C. F. D. Moule, *The Origin of Christology* (Cambridge: Cambridge University Press, 1977), pp. 58f., 64.

[43] Ibid., pp. 47-96.

[44] See Charles Villa-Vicencio, *A Theology of Reconstruction: Nation-Building and Human Rights* (Cambridge: Cambridge University Press, 1992) for an attempt to address some of these issues.

4

The Church and Genocide

Lessons from the Rwandan Tragedy[1]

IAN LINDEN

INTRODUCTION: Unlike many other African countries, Rwanda's borders are not simply artificial colonial constructs. They broadly correspond to the boundaries of a small precolonial kingdom in the Great Lakes region of East Africa, with a Hutu peasantry ruled by a king, the *mwami*, and a "feudal" nobility, the Tutsi. The people of this kingdom, the Banyarwanda, spoke a common language and lived in a complex society involving cattle vassalage, different forms of chieftaincy over land and people, and different forms of service to overlords.

The Rwandan kingship was sustained by a rich ideology expressed in myth and oral traditions of the royal court: the nobility was born to rule, the peasantry was ignorant and irresponsible, and the king was divine and above such distinctions. Close selective intermarrying among the aristocracy accentuated physical characteristics such as height, and differences in diet further emphasized the distinctness of the leading lineages and families.

German and then Belgian colonial rule interpreted the structure and history of this society as the story of an Hamitic race who invaded the territory in the distant past to rule over a Bantu people. The transformation of a complex "feudal" society with social mobility into a bureaucratic colonial state hardened social and economic differences into rigid class differences and finally resulted in "tribal" conflict. The full ambiguity of the terms *Tutsi* and *Hutu* was revealed by the Belgian system of ethnic classification, in which *Tutsi* was defined as "a Banyarwanda with more than ten cows."

After resisting the Catholic missions for several decades, the king and aristocracy converted in large numbers in the 1930s in a movement called *le tornade* ("the hurricane"). Rwanda became known as "the Christian Kingdom." But a postwar generation of priests with a growing commitment to social justice favored the emancipation of the Hutu and sponsored the formation of a Hutu political party. A political crisis in 1959 led to something reminiscent of the French Revolution and resulted, with Belgian connivance, in the flight of large numbers of Tutsi and formal independence under Hutu rule in 1962.

Raids across Rwanda's borders by Tutsi exiles and violent pogroms against Tutsi inside the country foreshadowed a politics of total exclusion. In July 1973 Major General Juvenal Habyarimana, representing northern Hutu, deposed Gregoire Kayibanda, a former seminarian from the central region. For many years the Habyarimana regime promised more harmonious Tutsi-Hutu relations. However, by the end of the 1980s, for a variety of reasons, his government, based on a small clique, had become autocratic and brutally repressive. Large-scale violations of human rights became increasingly common.

Tutsi exiles had gained in strength by participation in Museveni's guerrilla army in Uganda and formed the Rwanda Patriotic Front (RPF) in 1987. In October 1990 the RPF invaded Rwanda from the northeast, setting in motion international pressures for power sharing. Hard-line supporters of Habyarimana blocked him from implementing the Arusha accords, which called for a radical power-sharing formula.

In response, extremists around Habyarimana prepared for a final solution, the total elimination of their perceived enemy, the Tutsi. Youth groups that had initially appeared innocuous, "development" teams working together, known as *interahamwe*, turned into vigilante groups and death squads. Virulent and effective propaganda turned the old court and colonial myths on their heads: the RPF were alien tribal invaders coming to kill the Hutu and take their land from them. France trained and armed Habyarimana's army. The scene was set for popular participation in genocide.

It is not my intention to provide a historical account of the churches' role in the Rwandan tragedy of 1994. Perhaps it is even too early for any thoroughgoing assessment of the meaning of these events for the future of Christianity in Africa. What I should like to offer is a tentative framework for analyzing the news that emerged about the churches, along with some suggestions as to its implications both for African Christians and for missiology.

I write from a dangerously distanced perspective. As one of the few people in the U.K. with research experience on Hutu-Tutsi conflict,[2] the mass media called on me to comment when the news story broke. Through consultation with a wide range of people involved in Rwanda, I was able to respond, albeit with some difficulty. I was drawn into assuming the role of expert and followed events closely.

The designation of expert in my case seems somewat more spurious than usual; my analysis has relied on previous research and the judgment and integrity of my informants largely drawn from NGOs (Non-Government Organizations) and churches. But I am consoled by the truth that world historical events—among which the Rwandan genocide must be classified—are notoriously difficult to understand from within; partial knowledge is the lot of all bold enough to offer interpretation, whether outsider or insider.

The African Context

First of all it is necessary to say that the Rwandan genocide needs to be placed firmly in the world context of other violations of human rights, violations so prodigious that they call into question Christian anthropology.³ This is to universalize a horrific event that the mass media, with implicit racism, were all too willing to attribute to the heart of darkness understood as African "savagery." The Nazi holocaust and the Turkish genocide of Armenians are antecedents to the Rwandan genocide, realities of the twentieth century that can only elicit our silence and incomprehension. Like its antecedents, the Rwandan genocide took place within a larger slaughter; tens of thousands of Hutu opponents of the Rwandan regime died alongside their Tutsi compatriots. Any explanation of such human wickedness presents a daunting theological task, because it affirms the existence of an evil that deeply challenges the Christian gospel.

But to say that the Rwandan tragedy also occurs as part of a historical narrative more specific to Africa—a combination of ethnic, ecological, and economic pressures bringing about the collapse of the nation-state—is to move the question from the universal to the particular. Historical analysis raises a potentially answerable question: What were the necessary and proximate, the major and minor causes, of the events? Though the Rwandan genocide was complex in its causes, there are reasons why it occurred where and when it did. Though it may have been unavoidable, given the current nature of global ethics and the present world political configuration, it could have been checked. Repeated early warnings had been given, but they went unheeded or were ignored. Prompt and focused action by the world community through the United Nations would have at least significantly reduced the death-toll.

None of this is contended. Yet what was specific to Rwanda, so that genocide occurred here rather than elsewhere? The economic predicament of Rwanda was certainly a primary factor. Yet, most African countries are like Rwanda. First, they have meager possibilities for export, usually one or two cash crops (in the case of Rwanda, coffee), whose value dropped drastically in world markets after 1987. Second, during the 1980s many saw their national debt rise; Rwanda's rose from $189 million to $844 million, and some twenty other countries clocked in behind Rwanda in the U.N.'s classification of the poorest countries in the world. Third, like Rwanda, many were increasingly overpopulated, with huge populations of young men under twenty-five with no formal employment prospects. Fourth, several countries experienced annual declines of 2.4 percent in their economies during the 1980s and faced draconian structural adjustment programs.

What made Rwanda different economically was that it had significantly *improved* its economic condition during the early 1980s. But this rising curve turned sharply downward from 1987 through 1994 as a structural adjustment program rapidly aggravated problems of rising unemployment and rural poverty from 1990 to 1994. Two devaluations more than halved the value of the Rwandan currency and put even basic essentials such as cooking fuel out of reach for many.

In the past Rwanda had solved its economic problems by exporting its population, with wave after wave of economic migrants or refugees moving into neighboring countries. The Banyarwanda—Hutu, Tutsi, and Twa—were seen as skillful in establishing new lives and the wherewithal to live. The early 1990s, though, were characterized by the closing of a number of traditional safety valves. Neighboring states were becoming increasingly uncomfortable for immigrants as social tensions mounted or erupted in violence. No longer welcome, the Banyarwanda were pressured to return home.

At the same time the international community began to exert considerable pressure on the Hutu regime headed by President Juvenal Habyarimana to participate in the wave of democratization sweeping the African continent. The Arusha accords were signed in August 1993 after two years of frustrating negotiation. By any standard the accords were radical in the demands that they made on Habyarimana and his governing elite. They stipulated that rule by a repressive clique give way to a government of national unity, and that forces of the Rwandan Patriotic Front composed of Tutsi exiles based in Uganda be integrated into the national army. If the Arusha accords were implemented, many in the national army would face demobilization and unemployment. It seemed that Habyarimana was cornered and isolated by the East African states. Neither President Daniel Arap Moi of Kenya nor Yoweri Museveni of Uganda nor the Tanzanians held out any succor.

Democracy Aborted

Not surprisingly, Habyarimana dragged his feet over implementing the Arusha accords, as he had to contend with growing resistance to change from the extremists around him in the Committee for the Defense of the Republic (CDR) and in his National Republican Movement for Democracy and Development (MRND). For some, like Colonel Theoneste Bagosora in the Ministry of Defense, who would become ring-leaders of the genocide, the accords were the last straw.[4] Nonetheless, Rwanda signed the accords in August 1993, agreeing to a process of democratization. United Nations forces (UNAMIR) were present in the country by November to oversee implementation of the accords, and by then alternative political parties were forming and recruiting. At the same time, established human rights organizations began chronicling human rights violations.

Yet these developments were taking place in a country where the apparatus of tyranny was not only intact but highly active in the form of the Hutu militias and CDR youth networks. At no point did the repression relent. Indeed, it gained momentum from 1991 to 1992 in response to the success of the Rwandan Patriotic Front army under Major Paul Kagame, and by late 1993 it was characterized by widely monitored assassinations and repeated minor pogroms.[5] The democratization process was aborted by the horror of genocide and the massive systematic elimination of all opposition to the extremist clique. Genocide on this scale cries out for explanation; prior to the 1990s the Habyarimana government had not manipulated "ethnic" differences for political ends and had appeared to be a fairly typical one-party repressive regime.

Rwanda differed most clearly from South Africa—where a major transition took place successfully with the full apparatus of repression intact—in that the Rwanda regime could purport to represent the majority and hope to rely on its support. But since, in reality, it was a repressive clique that represented only a few groups in the northwest, it could claim to represent the majority only by creating an exclusive ethnic identity that it equated with the nation. Unfortunately, it had the historical preconditions and propaganda means to do so. As a result, the early 1990s were marked by a series of massacres of Tutsis numbered in the hundreds; from 1992 onward the massacres were instigated by the authorities, after extensive use of racist propaganda.

Historically, Rwanda was not a likely candidate for democratization. German and Belgian rule had transformed a feudal society based on cattle vassalage into a rigidly stratified social system with the strata identified as "tribes." A classic piece of Victorian anthropology, influenced by social Darwinism, placed the Tutsi aristocracy as part of a "Hamitic invasion" from Ethiopia and the northeast, supposedly superior to Bantu autochtones. The "Hamites," Tutsi aristocrats, with slender fingers and longer noses, were viewed as ethnically closer to Semitic stock than the Bantu; not surprisingly, they were deemed to be "natural rulers," like the Europeans who invented the classification. They were educated in elite institutions and assumed positions of power throughout the nascent colonial state.[6]

These poisonous fables lived on for a long time. During the Biafran War Henry Kissinger allegedly believed that the Ibo of Nigeria would win because they were "closer to Semitic races." In Rwanda, the Habyarimana clique turned the fable against the Rwandan Patriotic Front by presenting them as alien invaders. *Kangura*, a newspaper founded in 1990, elaborated on the myth by presenting the Habyarimana regime as a Hutu republic seeking to cleanse itself of the alien enemy within.

The Hutu revolt of 1959 had swept to power Gregoire Kayibanda, who emerged from peasant stock in central Rwanda. He drove the Rwandan *mwami* (king), and the court (all Tutsi) out of the country as refugees. Since that time capture of the Rwandan state from political opponents has been a violent game in which winner takes all. Political parties with mainly regional roots have intermittently attempted to wrap themselves in national colors as the ethnic-blind party of the Banyarwanda. The absence of the *mwami,* who was seen not as an elevated Tutsi noble but as a unifying symbol above the ethnic and political fray, made this more difficult.

Although the military coup led by Juvenal Habyarimana in 1973 initially attempted to widen the Hutu political base, by the 1980s rule was carried out by a narrow Gisenyi-centered clique. Military activity by Tutsi exile groups led to violent reprisals against the "ethnic minority" in the country, creating new waves of refugees. Today's ruling Rwandan Patriotic Front has made similar moves to widen its political base but appears to be refusing to incorporate prominent members of Habyarimana's MRND. Its capture of the government in 1994, of course, resulted in one of the greatest flights of refugees in African history.

Given this background, a process of democratization was bound to be exceptionally difficult to achieve. Indeed, democratization was guaranteed to be far more difficult than in a country like Tanzania, with its many but fairly equally sized language groups and cultural traditions. Yet, it was pushed very hard and very fast in the face of the Rwandan Patriotic Front's invasion, the dominance of Hutu extremist groups, and the risk of a wider civil war.[7]

Proximate Causes of the Genocide

Perhaps the single most important trigger in aborting the process of democratization was the assassination in Burundi on October 21, 1993, of the new Hutu president, Melchior Ndadaye. Tens of thousands died in the wake of the coup that followed, and some seventy thousand Burundian Hutu fled into southern Rwanda. These events signaled to many around Habyarimana that the Tutsi minority would never truly accept majority (Hutu) rule within the context of a government of national unity. In other words, the extremists were right: the Arusha accords called for too much, too fast.

There is much evidence to suggest that, at least from November 1993 onward, the Hutu extremists around Habyarimana systematically prepared for a "final solution." Death lists openly circulated. Unlike the Nazi version of genocide, which had a certain gratuitous, dysfunctional madness in the context of a war on two fronts against the Soviet Union and Allies, that of the Hutu extremists had a diabolical pragmatism based on fear. The Hutu felt that all the Tutsi, including exiles and their children who had returned, had to be eliminated, along with all other regional opponents, to prevent them from capturing the state. While the Nazis saw extermination of lesser races as a natural expression of Aryan power, the Hutu extremists saw elimination of the Tutsi as a practical solution to the political problem of retaining control of the state.

In early April 1994, because of the slow pace of change in Rwanda, neighboring heads of state and the international community called President Habyarimana to further rounds of talks. As a result, he seemed to agree to move rapidly toward implementation of the Arusha accords. By this time he had been called to task by the U.N. High Commission for Refugees, the U.N. rapporteur for human rights, and a variety of human rights organizations, national and international, that itemized massive human rights violations and warned of impending catastrophe unless rapid progress occurred toward democracy.

On April 6, several kilometers from the Kigali airport, which was heavily garrisoned by the Presidential Guard, as one story goes, two French-speaking soldiers of Caribbean origin carrying shoulder-held ground-to-air missiles took up position under the flight-path of the Rwandan president's Mystère Falcon jet as he returned home from Dar-es-Salaam. Also on board was the president of Burundi, Cyprien Ntaryamira. As the plane moved into its approach at 8:00 P.M. it was hit by two missiles, exploded in mid-air, and crashed, killing all on board. It is hard to tell whether or not the target was the Burundian president or the hapless President Habyarimana returning home to face his extremists. It matters little as the "final solution" would almost certainly have been implemented with or without his death.

The rest is history. Within hours of the plane crash, selective assassinations of Hutu opposition leaders, politicians, and key leaders in civil society began. Some of the first to die were Catholic church personnel at the Christus Center in Kigali. This was followed by the beginnings of a program of genocide against the Tutsi.

The response of the international community was muted and timorous. The killing of ten Belgian U.N. troops resulted in anxiety among Security Council member states, as it was feared that Rwanda was turning into a fiasco like that of Somalia. The limited mandate of the U.N. troops to oversee the Arusha accords did not permit their intervention. The U.N. mandate was modified to provide for seeking a cease-fire between the RPF and the Rwandan army but not to intervene in stopping genocide. After two weeks the Security Council reduced the numbers of UNAMIR forces from 1,700 to 270. The policy of the United States toward the growing violence in Rwanda could not escape the shadow of the debacle of Somalia.

Massacres undertaken by crowds of people, as well as the more systematic attacks by the Rwandan Army, the *interahamwe*, and youth mobs, produced a death-rate equal to the industrialized slaughter of the Jews by the Nazis. Government propaganda encouraged the massacres, with *Radio Télévision Libre des Mille Collines* playing a pernicious role in inciting mass murder. The withdrawal of the bulk of the U.N. forces, and the failure of the Security Council to send reinforcements or acknowledge that genocide was taking place, cost thousands of lives and will be recorded as one of the most culpable and tragic of the U.N.'s many failures.

Complicity of the Churches

As the news of the massacres began to break, initial media coverage about the churches was favorable. Journalists, reliant at first on church and NGO sources, were soon aware that church buildings, filled with crowds who sought sanctuary, were the scenes of major massacres. Priests and nuns were easily identifiable informants. Mission orders fleeing the country brought news of the killings, and the Society of the Missionaries of Our Lady of Africa, known as the White Fathers, produced several editions of a faxed newsletter. There was considerable sympathy as awareness spread of the degree to which the churches were targeted by the militias.

But by June the story had moved sharply to the theme of complicity. A press conference involving Anglican Archbishops Augustin Nshamihigo and Jonathan Ruhumuliza in Nairobi in early June ended as journalists walked out in disgust when the bishops refused to denounce unequivocally the Rwandan interim government, which was behind the genocide.[8] Evidence of complicity in the crude sense of priests and nuns being actively involved in the killings is meager. Nonetheless, later investigations by African Rights in London do provide evidence that some local Catholic, Anglican, and Baptist church leaders were implicated by omission or commission in militia killings.[9] The one widely disseminated story of a priest actually killing ten parishioners, reported by Isaac Samuel of the World Council of Churches in August, turned out to be false, based only on hear-say, according to reliable White Father sources in Belgium. Yet despite overwhelming evidence that the story was false, the newspapers that printed it never published retractions.[10]

Verified stories were about lower levels of leadership, such as catechists, directing or participating in mobs undertaking massacres. There is absolutely no doubt that significant numbers of prominent Christians were involved in the killings, sometimes slaughtering their own church leaders. This, perhaps more than any other aspect of the holocaust, has had a major impact on missionary congregations. "What," so many ask, "did we do wrong that this should happen?"[11]

At an entirely different level, but fundamental to the charge of complicity, was the earlier behavior of church leaders, such as the Anglican bishops in Nairobi. The most egregious example is that of the Roman Catholic Archbishop of Kigali, Vincent Nsengiyumva, who had become a member of the central committee of the MNRD in the mid-1970s and was confessor to Habyarimana's wife. He certainly moved in the circle of the hard-line fanatical anti-Tutsi clique around Habyarimana. Forced to relinquish his party position after a direct order from Rome prior to the pope's visit to Rwanda in 1990, he was still clearly identified with the regime. His death, along with two other bishops and the vicar-general of Kabgayi diocese, at the hands of four RPF soldiers on June 3, brought his former role into sharp focus.[12]

The conclusions of a joint delegation of the World Council of Churches, the All Africa Conference of Churches, and the Lutheran World Federation in early August 1994 added to the growing concern about the church's role. The language of the report—"tainted" and "discredited" are words used—was strongly condemnatory and reinforced the emphasis on complicity. What then can be made of this charge?

The danger is, of course, to assume unwittingly an apologetic role and, by seeking explanation, inadvertently to excuse. And it would be a simple matter to attempt to balance the record by itemizing the many incidents of martyrdom, heroic self-sacrifice, courage, and the kind of stubborn unwillingness to take the easy way out on the part of some Rwandan Christians. I am thinking particularly of people like Felicitas Niyitegeka at Gisenyi, who repeatedly refused to abandon her colleagues and save herself from the militia, of Cyprien and Daphrose Rugamba of the multi-ethnic Emmanuel Community, and many others now dead.[13] Whatever the judgment on complicity, it does not apply to all the church, which was also a church of martyrs.[14]

The Divided Church

The issue of complicity needs to be set in the context of a divided church, split by different views of the demands of simple justice *and* by ethnicity and regionalism. Put simply, the church and its clergy, both missionary and indigenous, were far from neutral in their sympathies. It is also important to note that neutrality was not a real option in Rwanda, given its repressive regime. The problem existed in a number of different forms: first, in society, where open criticism of the Habyarimana regime was dangerous and immediately labeled the person as a dissident, subject to repression; and second, in the church, where localized Tutsi domination polarized seminaries and many dioceses.

Growth in the Rwandan church had been saltatory and along class lines. For the first thirty years of the twentieth century, conversions had been virtually all from the Hutu peasantry. The inheritance of the *Tornade* in the 1930s swept large numbers of the Tutsi aristocracy into the church, partially fulfilling the dream of converting Africa through its chiefs. Rwanda became "the Christian Kingdom," with King Rudahigwa and the court supported by an ideology of Christian kingship that promoted the history of the Tutsi lineage as a second Old Testament leading up to the arrival of the New Testament gospel. In an extraordinary work Abbé Alexis Kagame, a court historian, inculturated the church symbolically and historically in court culture. Later, the social Catholicism of the postwar Belgian clergy and the Swiss Archbishop of Kabgayi, Perraudin, was taken up by the Hutu counter-elite, who saw in it an ideological weapon to emancipate the Hutu majority.[15]

After the 1959 revolt even individual church centers had a symbolic resonance, with Kabgayi being historically the "pro-Hutu" focus and Nyundo a "Tutsi diocese." Tutsi domination of the church's intellectual establishments was certain by the 1970s. In 1973, however, large numbers of Tutsi were chased out of schools and fled. Yet, by the early 1990s the quiet dominance of the Tutsi still existed, albeit localized, though only two of the country's eight bishops were Tutsi. The Hutu Archbishop of Kigali was at one extreme of a polarized church, which, on the whole, had found no way of talking openly about—let alone resolving—the system of exclusive ethnicity entrenched in Rwanda. What is summed up and rightly judged as complicity was in reality a complex reaction to social structures and historical events in a divided church.

The large-scale participation of Christians in the killings is to some degree, of course, a simple reflection of the fact that about 90 percent of the population were Christians of one denomination or another, with 62 percent baptized Catholics. Some distinction needs to be made among the instigators and planners of the genocide; the army and militia, who forced people to carry it out; and the ordinary people, who were coerced with varying degrees of reluctance to participate.

Fear

Fear seems to have motivated the "civilian" mobs doing the killing. I have heard mission personnel who observed massacres say that the mob looked more terrified than those being killed. Participants genuinely seemed to believe that they were involved in some kind of self-defense, to kill or be killed, either as a result of propaganda or because a refusal to participate would have resulted in becoming a target. This applies, of course, to the majority of peasants who were involved in the killing, but not to the same degree to the groups who organized the programs.

At another level, complicity was about the failure of many church leaders to dissociate themselves from, and work against, the stranglehold that ethnicity had gained in the church during the Belgian trusteeship. This failure was closely linked to their refusal to speak out strongly against the human rights violations of the regime. Inculturation seems to have meant no more than the immersion of the church in the divisions of society. The church had never seriously challenged Hutu or Tutsi identity as potentially open to being reimagined in a new Christian form, because ethnicity had always been taken as a given. But ethnicity is something that is interactively imagined and lived. Christianity had been adopted as a faith that was inculturated in exclusive identities and also as a set of ethics that left those identities unchanged. The same could be said, of course, for religious identities in the north of Ireland.

By the early 1990s the church had little recourse against the propaganda machine, which preached an exclusive Hutu identity that was defined in terms of a Tutsi invader, and, indeed, defined Hutus ultimately as killers of Tutsis. At a practical level, the church had no radio station with which to combat *Radio Télévision Libre des Mille Collines* or Radio Rwanda. It was hopelessly divided at its leadership level as well as at the parish level. And in the hundred years of its presence in Rwanda it had barely begun to call into question in the light of the gospel the two identities that dominated Rwandan politics. It had first blessed the Rwandan monarchy with the symbols of Christian kingship and then sought the political emancipation of the Hutu. As a historical force, it had reinforced those identities, though sometimes inadvertently.

Speaking Out

One bishop, Thaddee Nsengiyumva of Kabgayi (not to be confused with Archbishop Vincent Nsengiyumva), killed in June 1994, did offer a sense of leadership in the critical early 1990s. He was made president of the Bishops'

Conference, enabling the others to shelter passively behind him. In December 1991 he described the church as "sick"; called for multi-party politics, a negotiated end to the hostilities between the RPF and the Rwandan army, and a national convention; and pointed out the problems of human rights violations and ethnic discrimination.

To a great extent he reflected the widespread disquiet about government repression expressed in *Kinyamateka*, a socially conscious church periodical that had maintained a succession of (for Rwanda) radical editors, including Gregoire Kayibanda. Bishop Thaddee's description of a "sick" church in December 1991 led to the formation a month later of a ten-man church commission that he chaired, which sought to mediate the armed conflict by a classic "peace process." In January 1994 a popular peace movement involving several hundred Christians from different denominations held a rally in Kigali. By then, though, the key issue of the implementation of the Arusha accords was in diplomatic hands and the commission lost momentum. In February, in light of the growing repression and assassination by death squads, Bishop Thaddee again warned of impending catastrophe.

A key figure during this time was the apostolic nuncio, Monsignor Giuseppe Bertello, who had represented the Vatican at the U.N. Human Rights Commission in Geneva. Early in the 1990s, when human rights organizations formed in Rwanda, Bertello supported them and encouraged the president of the Bishops' Conference to speak out in the face of resistance or passivity from his colleagues, including two who were Tutsi. The Vatican put its weight behind the Arusha accords, and on five occasions Bertello met with Pope John Paul II to alert him to the impending crisis.[16]

Opening the African Synod in Rome on April 10, 1994, with news of the killings fresh in the international press, John Paul II was in a position to be particularly clear in his message to Rwanda: "I raise my voice to tell you: Stop these acts of violence. Stop these tragedies. Stop these fratricidal massacres." He described what was happening in Rwanda as an "overwhelming tragedy." Meanwhile Bertello had fled to safety through the back fence of the nunciature, having been warned that the militias were coming for him.

The response of Archbishop Vincent Nsengiyumva, a former member of the MNRD, was characteristically inadequate. He withdrew from Kigali with the interim government to Gitarama and issued a statement described by *African Rights* as "so mild that it could have been the work of the ministry of information." Finally, on May 13, he signed a statement with a group of Catholic and Protestant church leaders that began to hint at the horror of what was going on around them.

The death toll of church leaders, bishops, priests, ministers, and sisters was very high; between a quarter and a third of the leadership had been killed. This is explained primarily by the fact that Tutsi people had not been blocked from advancement in the churches as they had been in the rest of society, and thus had a disproportionate presence among the clergy. Indeed, their strength in the church in seminaries and the priesthood, and their behavior toward Hutu colleagues and pupils, had been a perennial and relatively unaddressed problem since the 1950s. But a great number of Hutu church leaders also died opposing the massacres, or they were killed as intellectual opponents of the Habyarimana regime. As foreigners, missionary clergy did not have the *locus standi* to address the problem of ethnicity or prophetically to denounce the government, though several tried. The greatest complicity was silence masquerading as prudence.

Toward a Culture of Entitlement

Throughout its recent history Rwanda institutionalized ethnic discrimination by a small ruling class through command of the state apparatus, legislation, and public policies. Power has essentially meant the power to deny a subordinate group access to legitimate and equitable entitlements; conversely, power has also meant giving privileged access to a small group, while holding out the false expectation of access to a larger group identified through patronage or regional identity with the rulers.

Likewise, during the last hundred years both the ruling groups and the large subordinated majority have sought ideological support from the church, either for their position or for ways of contesting monopolies of political power and asymmetrical access to entitlements.[17] The asymmetry of entitlement in Rwanda has been least notable within the church.

But it is not enough for the church to establish within itself more equitable forms of entitlements, for example, to education. Through its social teaching and leadership, it must seek equal entitlements for society at large and lay bare to what extent it has failed to do so within the institution of the church itself. In a society in which ethnic identity and entitlement are equated, this cannot be achieved without radically challenging the nature of these identities. And this cannot be done by pretending that entrenched identities are not socially and politically operational. The church must have the courage in situations like Rwanda to challenge the givenness of ethnic boundaries and to imagine new identities with new contents and so redefine inculturation in terms of social justice.

This courage will come only after the trauma of recent events has passed and healing has occurred. That amounts to a task whose time-line will be greater than the three generations since the church's implantation in Rwanda. And it will require leadership with something other than a proven record of uncritical conformity. It is very difficult to see how the Rwandan Patriotic Front government can break out of the ethnically bound policies that have bedeviled Rwandan history. The RPF shows little sign of doing so as far as land ownership and housing are concerned, and any political will to do so may wane sharply with time in power. If the church points this out, it is likely once again to become a church of martyrs. But it cannot do otherwise.

Notes

[1] This is a revision of an article that first appeared in *The Month* (July 1995). Revised by permission of the author. The editors gratefully acknowledge the editorial assistance of Sister Janice McLaughlin, M.M.

[2] Ian Linden, *Church and Revolution in Rwanda* (Manchester: Manchester University Press, 1977).

[3] S. Katz, *The Holocaust in Historical Context*, Vol. 1: *The Holocaust and Mass Death before the Modern Age* (Oxford: Oxford University Press, 1994). A review in the *London Review of Books* by Malcolm Bull raises some interesting issues about the definition of genocide and its ideological use (February 1993, p. 23).

[4] "Rwanda: Death, Despair and Defiance," *African Rights* (1994), p. 79.

[5] Ibid., pp. 42-92.

[6] See Linden, pp. 220-40.

[7] I am indebted to Bethuel Kiplagat, former secretary of foreign relations of Kenya, for discussions on this matter. See also OXFAM's *Insight Rwanda* (1994), pp. 28-30.

[8] *The Observer*, July 3, 1994.

[9] "Rwanda," *African Rights*, pp. 522-23.

[10] Rev. Guy Theunis, W.F., discussions in Brussels, January 4-7, 1995.

[11] Conversations with mission personnel in Brussels, January 4-7, 1995.

[12] My discussions with a wide range of sources all gave identical accounts of the position of the archbishop.

[13] *France Catholique* 22452 (May 20, 1994), pp. 22-23; Jef Vleugels, June 16, 1994, letter to Brussels from White Fathers, Rwanda region.

[14] *The Tablet* 8029 (June 25, 1994), p. 791.

[15] Linden, pp. 254-55.

[16] Conversations with Monsignor Giuseppe Bertello, January 5, 1995.

[17] Raimo Vayrnyen, "Towards a Theory of Ethnic Conflicts and Their Resolution," 1994 Inaugural Lecture at the University of Notre Dame (Ind.).

5

The Christian Ministry of Reconciliation in Chile

JOSÉ ALDUNATE, S.J.

Chile is one of the Latin American countries that has suffered the most from social conflict, polarization, and violence. As a result it has been one most in need of reconciliation. In this chapter we will take a look at how reconciliation, the ministry conferred by Christ on the church, has been at work in this country.

The History of Conflict

First we will take a look at Chile with its history of division and conflict, so that we can then examine how the churches, especially the Catholic church, has tried to bring about reconciliation, sometimes successfully, sometimes not. We will then conclude with a global evaluation.

We begin our exposition with the events of the last three decades, from the time when Eduardo Frei (the father) took the reins of power (1964). The following table presents these decades:

Date	Government	Characteristics
1964-70	Eduardo Frei M.	Christian Democrats; moderate social reforms; increasing political polarization; opposition from the Right and the Left
1970-73	Salvador Allende	Leftist government proposing radical changes: a democratic path to socialism; opposition from the Right and the center
1973	Military revolt	Military junta takes all power; coup is supported by the Right and the United States

1973-90	Military government headed by Pinochet	Political dictatorship, economically neo-liberal; supported by the Right; Christian Democrats move to the opposition
1990-	Patricio Aylwin (1990-94)	Christian Democrat government with renewed socialists; tries to move toward authentic democracy, overcoming the obstacles left by the dictatorship; attempts to promote justice.
	Eduardo Frei Ruiz-Tagle (1994-)	

Clearly the causes of the hostility and violence unleashed during recent years are very old. They have their roots in the Conquest and the domination of the continent by Spain and Portugal: the usurpation of sovereignty, of the lands and liberty of the indigenous people; exploitation and genocide; a legacy of misery and poverty. Over the years the distance separating the rich and the poor has grown, producing tension and violence.

In Chile ever since the beginning of this century there have been labor struggles in the nitrate fields and the mines of the north, which eventually fell under the direction of the Marxist parties. These and other social struggles soon extended into the political field, bringing about new parties and strong confrontations. The 1960s, under the influence of revolutionary Cuba, culminated with extreme political and ideological polarization.

In 1973 the dikes of the Constitution and the laws of democracy were breached. The military rose up and took power. The repressive violence of the dictatorship was loosed against its opponents; this, in turn, gave birth to the violence of the resistance. Even if there has recently been a turn toward democracy, the wounds still remain.

Chile has certainly suffered and continues to suffer from discord and enmity. Its wounds are rooted in the extreme poverty of vast sectors of the population; they are expressed in the political tensions that have arisen. Their impact is felt most vividly in the crimes perpetrated by a cruel dictatorship. This pain is expressed in three different dimensions.

The chronic poverty experienced by a great part of our population increased during the dictatorship so that, under the dictatorship, the "poor" increased from two to five million, some 40 percent of the population. The gap between rich and poor widened during the same period: in 1969 the poorest 20 percent of the population received 7.6 percent of the income and the richest 20 percent received 44.5 percent. By 1989, the poorest 20 percent received 4.6 percent as opposed to the 59.5 percent that went to the richest 20 percent of the population.

At the same time, political tension has been a characteristic expression of social tension, itself a product of the poverty. This has been expressed, on rare occasions, by the violence of revolutions against the country's leadership.

The military coup of 1973 was a very violent rupture of the democratic tradition. However, more serious yet were the grave violations of human rights for which the military authorities bear responsibility. The Rettig Report counted

2,279 unjustifiable deaths, the majority of that were executions or disappearances. The real figures are higher. Torture became an everyday occurrence, employed in the interrogations which frequently ended with the victims' deaths. On other occasions it was used to spread terror. As a result, hundreds of thousands of exiles and refugees fled the country, and for the most part, they stayed away for a long time.

To make matters worse, the authors of these abuses, almost all members of the Armed Forces, enjoy impunity. Nor has any help been given to the families of the disappeared in finding the bodies of their loved ones or learning their fate.

This leaves the country with a double injustice that causes tensions and enmity:
- the injustice of persistent poverty, even though the country has gone through a period of economic progress. In Chile a neo-liberal economic system prevails which tends to maintain poverty without eliminating or diminishing the distance between rich and poor.
- the injustice of not dealing with the human rights violations perpetrated by the Pinochet dictatorship. This has left many open sores.

It is here that the problem of reconciliation inserts itself. How does reconciliation work when unjust situations are at the bottom of the enmity and division? Can we overlook this situation, speaking only of the pacification of the spirit? Can the church ask for pardon from some without demanding reparation from others?

For this question we have the answer in the gospel: "So then, if you are bringing your offering to the altar and there remember that your brother has something against you, leave your offering there before the altar, go and be reconciled with your brother first, and then come back and present your offering" (Mt 5:23-24). One condition of reconciliation with God is reparation for offenses and injustices committed against one's neighbor.

The gospel strongly demands that Christians learn how to forgive and that they forgive effectively and always (Mt 6:12; 18:21-24). However, this forgiveness does not mean that Christians have to renounce reparations or the seeking of sanctions from the law; it means rather that they are called upon to include the offender or enemy in their love, that they do away with all hatred.

The church in its proclamation of reconciliation is accustomed to speaking out forcefully against hatred. Affective hatred, which often continues in the heart of the offended person, is to be discarded along with the rage against the offender, that is to say, the objective offense or the injustice caused by the offender's action. The transgressor must acknowledge his or her sin and make reparations for it as much as possible in order to enter into a relationship of love. The church, if it wishes to rescue transgressors for God and the community, must concern itself with this reparation and not leave them in their sin.

If we turn now to the national level, it is clear that if a state of law is to rule, crime must be punished and there must be equal justice for all. The institution of amnesty does exist, but it is up to the civil authority to decide whether the conditions exist to apply it in the name of the common good. In any case, there cannot be an amnesty declared by the guilty parties themselves. The military government passed a decree of self-amnesty in 1978. This is a moral aberration. The decree has not as yet been abolished, and its juridic effects constitute a major impediment to the application of justice.

In terms of reconciliation in matters of injustice and human rights violations there has been a lack of ethical and theological discernment on the part of certain leaders of our churches. Some of them have kept a guilty silence in the face of great crimes perpetrated by the constituted authorities. But the purpose of these pages is to be positive and to recount the exemplary acts of reconciliation that have occurred in this country.

Acts of Reconciliation by the Chilean Church

Socio-Economic Inequality and the Agrarian Reform

During the 1960s social tension, caused by inequality, increased throughout Latin America. Between 40 percent and 50 percent of the population was *poor* in the technical sense of the word and because of that suffered from hunger. Poverty and marginalization were even more widespread among the *campesinos*.

In rural Chile, according to the 1955 census, ten thousand large farms (haciendas) occupied 81.2 percent of arable land. On the other hand, some fifteen thousand family and sub-family holdings covered scarcely 7.4 percent of the land.[1] There was also the mass of tenant farmers who worked the fields of the land barons without owning even a square meter of property or the house they lived in.

The notion of agrarian reform was in the air, promoted by Marxist thought and the church's own social teaching. But this notion touched a raw nerve on the part of the Right, Catholics for the most part, which produced blind opposition. Bishops Manuel Larrain of Talca and Raul Silva of Santiago decided to proceed with the reform, dividing some church lands among small landholders and tenant farmers. This gesture, begun in mid-1962, caused a great stir and was imitated by other bishops and religious congregations.

National Agrarian Reform took root during the Frei administration and was strengthened under Salvador Allende. The bishops, through their joint statements, went to great pains to educate Catholics about the necessity of these changes demanded by justice and equity. It was justice for the landless tenants who for generations had been denied a fair recompense for their work. And it was equity for a whole social class: the *campesinos* received a just share in the ownership of the land that had been created by God for the benefit of all. So, in this way, a decisive step was taken toward reconciliation.

It is true that, at the time, the Agrarian Reform, for a thousand different reasons, was a source of scandal that soured the minds of many traditional

Catholics. But in the long run the church's action has remained as a sign that only through the road of justice and equity can we arrive at social peace. "We must kill hatred before hatred kills Chile" (Cardinal Silva).

We have talked about the end of the 1960s and the time of the Popular Unity Party (Unidad Popular, 1970-73), mentioning that it was a time of increasing political polarization giving way to hatred and violence. This development calls for a careful analysis: if we return to the Agrarian Reform, we will understand the character of this polarization. The Agrarian Reform had left a profound resentment among many of the land barons. Many felt that they had been unjustly wounded, and they thought only of reclaiming their lands, even if doing so meant violence. A growing number of them began to incite the Armed Forces to stage a coup d'état. Generally speaking, those privileged by the dominant system had not resigned themselves to the radical changes of the Popular Unity government, even though the changes were fundamentally just, and they decided to destabilize the regime.

This interpretation lays the responsibility for the hatred and violence principally on the most privileged, those situated on the economic and political Right. This was hard to accept by many Christian groups and members of the hierarchy, who thought that the violence should be attributed principally to sectors of the Marxist Left, which promoted class struggle. This prejudice was very deep-rooted and was the reason for the alarm caused by the triumph of the Popular Unity Party in September 1970. Yet the unwillingness to coexist with this regime dissipated during the following years, at least on the part of the church's hierarchy. This is seen in the pastoral letters of the hierarchy, many signed by the Permanent Committee of the Bishops, which expressed great alarm at the political tension and the climate of confrontation, but which also admitted the need for profound social changes. Together with a call for cooling passions, the letters urged the well-off to make sacrifices on the altar of justice and equality. But apart from this, the church did express great concern about the path many sectors of the government were taking.

The ecclesiastical documents from the end of the 1960s and the three years of the Popular Unity government testify to the church's efforts at reconciling the opposing forces. Unfortunately, they did not achieve their objective or manage to avoid the worst. The church's efforts were neither understood nor accepted by either side of the conflict. The largely Catholic Right rejected any social doctrine of the church that urged it to become involved in socio-economic matters. And the socialist and communist Left distrusted the church, felt distant from it, and did not pay attention to its appeals for moderation and respect. A group of priests and laity, which called itself Christians for Socialism, breached the wall of distrust on the part of the Left and the Popular Unity government, but they became too political, lost prestige, and created unnecessary divisions in the church.

A wide variety of documents testify to the church's prophetic word in support of reconciliation. We will note a few examples from the most critical years of 1972 and 1973[2]:

October 1972   "We Seek a Constructive and Fraternal Spirit."
December 1972   "Peace Is Possible."
February 1973   "Love One Another as I Have Loved You" (at the interna-
                tional Eucharistic Congress in Melbourne).
Easter 1973   "Feast of the Resurrection—Message of Resurrection."
June 1973   "Only with Love Can One Build a Country."
16 July 1973   "Peace for Chile Carries a Price" (Feast of Carmen).

Reconciliation under the Military Dictatorship

The military coup d'état on September 11, 1973, entirely changed the situation. Political polarization was succeeded by repressive polarization between
those who participated in or supported the coup with violence and those who
either suffered the violence directly or who opposed it.

The coup itself was hard and cruel. President Salvador Allende, who pre-
ferred death to abandoning the presidency, died. What followed the coup was
even more unjust and cruel. An arbitrary repression occurred that held no
respect for prisoners, tortured, shot people without trial, and caused disappearances. We have already referred to these crimes.

The first duty of the church was to oppose this violence. The second was to
reconcile the victims with their executioners. This meant a return to justice
and the law. Much of this huge task is left to be completed. The wounds are
very deep, and they have been festering for decades. They cannot be healed
by soothing words or the passage of time. Five acts of reconciliation merit a
brief commentary.

Letter from the Bishops to the Head of the Military Junta
concerning the Coup d'Etat

On September 13, two days after the coup, when Augusto Pinochet had already overcome all resistance in the country, he was sent a declaration of the
Permanent Committee of the Episcopacy on "The Situation of the Country."
This must have caused him profound displeasure since he was hoping that the
church would support, even rejoice, at what the military had done. We repro-
duce the entire document, complete with unfulfilled wishes and hopes:

1. Let the country be aware that we, the bishops, have done as much
as we could so that Chile would remain under the rule of the Constitution and the Law and avoid the violence that our institutional crisis has
experienced. This violence the members of the Junta Government have
been the first to lament.

2. We are in anguish because of the blood which has reddened our
streets, towns and factories—the blood of civilians and of soldiers—
and of the tears of so many women and children.

3. We ask for moderation in respect to those who have been defeated;
that there be no unnecessary reprisals; that the sincere idealism which

inspired many of them be taken into account; that hatred come to an end and the time of reconciliation arrive.

4. We ask for respect toward those who fell in battle, beginning with him who was President of the Republic until September 11.

5. We are confident that the labor rights which have been won by the working and campesino class not be revoked, but rather, be maintained and even increased until full equality and the participation of all in the life of the country is reached.

6. Trusting in the patriotism and lack of self-interest of those who have assumed the difficult task of restoring the institutional order and economic life of the country, so badly disturbed, we ask that, given the actual circumstances, Chileans cooperate to the last in dealing with this task. Above all, it is with humility and fervor that we ask God's help.

7. The prudence and patriotism of Chileans, together with the tradition of democracy and the humanitarianism of our Armed Forces, will allow Chile to return very quickly to institutional normalcy, as has been promised by the members of the Junta Government, and to take again the road to peace.[3]

The Vicariate of Solidarity

A Peace Committee, followed by the Vicariate of Solidarity, were the institutional answers of the churches to the cruel and criminal situation imposed by the regime against its adversaries. The Catholic church through Cardinal Raul Silva Henriquez, the Lutheran church through Bishop Helmut Frens, and the Jewish community through its rabbi, all participated in the Peace Committee.

The idea was to create an institution that would support victims in the legal defense of their rights, especially through "Appeals to Protection," "Habeas Corpus," and other legal resources in favor of the assassinated, kidnapped, and disappeared.

These judicial actions, which sought to bring about justice, were condemned to failure. Although the military government from the very beginning promised to respect the judiciary, the latter submitted servilely to the junta, supporting its procedures. Thus "Habeas Corpus" lost all its efficacy as a defense against abuses of power. Nevertheless, these legal actions did constitute a protest and legal evidence.

The Vicariate of Solidarity, since it was a church institution, enjoyed a certain immunity, and its pronouncements carried a great deal of authority on the international level as well as in Chile. The Vicariate became a watchdog that denounced the abusive acts of the regime, which the latter wanted to keep hidden.

Since our theme is reconciliation, we must ask whether and in what way these actions in support of justice and truth can be qualified as a work of reconciliation. Reconciliation in the true sense takes place when victims and transgressors come together in justice to repair the injustices. If the transgressor offers just compensation and the victim accepts it, thereby rooting up vengeance and hatred (this can include pardon where the reparations have been remitted), then the opponents are reconciled with justice, with God, and with each other.

Later, after 1990, the arrival of democracy permitted better opportunities to get to the truth about what had happened. The archives of the Vicariate of Solidarity helped the Commission for Truth and Reconciliation, the so-called Rettig Commission, draw up a report. This report gives an account of the graver crimes committed by the military regime. It was done with such care and prudence that it elicited the consent of many who were in favor of the Armed Forces and the coup. It even elicited the respect of the injured parties who were seeking not only the truth but also justice. The Rettig Report has certainly been an important step on the long road to reconciliation.

An Initiative in the Political Field
Bishop Francisco Fresno succeeded Cardinal Raul Silva as archbishop of Santiago. The 1980 Constitution promulgated by the military regime foresaw a transition to democracy and elections. It was hoped that in 1988 General Pinochet would be a candidate and, if triumphant, would govern another eight years. Sectors on the Left began a protest campaign, and certain resistance groups even prepared armed activities (in 1986 there was an attempt on Pinochet's life). In this situation Bishop Fresno took the initiative in a political fashion that was unusual both for the church and for a bishop not known for his political involvement. He called together the leaders of the various political parties that had been reestablished by the Constitution and spoke with them about working together to prepare Chile for the coming of democracy. The parties of the Right, which wanted to keep Pinochet in power, and the Communist Party were excluded—for reasons of principle and tactics. It was clear by then that the Communist Party after 1980 was turning to violence, something that was new for Chilean communism.

The conversations starting at the beginning of 1985 were successful. In July/August of that year a document called "The National Agreement for the Transition to Full Democracy" was published. The introductory paragraph well demonstrates its tone.

> As a contribution to the call for National Reconciliation, made by His Eminence the Cardinal Archbishop of Santiago, and as evidence of the disposition of many sectors of the country for a National Agreement that will assure the peaceful evolution toward a full and authentic democracy, all who subscribe to this document express their support of the political, economic, and social principles it enunciates.

This agreement received much publicity but was rejected by the military government. However, it was an initiative that was to succeed later when, in preparation for the 1988 plebiscite, a coalition was formed with a wide range of parties. It was this coalition that triumphed over Pinochet and brought Patricio Aylwin to the presidency.

Sectors on the extreme Left, which had been looking toward the violent overthrow of the dictatorship—in our opinion, a great illusion—objected to this church initiative. We, on the other hand, think that it was a reconciling gesture.

The Sebastian Acevedo Movement against Torture

A movement of active nonviolence arose in 1983, during the time of greatest violence and repression. The police at that time resorted to torture to intimidate a population that had begun to react against the prolongation of the dictatorial regime. This movement differed from the preceding initiatives in that it arose out of the base communities and their pastoral workers, priests, and religious. Some bishops, who were not accustomed to seeing their priests and religious protesting in the streets or being detained in police stations, had difficulty accepting the movement.

The movement sought to awaken public opinion, the ordinary people on the streets, the news media, and the church itself in regard to the unspeakable acts of torture common in Chile at that time. The practice of torture, together with that of making people disappear, were perhaps the most characteristic features of the repression in Chile. Torture created fear and intimidation. One did not talk about it. First it created an atmosphere of silence, then of acquiescence. It was imperative for a group of Christians to demonstrate in the streets in front of the buildings where torture was practiced, defying fear and showing that torture must not be tolerated.

In response, the church, in the person of its communities, ministers, and leaders, suffered repression, blows, tear gas, prison, and exile. These were offered on the altar of solidarity with the victims of torture.

The movement mobilized hundreds of participants. It acted 180 times in its seven years (among the dictatorship's most cruel) and received international awards. Its greatest merit was the affirmation that human beings are untouchable in their fundamental rights and that only on this foundation can one construct a democratic consensus. The movement thus complemented what the Vicariate for Peace was doing, making more credible the commitment of the church to human rights and raising the flag that was at the same time a flag of convocation for all Christians and of reconciliation for all citizens, whatever their political differences.

A Projected Meeting

Juan Luis Ysern was bishop of Calama, a city in northern Chile, situated in the desert near the country's largest copper mine, Chuquicamata. When the coup took place, the military governor, as a precaution, imprisoned the authorities and bureaucrats of the previous government. There had not been any conflict or violence in the zone despite it being a labor center of some importance. On October 19, 1973, a military mission that would later be called the Caravan of Death arrived by helicopter. It came to visit the various jails and to execute people and instill fear. It was directed by General Arellano Stark. In

Calama it accomplished its mission: while General Arellano conferred with the governor and visited Chuquicamata, his companions "by higher orders" arbitrarily chose twenty-six prisoners and without further ado killed them. The execution was accomplished with incredible ferocity; the victims were not only shot but also cut open with knives. Their bodies were not returned but were buried in a nitrous bed in a secret place and later blown up with dynamite to remove all evidence.

This criminal action remained unpunished. The complaints brought before the courts were, like so many others, passed on to the military courts and simply suppressed. General Stark, a professed Catholic, denied any responsibility. Unbelievable as it sounds, he pretended not to have known about the killings. In response, Bishop Ysern proposed bringing together the presumed transgressors and the families of the victims to create a human space for listening, admitting faults, understanding, and pardoning. Bishop Ysern received the agreement of all involved, but at the last moment the meeting was called off because the soldiers refused to attend.

Yet Bishop Ysern's initiative appears to many of us to be quite valid. The ministry of reconciliation conferred by Christ upon his church cannot be reduced to the administration of a sacrament, but rather takes many forms.

It also seems symptomatic that the obstacle in this case arose from the military. In Chile the major impediment to reconciliation lies with the military leaders who contemptuously refuse to acknowledge their faults and to offer restitution.

Epilogue: Reconciliation Still to Be Accomplished

Despite some successful advances in which the church has played a part, Christians must face the fact that in Chile the important task of reconciliation still remains largely unfulfilled.

The reconciliation between rich and poor has been left unresolved. It will not be attained through facile preaching but only through basic economic changes infused with a spirit of justice. Also unfulfilled is the reconciliation of political activists. This does not demand a common program, but it calls for a *metanoia* through adherence to democracy and service to the common good. Reconciliation needs to move forward among groups of people who are still imbued with ideologies. They must learn to acknowledge the human dignity of those they have injured, make restitution, offer forgiveness, and accept that no one is deserving of hate or ought to be excluded from fraternal coexistence.

We would like to see our churches, which on occasion have motivated fanaticism and violence, turn to these challenges by going beyond the restricted world of parishes and sacraments. They have been called by Vatican Council II to defend and promote human dignity in a new world that is entering the third millennium. As we have seen, they have already been active in this field.

We look forward to the day when, as churches of reconciliation, they will be able to more fully participate in this work for the salvation of the world.

—Translated by Ernest Schibli

Notes

[1] *Memoirs of Cardinal Raul Silva*, I, p. 243 ff.
[2] See *Documentos del Episcopado de Chile, 1970-73*.
[3] Ibid., document 62.

Recommended Reading

Pamela Lowden. *Moral Opposition to Authoritanian Rule in Chile, 1973-90*. New York: St. Martin's Press, 1996.

William H. Swatos, ed. *Religion and Democracy in Latin America*. New Bruswick, N.Y.: Transaction Publisher, 1995.

6

The Tozanso Process

Ecumenical Efforts for Korean Reconciliation and Reunification

ERICH WEINGARTNER

Most historians have already written the Cold War into the past tense. The collapse of communist regimes in Eastern Europe, the reunification of Germany, and the dissolution of the Soviet Union seem ample proof that the bi-polar world of the past half century has come to an end. In one corner of the globe, however, the anachronism of division persists unabated, a stark reminder that the twentieth century's major ideological conflict continues to persecute its victims.

The insanity of the divided world we have lived in for half a century is nowhere more apparent than at the thin line that runs through the middle of four pale-blue barracks in a place called Panmunjom. Almost invisible, this line continues to be the world's most impenetrable. It separates two systems, two ideologies, two world views. It fortifies two governments and justifies two of the world's largest military machines. It divides a people who have shared the same culture, language, and history for thousands of years.

Few have crossed this line in either direction and lived to tell about it. For fifty years, all communication has been severed. Neither electric wires nor telephone cables connect the two sides. Radio and television broadcasts are jammed both ways. Highways that were once bustling with traffic are overgrown with weeds. Tall trees decorate rusting railway links. Large, ominous signs warn would-be trespassers of mines.

The pale-blue structures house offices and meeting rooms used by the guardians of an uneasy truce that has held for more than four decades. The line bisecting the central conference table is the military demarcation line, which extends through a four-kilometer-wide strip of land known as the DMZ, the demilitarized zone that extends across the entire Korean peninsula at the 38th parallel.

Panmunjom, the place where this "Joint Security Area" is located, has been deceptively misnamed "Peace Village." It is not peace that is maintained here. The Korean War, having claimed millions of lives between 1950 and 1953, was frozen in time with the signing of an armistice agreement, a cessation of hostilities. Technically the war never ended. The military of the Democratic People's Republic of Korea (DPRK) on the northern side, and the United States, under the flag of the United Nations Command on the southern perimeter, are still at war, content in the conviction that the price of security is readiness to resort to arms, and that justice is irrelevant to peace.

For the sake of this false peace, sixty million Koreans continue to long for genuine democratic freedom. In the name of security, ten million Koreans are prevented from knowing the fate of mothers, fathers, husbands, wives, sisters, brothers, from whom they have been separated for close to fifty years.

Although the pain of this tragedy is borne primarily by Koreans, the illness which caused it is global. Korea has been the victim of geopolitical greed and manipulation since the nineteenth century. The United States, Russia, China, and Japan not only share the guilt but continue to benefit from Korea's division.

Socio-pathological research confirms that individuals often manifest psychological or psychosomatic disorders whose causes are in fact communal. Successful treatment often necessitates the healing of the entire family group or a change in the patient's social environment. It is quite common, moreover, that families resist therapy to the point of withdrawing patients from therapy when healing begins to take place. The illness of the individual, it would seem, absorbs the family group's pathology, allowing the group to function in apparent health.

Korea has served this function for the world community, whose trauma, stemming from two "hot" wars followed by the nuclear terror of a Cold War, has never been truly healed. The division of Korea is the incarnation of a divided world. The two parts of Korea embody the best and the worst of the twentieth century's social, political, and economic systems.

World Council of Churches Initiatives

When the World Council of Churches embarked on its mission of reconciliation—originally a modest attempt to seek lines of communication between North and South Korea—that act in itself challenged the sanity of the bi-polar world that had brought about Korea's rupture. Opening lines of communication with an isolated North Korea meant suspending judgment and accepting responsibility. And the WCC bore a special responsibility. Its support for the United Nations action during the Korean War had led to the forced withdrawal of Chinese churches from WCC membership.

I have the dubious privilege of being one of the few mortals to have seen the suture line of Panmunjom from both sides, guest each time of respective government agents.

The first time was in 1980. My colleague Victor Hsu and I were negotiating with the South Korean government for permission to send a high-profile WCC delegation to Korean churches during a period of strict martial law in the wake of General Chun Doo Hwan's coup d'état and the Kwangju massacre. One of the conditions imposed for our visit was an educational trip to the DMZ to learn firsthand about "the dangers of an invasion by communist troops from the North."

The surrealistic exercise to which we were subjected would have been more entertaining had we not known that this morose display of paranoia was backed by the nuclear arsenals of both superpowers. So we sat in morbid fascination—the two of us alone in a theater built for five hundred—as a South Korean military officer lectured us on the need for vigilant anticommunism. We allowed ourselves to be led, wearing standard issue military helmets, down a narrow corridor into the mountain's interior to view one of the tunnels allegedly dug by North Korea to invade the South. We mingled with a group of noisy Italian tourists, guided by a young American soldier whose memorized dialogue might have been written by horror movie script writers. By the time we reached the Joint Security Area of Panmunjom, to stare at and take photos of North Korean soldiers, the tourists were so frightened they spoke in whispers. In strict obedience to instructions, they avoided gesticulating lest they inadvertently "create an excuse for an incident."

What was indeed frightening and not in the least amusing was the realization that this theater of the absurd was being played out in such deadly earnest by youngsters who had not even been born at the time of the Korean War. It took an act of conscious determination to keep in mind that we were standing at one of the most dangerous spots on the earth—the hair trigger, quite possibly, of a global conflagration.

I had been aware of a vivid debate among South Korean peace and human rights activists regarding priorities for their actions. One faction held that democratization would have to be achieved in the South before Korea could be reunified. Others insisted that only after reunification could both parts of the country be democratized. At Panmunjom the South Korean government inadvertently convinced me that it is not possible to have the one without the other. Peace and justice are inseparable and must be worked for together.

Exactly five years passed before I returned to Panmunjom from the northern side, this time with my colleague Ninan Koshy. We were the first WCC delegation to visit North Korea. We were also the first delegation to do so in the name of South Korean churches.

Here too we heard lectures in empty theaters, saw films and photographs describing the same history, the same incidents. The only difference was that the good and the bad, the heroes and the villains, were presented in mirror-image reversal.

Instead of a tour inside a tunnel, we were taken to a hillside overlooking the DMZ. Through a pair of binoculars we were able to see a barrier whose dimensions dwarf those of the infamous Berlin wall. The United States constructed it as a bulwark against invasion from the north. It is the largest rein-forced concrete structure ever built. Ten meters high and five meters thick at the base, it stretches more than two hundred kilometers across the Korean peninsula. Even fish and animals are denied passage between north and south. All for the sake of security,

By the time we came to the same pale-blue barracks, I felt like Alice in Wonderland, looking out from inside the mirror. Just as we arrived on the balcony of the North Korean building, a sightseeing bus was disgorging tour-ists on the southern side. I would have loved to hear the American soldier's explanation of our presence.

What brought me to Panmunjom this second time was the first leg of what in ecumenical circles has come to be called the Tozanso Process. At the end of October 1984, the YMCA retreat center at Tozanso (a small town near Tokyo) served as venue for an extraordinary meeting. It was here that top-level repre-sentatives of the WCC's member churches in the Republic of (South) Korea first encouraged the Commission of the Churches on International Affairs to forge contacts with North Korean Christians.

To anyone unfamiliar with the Korean trauma, this may seem mundane. From the very beginning of Germany's division churches had uninterrupted and intense East-West contact. The case of Korea is quite different. The vast majority of Korean Christians fled south before and during the Korean War. Decades of intensive anticommunist propaganda, combined with a total infor-mation blackout about life in North Korea, led to the broadly held conviction that Christianity had effectively disappeared on the northern part of the pen-insula.

Stories about the existence of a worshiping community in the DPRK—meeting in private homes, much like the Chinese "house churches"—were met with extreme skepticism. Expatriate Korean Christians and pastors who visited the North were regarded as dupes of communism.

One such pastor visited my office at the WCC and offered to write a report of his visit to the North. I gratefully, if naively, accepted. Swift and emotional reactions caught me by surprise. South Korean ecumenical friends accused me of conspiracy and collaboration with the enemy. I learned quickly that even the smallest step taken by the WCC with regard to North Korea impli-cated nervous South Korean member churches and therefore required intimate dialogue and acquiescence.

The danger of North-South initiatives for churches in the South was clear. Under South Korea's National Security Law, punishment for contact with the North continues to be draconian. Meetings on the theme of reunification—for example, those planned by the National Council of Churches in Korea (NCCK)—were consistently blocked by police action. Christian teachers who merely discussed reunification proposals with their students were arrested and severely tortured.

Church leaders told government officials that if South Koreans continue to be barred from discussing reunification inside Korea, organizations such as the WCC could not be prevented from convening meetings outside. Korean churches could not, of course, make this an official request. The WCC would have to "go it alone" and take full responsibility for the outcome.

Since the purpose was to begin a process of open dialogue, we had to convince both Korean governments to see the WCC's initiative in a positive light. We had to be reasonably sure that Korean church leaders could participate without fear of reprisal.

Dealing with Korean officialdom, South or North, is the stuff of spy novels. Example: A luncheon encounter in a private suite on the fifteenth floor of one of Seoul's many luxury hotels. Plainclothes guards check us over in the hallway. The man who welcomes us declines to give his name or rank, though we understand he is second-in-command of the disreputable Korean Central Intelligence Agency. It is the spring of 1984. Victor Hsu and I had asked for the meeting, ostensibly to seek protection for WCC General Secretary Philip Potter's high-profile visit to Korea.

"This meeting," the man said with a friendly smile, "does not exist. Any reports of it outside this room will be categorically denied by every agency of my government."

Having been assured that the General Secretary's well-being is in the interest of the Korean government, we "rewarded" our host with advance warning of plans to hold an international ecumenical consultation in Tozanso. The topic would be "Peace and Justice in North-East Asia: Prospects for Peaceful Resolution of Conflicts." We explained that though the context is the wider region and participation global, Korea's division would be a central concern. Apart from South Korean member churches, representatives of the North Korean Christians Federation (KCF), as well as churches in China, Hong Kong, and Taiwan, would be invited. We suggested that the South Korean government could avoid international embarrassment by allowing its church leaders to attend.

Since the luncheon "never happened," we could not have received assurances that church leaders would be given exit visas to come to Tozanso. Nor could we communicate these assurances to the invitees. Suffice it to say that the highest officials of each WCC member church and of the NCCK did attend. This was a key factor in the success not only of the meeting, but of the even more spectacular follow-up.

The consultation that gave birth to the Tozanso Process was the most tension-filled event of my WCC experience. Korean participants were extremely nervous, illustrated by a conflict among themselves that left the rest of us in puzzlement.

Unable to send a delegation, the North Korean KCF had transmitted a cable of greetings to the consultation. The fact that this cable arrived through the mediation of a pro-North political group in Japan caused an emotional debate over whether it should even be mentioned, let alone reproduced, in the final report. So great were suspicions that the routing of the message was enough proof to some that the KCF was a communist front organization.

Those of us responsible for drafting the concluding document decided that the time was not ripe to make any mention whatever of initiatives relating to North Korea. We began to consider the implications of a failed meeting.

During the final plenary, the Korean church leaders themselves achieved the breakthrough. They insisted on the inclusion of operative paragraphs relating to contacts with North Korea. Laconically worded—though breathtaking in its implications—was the following sentence: "The WCC, in collaboration with the CCA [Christian Conference of Asia] [should] seek to facilitate opportunities where it would be possible for Christians from both North and South Korea to meet in dialogue."

The Tozanso Process

As we celebrated the successful conclusion of the consultation that evening, I could not have guessed that the name Tozanso would soon be inscribed in Korean church history—on both sides of the military demarcation line—as a symbol of openness, dialogue, conversion, hope, healing, and reconciliation.

Christians in North Korea, as we discovered when we made our first visit there, had waited prayerfully for news from Tozanso and had welcomed with relief and thanksgiving the results. They felt that their severe isolation finally had been broken. It was their acceptance of the Tozanso conclusions that has made possible the Tozanso Process.

Repeatedly over the decade since Tozanso, barriers have been overcome, doors have been opened, and, as a result, misunderstandings have been removed. A series of "firsts" have been added to historical chronologies. Each breakthrough was an emotional highlight, not only for Koreans, but for all of us in the ecumenical community who have had the privilege of sharing their joy.

Exactly a year later (November 1985), after a period of negotiation with North Korean government officials and constant communication with the South Korean embassy, Ninan Koshy and I visited the DPRK. We established the first direct contact with the KCF and worshiped with local Christians in a house church. We brought gifts of bibles and hymnbooks from the NCCK and expressed their desire for a face-to-face dialogue.

Two years after Tozanso (September 1986), the dream of a direct encounter between North and South Koreans became a reality at a CCIA-sponsored meeting in Glion, Switzerland. The meeting was camouflaged as a worldwide gathering around a general biblical subject. To this day, South Korea's National Security Law prohibits its citizens from contact with the North. For the North, too, this fiction helped to expedite agreement to participate in an event of unknown international repercussions.

Glion 1, as it came to be called, began with fear and trembling. Each side tested the other, openly confessing mistrust. Both were keenly aware that they would have to account for their words and deeds back home. At the conclusion, it was the celebration of the Eucharist—that powerful symbol of the unity of all children of God—which broke down the invisible walls of separation that have tormented the Korean nation for too long. Participants, North and South, dissolved into tears and embraces. The Tozanso Process began to take root.

Three years after Tozanso (November 1987), a second, larger CCIA/WCC delegation visited North and South Korea. Part of its mandate was to discuss the contents of an eventual WCC statement on reunification. In South Korea, the delegates were able to report to a larger audience about the life of Christians in the North. Government spokespersons whom they saw continued to insist that the WCC was being duped by North Korean government agents.

Four years after Tozanso (November 1988), Glion 2 was held, this time expanded to include women from both parts of Korea. The two delegations agreed on a common "Glion Declaration on Peace and the Reunification of Korea." Among its recommendations was a decision to observe 1995 as the Year of Jubilee for Unification and to designate the Sunday before August 15 each year as a common day of prayer for peace. To this end, a common prayer text was adopted. For the first time since division, Christians throughout the Korean peninsula would use the same liturgical element on the same Sunday.

Five years after Tozanso (July 1989), the WCC Central Committee issued a policy statement on peace and the reunification of Korea, committing the worldwide ecumenical community to the search for peace and justice in Korea. For the first time, a North Korean delegation attended as observers.

Six years after Tozanso (December 1990), Glion 3 was held; its purpose was to prepare a five-year plan for the "Jubilee Year of Peace and Reunification of Korea." It called for a broadening of contacts and exchanges between North and South, involving a greater number of people from both sides. To this end, delegates agreed that future meetings in the Glion series should be held on the Korean peninsula, first in Pyongyang, then in Seoul.

Seven years after Tozanso (February 1991), a KCF delegation for the first time attended a World Council of Churches Assembly in Canberra, Australia.

Other ecumenical partners meanwhile played their own part in following up Tozanso. Most important in this respect (considering the crucial role of the United States in Korea's predicament) have been the activities of the National Council of the Churches of Christ in the United States. Delegations visited both parts of Korea in 1986 and 1987. A policy statement was adopted and a campaign launched to encourage the U.S. government toward a comprehensive peace settlement in Korea. In 1989 a KCF delegation was hosted by the NCCCUSA, the first time since the war that members of a North Korean group were granted visas to visit the United States.

Church delegations from other countries have visited the DPRK. A Canadian delegation visited North Korea in 1988, and a KCF delegation visited Canada in 1991. Churches in Europe have created an Ecumenical Network on Korea. In 1989 a KCF delegation attended the German "Kirchentag" in Berlin/West.

Within Korea the NCCK organized a Jubilee Preparation Committee for Peace and Reunification, with a membership of forty-six South Korean denominations. It issued a courageous "Declaration of the Churches of Korea on National Reunification and Peace" in February 1988. In April 1988 a major international consultation was convened in Inchon, the first such event to deal openly and publicly with this question. Since then there have been yearly conferences, attracting as many as three hundred fifty participants from a dozen countries, including numerous overseas Koreans. The NCCK invited the KCF to attend its 1990 Assembly in Seoul, but obstructive demands by both governments prevented attendance.

The South Korean government continued its opposition to informal contacts with the North. In 1989 Rev. Moon Ik-Hwan, Ms. Im Su-Kyong, and Fr. Moon Kyu-Hyon made unauthorized visits to North Korea and were imprisoned under the National Security Law when they returned to the South. In 1990 Rev. Cho Yong-Seul, Rev. Yi Hae-Hak, and Cho Sung-Woo were arrested on their return from a meeting in Berlin, where they met with North Koreans. In February 1991 Rev. Hong Keun-Soo was arrested for "praising" North Korea in his sermons.

Christians in North Korea meanwhile gained political importance and influence. Alongside the KCF, which has existed since 1946, a Korean Catholic Association was formed in 1988. In the same year, two churches (Protestant and Roman Catholic) were consecrated, the first to be built since the DPRK was created in 1948. A year later a second Protestant church was under construction in Pyongyang.

Signs of Uncertainty

Not all observers of the Tozanso Process are convinced that progress has been genuine. Skeptics both inside and outside Korea are numerous and influential. When the KCF delegation visited the USA, dissenting Korean-American pastors protested, demonstrated, and collected thousands of signatures to oppose NCCCUSA plans. Analysts are quick to point out that North Korea is using Christian channels to create a positive image for the sake of attracting Western business and technology. Doubters have been eager to put North Korean Christians through a test of faith, to the absurd extreme of inspecting whether they pray before meals.

Thankfully, the Tozanso Process does not depend on the certification of true believers. Were that the case, there would be little hope of reconciliation. Reconciliation is a two-way street, as the NCCK recognized in its 1988 declaration, which includes a "Confession of the Sin of Hatred within Division." Reconciliation is a process of confidence-building, of tearing down fabricated enemy images, of daring to love—and to trust that God can manage the final judgment without our help.

The ecumenical family has contributed to the unraveling of the rationale for the division of Korea. But this may well produce more distress in the short term. The realization that healing is possible includes the devastating awareness that long years of suffering could have been avoided.

My wife's *Pocket Medical Dictionary* defines mental health in part as the ability to form lasting, intimate, interpersonal relationships. This may be relevant to the experience of Korea's pain. But the re-establishment of relationships between North and South cannot be a matter of indifference to the rest of the world.

In *The Voice of Illness* Finnish-Canadian theologian Aarne Siirala shows that the illness of an individual is a message to the community as a whole. The way in which the community deals with illness constitutes a choice between true and false prophecy. The ecumenical community's involvement in Korea's reunification is not an exercise in altruism. It is the prophetic acknowledgment that reconciliation is the key to curing our global schizophrenia.

That cure unfortunately remains elusive. The simplistic dualism of the Cold War has vanished, revealing a world whose conflicts are much more complex than heretofore imagined. Nostalgia for a clearly defined enemy led to the Gulf War, and North Korea was soon targeted as the next pariah state. Years of gradual progress in relationships came suddenly to an end.

It is a Korean peculiarity that each major breakthrough is followed by a major setback. 1991 was a year of dramatic developments. South Korea began to review its attitude to reunification. It began to promote "three openings" (trade, communications, civilian travel). The two sides applied for and in September received simultaneous membership in the United Nations. On 13 December they signed an "Agreement on Reconciliation, Non-aggression, Exchange and Cooperation," committing themselves to a formal end to the Korean War. They agreed to rebuild railway and road links, telephone lines and mail service, as well as promote economic exchanges and the reunion of some families. They agreed on a number of confidence-building measures and an emergency hotline.

On the last night of 1991 the two sides signed a "Joint Declaration for Denuclearization of the Korean Peninsula." The six-point statement requires the two Koreas to abstain from making, owning, deploying, and using nuclear weapons. The breakthrough came with a private deal that the North would allow inspection of its nuclear facilities by the IAEA in exchange for the South's withdrawal from the U.S.-sponsored annual "Team Spirit" military exercises.

In all these areas the Korean churches were far in advance of their government. Already in its 1988 statement the NCCK outlined policies similar to those later adopted in the agreements. In the wake of the December breakthrough, NCCK General Secretary Rev. Kwon Ho-Kyung made a historic visit to Pyongyang in January 1992. Among activities prepared for him by the North Korean Christians Federation was a luncheon with President Kim Il-Sung. The Federation accepted an invitation to attend the NCCK's General Assembly in Seoul in mid-February and discussed plans for a larger North-South church meeting to be organized in Pyongyang later in the year.

Unfortunately, none of these plans materialized. It is open to speculation whether either of the governments was prepared to follow up on the agreements both had signed. What is clear is that the world community gave no encouragement to a negotiated rapprochement. The United States in particular used the nuclear inspection issue to apply extreme pressure on North Korea, already weakened by the loss of its economic allies in Eastern Europe. In the summer of 1994 Kim Il-Sung died, further compounding uncertainties on the peninsula.

As might have been expected under these circumstances, church efforts for reconciliation ground to a halt. Meetings of any kind between North and South Korean Christians became impossible. Glion 3's hope for the first inter-Korean gathering on the peninsula evaporated. The WCC—which had planned to withdraw from its intermediary role—was once again summoned to convene the two sides.

After an hiatus of nearly five years, Glion 4 was finally held at the end of March 1995. In order to give some semblance of proximity to Korea, as originally planned, the meeting was held in Kyoto, Japan. The "Jubilee Year of Peace and Reunification of Korea" had arrived, but the goals the churches had set for themselves seemed more remote than ever. A shadow of disappointment dogged the meeting from the outset. The North Korean delegation was able to come only because the organizers had agreed to a certain number of conditions. The South Korean delegation, already badly divided among itself, was in no mood for compromise.

On both sides there was a new, less confident leadership. Despite the fact that it was a closed meeting, South Korean journalists dogged participants, ready to report any "weakness" in their positions.

The meeting erupted in acrimony. The concluding document fell far behind that which had already been agreed upon in Glion 2 and 3. The only tangible result was a plan to hold a joint worship at Panmunjom on the fiftieth anniversary of the liberation of Korea from Japanese rule in August 1995. Immediately upon their return, South Korean church leaders were harassed by their government and told that joint worship at Panmunjom was out of the question, since this would merely be used as a political propaganda ploy by the North.

Concluding Reflections

My lengthy experience in promoting inter-Korean Christian dialogue has taught me a number of lessons:

• The global ecumenical community has a responsibility for reconciliation between North and South Korea, because the world community is responsible for Korea's division. As one of the last, most dangerous remnants of the Cold

War, Korea's illness confronts us prophetically with our own unresolved global schizophrenia.

• Reconciliation work is never purely humanitarian. Where the origin of a conflict is political, solutions cannot ignore the political aspects. Rather than choosing between opposition and acquiescence to political authority, churches must learn how to guide and, if necessary, manipulate governments into positive, peace-promoting conduct.

• It cannot be taken for granted that churches or Christian organizations are truly independent from political or ideological prejudices, or operate free from the control of their governments. In circumstances like Korea, it is better to involve political authorities in an open process than to try to bypass them.

• Reconciliation can proceed only to the extent that the parties in question are willing to suspend judgment of the other side's guilt and open to see guilt on their own side. If this insight is not apparent to the parties at the outset, it should become a goal of the process. The tendency to see North Korea as the absolute evil and South Korea as the ultimately victorious model makes it difficult to find common ground upon which to build a relationship.

• Intermediaries become necessary when the parties themselves are prevented from or unwilling to engage in direct contact. Sometimes intermediaries have to take an active role, "kick-starting" a process by convincing the parties in conflict of the benefit of opening channels of communication.

• The role of intermediaries is to facilitate direct contact and communication between the conflicting parties, not to dictate the terms of that contact. This may mean adding support to the weaker side or absorbing criticism from both sides, if this will maintain the dialogue between them. The WCC, the NCCCUSA, and the CCC have been accused of naivete whenever they sought to interpret North Korean Christianity to the outside world.

• In the first stages of an initiative, confidentiality is paramount. Only a limited number of actors may usefully become involved. Ultimately, however, the goal is the reconciliation of an entire people. The transition from "advance party" to "mass movement" is the most difficult to accomplish, since the arduous learning process undergone by the few will have to be made accessible and acceptable to the many.

• There is a contradiction between the need for continuity—the need to build confidence in specific people over time—and the need to broaden the base of reconciliation. Continuity requires the involvement of the same people in meetings which of necessity have limited participation. But in the case of Korea, there are voices that have been excluded in these encounters—specifically women and youth. Korean culture has not yet made a breakthrough in sexual equality, so continuity becomes the enemy of inclusiveness.

• Ecumenical work for peace and reconciliation requires ecumenical discipline. The greater the disunity of purpose on any one side, the greater the potential for sabotage or political manipulation. At Glion 4, a conflict within the NCCK reduced the southern room for maneuver, with the result that meaningful compromise or accommodation became impossible.

• The word *compromise* is itself suspect, although there can be no reconciliation without compromise. Too often compromise on nonessentials is confused with compromise on principles. But to be uncompromising on principles requires that the principles themselves be carefully chosen and agreed to by both sides. Is continued and expanded contact between North and South Korea of paramount importance? Then it stands to reason that any roadblocks to such contact must be compromised.

• Neither the parties in conflict nor the mediators are infallible. All are composed of personalities with ambitions, personal agendas, and preconceived expectations. Work for reconciliation requires open acknowledgment of this fact—and humility in one's personal assessments. This includes an acknowledgment of limitations, including financial ones. It is doubtful, for example, that the WCC will be able to continue to devote the amount of energy to the Korean situation as it has in the past.

• Work for peace and reconciliation is a very long process, requiring patience and long-range plans. It is impossible to "solve" in a few years problems that have a history spanning decades or centuries. "Quick fixes" often create more problems than they solve. By the same token, ultimata and win-lose options should be avoided. These simply pave the way for disappointment or later retaliation.

• Breakthroughs can be ephemeral and setbacks are inevitable. They are both part of the process. Rather than thinking in terms of a conclusion to reconciliation, it is better to think of it as an ongoing process that needs to be nurtured. Although the "Year of Jubilee" idea seemed theologically and psychologically appropriate, its "deadline" character set the stage for feelings of disappointment and deception.

Despite the present deadlock in the Tozanso Process, the movement for reconciliation and reunification has grown into a force to be reckoned with. A new generation, for whom the Korean War is ancient history, has grown to adulthood. These adults see division as an anachronism, a drain on resources, and an obstacle to self-determination and progress. They are a force politicians will not be able to ignore for long.

Hopefully the churches will have learned enough from the Tozanso Process to be ready for the inevitable next breakthrough.

7

The Church and Reconciliation in Ethnic Conflicts

The Case of Fiji

RALPH R. PREMDAS

Religion is involved in ethnic conflicts in many parts of the world, especially in countries of the so-called Third World. Since religion is an ambiguous historical phenomenon exerting cultural power of different kinds, it reinforces these conflicts in some situations while it acts as a reconciling force in others.[1]

This article is a case study of the role of the Christian churches in the conflictive political situation of Fiji Island. I shall offer a brief discussion of the tension between culture and religion as it pertains to the Fiji case, and a brief overview of the christianization of Fiji and the making of a multireligious, multicultural society. Then I shall discuss the split that is taking place in the main Christian church and the challenge of reconciliation versus domination. I shall delve into the military seizure of power and the ensuing debate over the role of the church as instigator of communal conflict or reconciler of peoples in justice. The final part is devoted to critical reflection on the Christian challenge to reconciliation in the context of the claims of culture.

Fiji: Discovery, Christianization, and the Making of a Multi-ethnic Society

Fiji is an archipelago in the South Pacific. Although European intrusion in these islands first occurred in 1643, missionary activity did not commence until the beginning of the nineteenth century. The Methodists, who were the first to arrive in Fiji on October 12, 1835, not only faced the problem of warring tribes but also the practice of cannibalism. Among the Fijians, the most powerful subgroup came from the tiny island of Bau, ruled by King Cakabau.

Cakabau resisted Christian conversion for a long time, and when he finally succumbed, this momentous event marked "the turning point in Fiji's missionary history."[2]

The Methodist missionaries were a disciplined and determined group. Their persistence in the face of many daunting adversities was uncompromising. A noted historian writes: "The missionaries' objective was nothing less than the complete change of the Fijians' beliefs and behavior, replacing barbarism with Christian knowledge and faith. They followed John Wesley's threefold method of preaching, teaching, and pastoral care."[3] As in the Polynesian cases, the target of conversion was the "chief" or "king" in those parts of Fiji where such an institution existed. An incentive that attracted kings to convert was the participant role they played in church affairs, where their prestige was partly upheld and generally remained undiminished. Over the years, after conversion by the Methodists, the entire Fijian cultural system became intertwined with the Wesleyan church so that "the Wesleyan Church became the Church of the Fijian nation and this, very largely, is still true to this day."[4] While the early Methodist missionaries operated in the Fiji islands, the archipelago was still free from direct European colonial control until the latter part of the nineteenth century. When the British accepted the Fiji islands as a colony in 1874, on the request of the major chiefs, including Cakabau, they came upon a scene where Methodism had already triumphed. The new colonial administration decided, therefore, that it was expedient to work hand-in-hand with the church and the chiefs. To satisfy the Methodist missionaries, the British colonial authorities forbade religious ceremonies of the pre-Christian Fijians and "sometimes jailed those convicted of practising them."[5] This sort of collaboration between church and state since 1874 under British rule "tended to support the same leaders and same religion (Methodism)" among Fijians to the virtual exclusion of other claimants.[6] Because of this, the Methodist church in the villages came to be regarded, as church historian Forman pointed out, as "the Chief's church."

Today, the main Christian denomination in Fiji is the Methodist church. About 51 percent of all persons in Fiji are Christians. About 78 percent of all Christians are Methodists. About 85 to 90 percent of all indigenous Fijians are Christians. The relationship between the Methodist church and the traditional chief has become so interlocked that Methodism and Fijian culture appear inseparable. Fijians have intermixed their traditional cosmic beliefs with the Christian message. The new synthesis elevated Christian spiritual symbols and ethical guidance, placing them at the very center of Fijian cultural expression. Culture and religion became meshed, and the new identity seemed for the most part to preserve the basic Christian message within the cultural idiom.

Catholics, who first came to Fiji in 1844, number about 8 percent of the Christian population. Anglicans also came to Fiji, but their entry in 1870 was originally intended to serve the European settlers. Today, Anglicans number about 1 percent of the total Christian population. Finally, the Presbyterians maintain only one church, St. Andrews, in Fiji. In recent years Fiji's traditional mainstream Christian churches—Methodist, Anglican, and Catholic—have been joined by a proliferation of Pentecostal churches as well as by the Mormons and Adventists. No one knows precisely the membership in these churches, except it is widely believed that the Pentecostal churches are making many converts, especially from among the Methodists.

The colonization of Fiji was legally formalized on October 10, 1874, when Chief Cakabau and other chiefs ceded Fiji to Britain.[7] The Deed of Cession of 1874 bound Britain to protect the Fijians from European commercial interests and to preserve the Fijian way of life. To halt the steady decline of Fijian customs, Sir Arthur Gordon, the first British governor of Fiji, initiated a major policy that laid the cornerstone of communalism. To meet the demand for cheap and abundant labor for the European plantations, he recommended the importation of Indian coolies from India, as had been done successfully in British Guiana, Mauritius, and Trinidad. From 1879, when the labor indentureship system was inaugurated, to 1916, when it was terminated, 60,537 Indians from India were introduced into Fiji.[8] About half of these Indians returned to India, the rest remaining under a scheme that allowed them to become legal residents "with privileges no whit inferior to those of any other class of Her Majesty's subjects resident in the colonies."[9] The Indian population grew steadily, so that by 1945 Indians outnumbered Fijians for the first time.

Through the establishment of a separate Native Fijian administration, the British governed the indigenous Fijians indirectly. The Fijian hierarchical political structure was recognized and Fijian chiefs continued to govern their own people. While this policy did preserve to some extent the traditional Fijian political structure by virtually establishing a state within a state, it so protected the Fijians that they would be almost wholly unprepared to compete effectively with the Europeans, Chinese, and Indians once their circle of interaction had enlarged beyond the village. The upshot was the institutionalization of Fijian economic inferiority.[10] A recent census indicates that about 30 percent of the Fijians still live from a subsistence economy, mainly in the villages. While the main drift has been toward an urban monetary economy, the Fijian community continues to own about 83 percent of the land in the country.[11] The land is held communally by over seven thousand *mataqali* patrilineal groups, which can only lease the land with the approval of the Native Lands Trust Board. Over 60 percent of the Fijian leases are held by Indians, who demand more land to meet the needs of a growing Indian population. Fijians who no longer rely on their villages for their income are employed by the government as policemen, army officers, teachers, nurses, medical officers, office workers, and so on. From the government services has sprung a well-to-do Fijian middle class. Many regard the government bureaucracy as their preeminent domain, much the same way many Indians regard the commercial and sugar sectors as their own. Fijian penetration of the business sector has been generally unsuccessful, even when special programs have been established to initiate them into the commercial world. The nature of Fijian culture, which is communal, noncompetitive, and nonprofit oriented, has been blamed for the poor performance. To date, Fijians own very few businesses. Commerce is almost totally in Indian, European, and Chinese hands.

Most Indian immigrants to Fiji came as indentured laborers.[12] About 85 percent were Hindus and 15 percent Muslims; a small group consisted of Sikhs. Today, some 80 percent of cane farmers are Indians. However, most of the lands are leased from Fijians, rendering what would normally be a powerful political base into a tinder box of communal conflict.[13] Sugar is the most significant crop in the Fijian economy, providing more than half of Fiji's foreign reserves. When the Indians came to Fiji, they brought with them their religious affiliation as part of their cultural inheritance. Nearly all Indians (except about 3.5 percent) have remained Hindus, Sikhs, and Muslims. Of the 3.5 percent, many have converted to Christianity. Among these Indian Christians are a curious group of some twelve hundred persons who became Methodists.[14] By mutual consent, this community exists separately from the indigenous Fijian Methodists as an Indian Methodist Division with its own Indian Methodist churches and schools.

Europeans, although numerically insignificant, have directly or indirectly dominated the direction of the colony. Yet in 1970 Fiji received its independence from Britain. Thereafter, the contest for power devolved to the two main groups, the indigenous Fijians and the descendants of the Asian Indians. The remaining population is made up of Chinese, Mixed Races, and other Pacific Islanders. The following table gives a demographic breakdown of Fiji.

	Total	Percent of Total
Fijian	263,694	43.41
Indian	277,248	50.85
European	3,477	.64
Part-European	9,673	1.77
Chinese / Pt. Chinese	4,263	.78
Other Pacific Is.	13,850	2.55

The Coup and Its Links to the Church

In early 1987 a political coalition group called the Labor-Federation Party won the April general elections and in so doing defeated the predominantly indigenous Fijian-based Alliance Party, which had governed Fiji under a Fijian Prime Minister (Ratu Mara) since the country attained its independence in 1970. The victory ushered in a new government that, although multiracial in composition, was predominantly supported by Indians, although led by an indigenous Fijian prime minister, Dr. Timoci Bavadra. The fact that the new prime minister was a Fijian and that half of the cabinet posts went to indigenous Fijians did not seem as significant to many indigenous Fijians as the fact that the predominant popular base of the Labor-Federation Party was constituted of Indians.

The overthrow of the legally elected government in Fiji was carried out by Lt. Col. Sitiveni Rabuka on May 14, 1987, and about a year later it became known that the instigators of the event were people deeply steeped in Christian religious practice who openly invoked their faith as the guide of their action. In a startling admission following the coup, Rabuka declared that the primary motivation of his action to remove the duly elected civilian government of Fiji was an instruction from God. It was "a mission that God has given me," he said.[15] Rabuka, who had served periodically as a lay preacher in the Methodist church, claimed that "his principal driving forces are God, the Bible, and Christianity."[16] His Methodist religious faith influenced the way in which he saw his country and culture in relation to other communities. For him, religion, country, and culture were intimately intertwined so that their boundaries became blurred. He believed that according to God's providence Christian missionaries and the British government arrived in Fiji to make it a Christian society. This religious reading of Fiji's colonial history had a significant influence on Rabuka's execution of the coup in May 1987. To him, the elected government defied God's will and intent for Fiji.

Listening to the results of the fateful April 1987 election, Rabuka decided that "as it became clear that Fiji was in the hands of the immigrant race, the only option was . . . the military option."[17] To Rabuka, the Indians were "heathens," an "immigrant race," who threatened to dominate Fiji and make it a non-Christian country. For him, the choice was cast in uncompromising terms. The removal of the new government was to him "essential to the survival of the Fijian race." Hence, the slogan of the coup was "Fiji for Fijians." Said Rabuka: "In the simplest terms, the May 14 coup had been staged to restore control of the country to the indigenous Fijians." Rabuka wanted Fiji to be governed by Fijians alone, and not by descendants of immigrants, regardless of the fact that they were born in Fiji, numbered over 50 percent of the population, and had contributed to Fiji's development. He denied equal political rights to non-Fijians, designating them second-class citizens. He wanted Fiji to be Christian. Fiji was to be declared officially "a Christian democratic state." Rabuka saw no contradiction between his Christian faith and his politics of discrimination. His plan was not to evict or deport Indians and other non-Fijians, but to start a missionary drive to evangelize these non-Christians. He was unequivocal about the Christian purpose of the coup, insisting "that Christianity must be the official religion of Fiji because that is the religion chosen by the Fijians."[18]

Impact of the Coup on the Religious Communities

The coup d'état created an immense split in the country, especially in the Christian churches.[19] The Methodist church, which accounted for about 90 percent of all Christians in Fiji, was divided right down the middle. Not surprisingly, the non-Christian religious communities—Hindu, Sikh, and

Muslim—were fully united in condemning the coup. But for the Christian churches which drew their congregations from the indigenous Fijian community, the coup was a cause of concern. While their Fijian members celebrated the restoration of unequivocal Fijian paramountcy in government, many of the clergy agonized about the "rightness" of the coup. The question whether the coup was ethical and in keeping with Christian teaching summoned forth a vigorous debate among Christian ministers. Many indigenous Fijians were deeply troubled and torn apart by their loyalty to land and culture on one hand, and the use of questionable means to satisfy the demands of their faith on the other hand.

The Christian churches separately and collectively reacted to the coup. The president of the Methodist church contacted leaders of several Christian denominations, and together they issued a joint statement on behalf of the Methodists, Anglicans, Presbyterians, and Assemblies of God (they would be later joined by the Catholic church). The statement reads:

> We, the Churches, would like to appeal for and place before you the people of Fiji, the Christian values of justice, peace, tolerance, goodwill, freedom and love, patience and forgiveness, sacrifice and obedience. To promote and uphold these values, we appeal to you today. By adhering to these values, we look forward in hope to further progress and future prosperity. We the heads of Christian Churches have been informed of the military takeover of our Government on this day. We call on the Royal Fiji Military Forces to release the hostages immediately and to surrender to the sovereign authority of the land. We call on the people of Fiji of all religions to join us in prayer for an end to this most grievous situation and for the restoration of our duly-elected Government immediately.[20]

The leaders of the churches, which accounted for over 90 percent of Christians in Fiji, unequivocally called for the restoration of the duly-elected Labor-Federation government. The basis of this collective appeal was the conviction that the military take-over violated Christian values that were fundamental to Christian teaching. Yet the churches had no practical way of compelling the soldiers to return to their barracks. Still, the prompt declaration by the churches made it quite clear that the coup-makers' claim to divine guidance was not shared by the leadership of the Christian community.

In the week following the coup, demonstrations, protests, and prayer meetings, some sponsored by Christian communities, were held against the coup-makers. The *Fiji Times* and *Fiji Sun*, which were not immediately closed down by the military junta, published on the front pages a barrage of opinions against the coup-makers. Several clergy from the Christian denominations who organized collective prayer vigils in protest against the coup were arrested and jailed. Among them was Father Rouse, a prominent Catholic priest, whose work among the urban poor had made him famous in Fiji. Some time thereafter, Father Rouse was forced to leave Fiji, since his work permit was not renewed.[21]

The anti-coup activism of many Catholic clergy raised the question of the official position of the Catholic church. It had not joined the Christian churches that issued the statement against the coup. On 24 May, nine days after the coup, Archbishop P. Mataca, an indigenous Fijian, issued a joint statement based on his own initial draft and endorsed by the president of the Methodist church, the Anglican bishop, the leaders of the Presbyterian church, and the Salvation Army. The statement condemned the coup outright, declaring it illegal and "an attack on our Constitution and democracy."[22] The archbishop hinted at the churches' role as "healer and reconciler."

On May 22, 1987, two days prior to the publication of the joint statement, the archbishop had expressed his own position on the coup. He recognized that the election of a new government had unleashed "fears in one section of our society that their rights, aspirations, and position were now seriously at risk."[23] The archbishop sought to reassure the indigenous Fijian people, especially those belonging to the Taukei Movement, that they had nothing to fear from non-Fijians because "our diversities have been seen as an asset rather than a hindrance."[24] He called on all citizens "to celebrate our ethnic and religious diversities rather than regard them as problems." Regarding the issue of Fijian land, an issue made central by the Taukei Movement, he acknowledged "the rights, aspirations and fears of the Fijian people, especially in view of the unique traditional link there is between people and land." But he also recognized "the rights, aspirations and fears of the Fiji-Indian people who take pride in themselves as Fiji-born and Fiji-citizens and who have labored to build Fiji."

Having conceded that both Indian and Fijian fears and interests should be acknowledged in any settlement of the crisis, Mataca proceeded to condemn the coup as not the appropriate method by which these fears were to be assuaged. He called the coup "illegal" and deemed it "an attack on basic democracy based on our Constitution." He believed that the coup was an act in "violation of the right of people to be governed by the government of their choice expressed by their vote in a National Election." He condemned the ethnic violence against the Indians that followed the coup, calling it unchristian. He called for fear to be replaced by love.

Archbishop Mataca believed that the manner of resolving differences in Fiji's multilingual, multicultural, and multireligious society was through the *tanoa* approach or dialogue. The *tanoa* is an indigenous Fijian wooden four-legged repository (a bowl) into which *kava*, the local ceremonial drink, is poured and shared by everyone who sits and discusses the issues and disputes that may arise. Again, he stressed that the churches were to be "healer and reconciler," helping to resolve the crisis. He stressed that "a way has to be found to accommodate each group with justice and fairness so that Fiji can be a place where all can live in harmony and peace." At the end of his message he invoked Philippians 2:3-7 to persuade Christians to set aside selfishness, recognize the interests of others, and see themselves as servants of national unity.

With the Catholic church firmly in league with the other major Christian denominations in condemning the coup and calling for restoration of the Constitution, it seemed that practically all Christians would act in accord to pressure the military to surrender power. There appeared to be near unanimity among the major Christian churches in Fiji on the coup. Yet that apparent unity was soon shattered. The major Christian denomination in Fiji, the Methodist church, was internally split, with most Methodists supporting the coup. This was almost inevitable since nearly all Methodists in Fiji were indigenous Fijians, the overwhelming majority of whom enthusiastically supported Rabuka's call, "Fiji for Fijians." The Methodist church was for all practical purposes a Fijian church, even though there was a small faction of Methodist Indians who belonged to separate ethnic congregations. The ultra-nationalist Taukei Movement had its base in the Methodist membership.

How, then, does one explain the public statement by the president of the Methodist church against the coup? When the Rev. Koroi condemned the coup, he discovered subsequently that he had espoused the minority position in his church. Soon a movement was organized among a large number of Methodist clergymen and congregations to depose Rev. Koroi, even before his term of office as president of the Methodist Conference was over.

The person around whom the opposition against Rev. Koroi was organized was the Rev. Lasaro, the charismatic secretary of the Methodist Conference. The Rev. Lasaro was an open supporter of the coup and a close friend of Lt. Col. Rabuka. Lasaro saw the coup in larger Fijian terms in which the Methodist church was an integral institutional pillar of Fijian culture. Said Lasaro:

The issues and events involving the Church now are part of the national crisis that we have been facing over the past two years. The crisis has got to do with Fijians as a people who are trying to keep their own identity, who are trying to see what their future is in their own country.

And when you are talking about the Fijian people you are really talking about the Methodist Church. The personalities who are involved are the grassroots on the one hand and the well-to-do Fijians on the other.[25]

The view of Lasaro closely approximated that of Lt. Col. Rabuka, who saw the coup as a means to nullify the perceived threat to the survival of Fijians as a people. Apart from the threat of Indian dominance, Lasaro and Rabuka complained against the erosion of Fijian traditional and Christian values. After the coup Rabuka had turned over the government to the governor general, yet he later decided against this interim civilian arrangement, fearing the continued Indian presence in it, and seized the government on September 26 in a second coup, made himself president of Fiji, and proceeded to rule personally by decree. One of the decrees that President Rabuka issued was the Sunday Observance Decree, which made Sunday a day of rest for everyone regardless of religious affiliation. The Sunday Observance Decree would further plunge the Methodist church into controversy and deepen the cleavage between the two schismatic parts, one headed by the moderate President Koroi and the other by Secretary Lasaro.

Nothing could be done immediately to remove Rev. Koroi. The opportunity to do so, however, availed itself with the issuance of the Sunday Observance Decree. The moderate Koroi faction opposed the decree. Koroi and his supporters did not deny the significance of setting aside a special day for rest, thanksgiving, and worship, but they opposed imposing such a decree on other religious communities in a culturally plural society. "The Sabbath is for people and not people for the Sabbath," argued the Koroi position. In concert with the Fiji Council of Churches, Rev. Koroi endorsed the following view on the decree.

> We believe that under God, governments have the responsibility of seeking the welfare of all their people in their individual, family, and community lives. This includes the responsibility of ensuring freedom of religion and freedom of conscience in matters of faith and personal morality. This implies freedom from having the tenets of a religion forcibly imposed on any section of the population. In addition, we believe that states should be very slow to be involved, and very reluctant to legislate in the area of religious faith and personal morality. Some of the darkest moments in Christian history are associated with times when the state enforced a particular religious tradition. The Sunday Observance Decree crosses over the limits of state authority. It decrees that "Sunday shall be observed in the Republic of Fiji as a sacred day and a day of worship and thanksgiving to Christ the Lord." To legislate for the worship of Christ the Lord is to go against the whole spirit of the Gospel which sets people free from the bondage of the law. Worship cannot be enforced by threat of punishment and force or arms. We would ask the present government to take great care in making decrees and legislation in this area. In particular, we would request that it immediately revoke the Sunday Observance Decree.[26]

To this argument, Lasaro would counter that Sunday observance was vital for the preservation of the Fijian way of life and that permitting non-Christian groups to work and play during Sunday distracted and interfered with Fijians exercising their freedom of worship. Said Lasaro:

> This has always been the stand of the Methodist Church in Fiji: Sunday has to be observed, which does not mean a total ban of activities on Sunday. Special provisions are made for essential services like hospitals and the Public Works Department that controls the transport system to facilitate worship in the urban centres. Sunday has its additional special significance to Fijians and its observance helps Fijians maintain values

which set them apart as a people. There are certain human values which we need to hold on to keep us sane and human. The Fijians look to the observance of Sunday as a means of maintaining these values. People ought to be free to worship on Sunday and not being interfered with. We have got instances where people are worshipping and in the next building people work on a construction programme. In the rural areas where some Fijians have moved away from their villages to settle on their farms, Sunday brings them back to their villages, to their communities, to their families to worship together.

So Sunday is very important to Fijians as a uniting influence. This is nothing new and the fight to observe Sunday is not new either. It has been going on for years. . . . In view of the presence of people in Fiji who have other beliefs, is there a common ground for compromise?

The common ground through which we can exist together in this country is that we are asking the people of other faiths to respect us and respect our faith. We are not asking them to believe in what we believe, but to respect what we believe in the same way we respect their holy days and the way they worship. And for us as Methodist Christians we ask them to observe Sunday and not to interfere with Sunday.[27]

The Reaction of Church Councils

When the coup occurred in May 1987, two institutions representing Christians both within Fiji, the Fiji Council of Churches (FCC), and throughout the Pacific Islands region, the Pacific Conference of Churches (PCC), had already emerged as bodies with influence on public opinion. In particular, the PCC had grown since its inception nearly three decades before into a widely known and fairly powerful opinion-maker not only on traditional church issues but also on secular and political matters.[28] The FCC was a more recent body, but its voice and role in Fiji were beginning to gather strength. Together, these two bodies were drawn into the implications of the coup, in particular offering interpretation and guidance from a Christian perspective. In fact, the coup not only deeply embroiled the PCC in worldly matters, but its policy positions became controversial causing one major denominational group within the PCC to threaten withdrawal from membership.

The PCC was founded in 1961, becoming one of a similar set of regional organizations that had proliferated around the world: the Christian Conference of Asia established in 1957; the All Africa Conference of Churches in 1958; the Conference of European Churches in 1964; the Caribbean Conference of Churches in 1973; the Middle East Council of Churches in 1974; and the Latin America Council of Churches in 1982.[29] The programs that would soon become the preoccupation of the PCC ranged from matters pertaining to the family to politics.[30] It is with the latter we are concerned here, for it is under this ambit that the PCC approached the problem of the coup in Fiji. The

Fiji coup fell into a category of problem unprecedented in the political experience of the PCC. It involved a new issue, the forcible removal from office of a legally elected democratic government. There was one complication that made what would ordinarily be a straightforward issue into a complex one involving the choice of conflicting fundamental values. More specifically, while the PCC advocated democracy and equality symbolically represented by free and fair elections, it was also committed to protecting indigenous peoples in the Pacific from domination and genocide. The PCC held and expressed strong pro-indigenous positions with regard to the plight of the first peoples of Australia (the Aborigines), New Zealand (the Maoris), New Caledonia (the Kanaks), and of Irian Jaya and East Timor in Indonesia. The coup-makers had invoked the slogan "Fiji for Fijians," clearly arguing that the justification of the coup was the protection of the indigenous people of Fiji. They spoke the familiar language of indigenous rights. But the crux of the problem included not only indigenous rights but also the status of the Indians in Fiji, nearly all of whom were born and raised in Fiji and had lived in no other country and possessed no other citizenship. In a way, the choice of values was between collective indigenous rights and individual human rights. In its first declaration on the coup, the PCC joined its members, who had already expressed condemnation of the coup, and proceeded to say "that we admire the courageous way we know some of you spoke out against the violations of human rights by the military regime."[31]

The PCC chose to focus its argument against the coup on the basis of the violation of human rights. It took cognizance of the collective indigenous claims of the coup-makers' arguments but clearly stated that to invoke the word *indigenous* was not to make a morally wrong act right. Said the PCC: "We are all mindful of the mistaken tendency to consider that all that is indigenous, all that is traditional or cultural and even the chiefly systems are right. All these have their good points but all are in need of purification or redemption in Christ."[32]

The PCC was aware that certain aspects of indigenous Fijian culture which the coup-makers had extolled were in fact structures of domination within the Fijian community, that is to say, institutions by which the higher-status Fijians exploited the poorer sections. In this respect the PCC would find itself on a collision course with Rabuka. Rabuka had declared that one of the reasons for the military intervention was "a growing materialism which deeply worried the Fijian traditionalists—young Fijians were ignoring or defying old values, their chiefs and their elders."[33] Rabuka regarded the indigenous chiefly system with reverence and saw in social change "the breaking down of standards" in "a growing lack of respect for their chiefs."[34]

For some Fijians the traditional Fijian chiefly system was worthy of unmodified retention. But many others saw in the system a source of corruption and unjust practices. Hence, during the 1986 election campaign, the Labor-Federation coalition leveled strong criticisms against alleged malpractices of the chiefly system including the failure of chiefs to distribute to ordinary Fijians the millions of dollars paid annually in land rents by Indian tenants.[35] Under the traditional formula, only about one-tenth or less of all rents for collectively owned lands ever got to poor and needy Fijians. The Labor-Federation coalition pounded on this issue during the election campaign and pointed to alleged "corruption" in the Mara government (Ratu Mara was one of Fiji's highest chiefs). To Rabuka, such an attack on the chiefly system during the election campaign was intolerable. Said Rabuka: "The chiefly system was ridiculed as being out of date and out of touch. We Fijians cannot stand by and listen to our chiefs being ridiculed and called names."[36]

The PCC was aware that the question of indigenous tradition and especially chiefly rights had become part of the election debate. It was also aware that the issue was less a debate between Indians and Fijians than it was a debate among indigenous Fijians themselves. More specifically, the more educated and the more liberal to left-wing indigenous Fijians tended to oppose the chiefly system.[37] These persons often cited the record of colonial rule to show that the chiefly system as bequeathed by Britain to Fiji at independence was substantially a colonial creation.[38] The British made chiefs of those who favored them; they froze a changing situation of ongoing conflict among warring Fijian tribes to favor those groups and chiefs who supported British colonial control.[39]

Hence, "the indigenous issue" was caught in deep historical controversy. Rabuka was seen as a defender of a particular position in favor of chiefs. By contrast, the PCC was very committed to a position of equality, and in its declaration on the coup underscored this point: "Please allow us to share with you our hopes and expectations that the Churches in Fiji will have a special concern for the weak and poor."[40] Turning more specifically to the indigenous justification of the coup, the PCC argued that "as followers of Jesus, his ways as expressed in the Gospels now become our measure of what is right and what is wrong." The PCC was unwilling to buy the indigenous argument advanced by Rabuka and his supporters and underscored the point that the slogan "Fiji for Fijians" was emotionally manipulative and unchristian and lent itself to racism and intolerance in a multicultural and multireligious society. Said the PCC: "We deplore not only the military coup in Fiji but also the violations of human rights, the violence, the tendency to racism and subtle persecution of peoples who do not share with us the same Christian faith."[41]

To the PCC, the military coup was racially divisive. Its claims tended to destroy whatever amity existed between Fijians and Indians. The PCC sought to restore an environment of equality in dignity for social harmony. During the post-coup period, nearly all of the violence committed by the military was aimed at the Indian community. Many were hauled out of their homes by Rabuka's soldiers and taken to jail. Many were detained and beaten. The PCC could not see how an indigenous claim could justify such actions. What made it even more difficult to bear was the claim by Rabuka and his followers that they were Christians and that this in part justified their action against the Hindu and Muslim "heathens" in Fiji.

On the issue of the Sunday Observance Day, the PCC was equally forth-right. Rabuka's fundamentalist understanding of the Christian message required him to observe the Sabbath as a day of prayer and rest. In a multireligious society, he did not see anything contradictory between forcibly imposing Sunday observances on other faiths on the one hand and Christian tolerance and love on the other. The PCC articulated its own understanding of what the Sabbath meant. It began by admitting that "we [should] be very concerned about the Sunday Laws in Fiji." However, it argued that "we are now in the New Testament, and Jesus tells us that man was not made for the Sabbath." The PCC then proceeded to point out that Sunday Observance must be voluntary and in a multicultural plural society "our respect for the Christian Sunday makes us also respect the belief of other religions. We do not enforce our belief on them; they are free to follow their conscience."

It must be remembered at this point that the PCC contained among its membership the Methodist church of Fiji. There existed at this time a discernible split between the views of the Methodist representative on the PCC executive council and the broad base of Methodist parishioners. As we noted earlier, this split in sentiment in the Methodist church over the coup led to a change in the leadership of the Methodist Conference. Once this change had occurred, Rev. Lasaro and his group proceeded to withdraw the Methodist church from the PCC. But the Methodist church was now split between two groups and two separate conferences emerged. One faction of the Methodist church would remain in the PCC, albeit the minority part.

The Fiji Council of Churches was a more recently formed body, created less than five years prior to the coup. It was an ecumenical body that envisaged interreligious dialogue among the various faiths in Fiji. Despite its internal organizational weakness, the FCC quickly acquired public visibility. With the occurrence of the coup the FCC became a focal point of collective church discussion. Frequent meetings were convened, at which Christians of different churches—Catholics, Methodists, Anglicans, and combinations of these—issued their positions on the coup. This meant that while the FCC did not issue a statement on the Sunday Observance Decree until March 1988, it had organized under its auspices public discussions with a number of Christian churches which, as a result, took their own action.

On March 11, 1988, the FCC issued a statement aimed at the Sunday Observance Decree. It began by describing what it felt should be the proper relationship between church and government:

> We believe that under God, governments have the responsibility of seeking the welfare of all their people in their individual, family and community lives. This includes the responsibility of ensuring freedom and personal morality. This implies freedom from having the tenets of a religion forcibly imposed on any section of the population.[42]

The FCC pointed to the destructive effects that have in the past besmirched Christian history when the faith became bonded with state power. It warned that "some of the darkest moments in Christian history are associated with times when the state enforced a particular religious tradition." Accordingly it declared that:

> The Sunday Observance Decree crosses over the limits of state author-
> ity. It decrees that "Sunday shall be observed in the Republic of Fiji as a
> sacred day and a day of worship and thanksgiving to Christ the Lord."
> To legislate for the worship of Christ, the Lord, is to go against the
> whole spirit of the Gospel which sets people free from the bondage of
> the law.[43]

Apart from depicting the observance of the Sabbath as a voluntary act, the FCC proceeded to point out that in practice the Sunday Observance Decree tended to favor the rich and powerful and make things more difficult for the poor and needy, for example, in the area of transport to church or visiting relatives and friends or the sick in the hospital. Further, the FCC condemned the inconsistency in the decree which permitted—for economic gain—tour-ists to engage in acts that were prohibited for the local population.

In a second message, this time issued at Christmas 1988, the FCC assumed the role of conciliator in a social context that was marked by intercommunal animosity caused by the discriminatory behavior of the military regime. Indi-ans were migrating to other countries in droves. Some indigenous Fijians were also victimized because of their support of the overthrown prime minister, Dr. T. Bavadra. The atmosphere was fraught with fear and resentment in a society that was strained to the utmost at its ethnic seams. In this context the FCC noted that "the way of Christ is not the way of fear and domination but the way of love." In the main part of the message the FCC appealed for peace and goodwill saying:

> At this Christmas time Fiji is being severely tested. Many people are
> seeking to show the peacemaking, reconciling and loving way of Jesus.
> Yet others act in a way that defeats the whole message of Christmas. To
> our fellow Christians we say: we are called to be peacemakers and a
> people of goodwill. Let us work with all peoples of goodwill to break
> down barriers and create a lasting peace. To all people of Fiji we say:
> We Christians have failed to live up to what we profess to believe. But
> the promise of the holy child of Bethlehem is that failure and wrong are
> not the last word. A new beginning is possible. We call on all people of
> goodwill to reach out to one another across the walls that divide us. May
> we all be bearers of good tidings of peace, joy and love.[44]

The FCC, invoking the Christian message of love and peace, embarked upon the role of reconciler between races in Fiji and between Christians of different denominations. Yet because of the stand taken by the Methodist church, Christians remained deeply divided. The new leadership of the Methodist church decided to withdraw its members from the FCC, even if a faction remained, as they had remained in the PCC.

The Methodist Conference under the divisive rule of Rev. Lasaro, and indirectly under Rabuka, did not hold a conciliatory position toward Indians. Indians were regarded as heathens and deserving of discriminatory treatment in the new Fiji. While most of these Methodists wanted Indians to remain in Fiji, they held that the Indians should be denied equal status to Fijians. They demanded that the paramountcy of Fijians over the non-indigenous races in Fiji be inscribed in the Constitution.

Conclusion

The evidence on the role of the churches in the communal strife in Fiji underscores the ambiguity and contradictions present in religious traditions. The church may be split, with one part serving as instigator of conflict and another acting as reconciler. This can be accounted for in part by intervening variables such as the political ambition of church leaders, the institutional interests of the churches, and the claims of culture on the allegiance of Christian adherents. In this chapter we have seen all these factors at play in creating deep divisions among the churches in Fiji. The conflict among Christians tested the authentic meaning of the Christian message against the more narrow claims of culture and political ambition. In Fiji, the temptation was strong to align the church to the interests of chauvinist politicians who seized control of the state and sought legitimation of their rule that pitched one ethnic community against another. It fell upon another set of church leaders to defy the military and secular authorities in advocating an alternative course of reconciliation, more consistent with the Christian message.

Notes

[1] The ambiguity of religion is a theme developed in G. Baum, *Religion and Alienation* (Toronto: Paulist Press, 1975).

[2] Charles W. Forman, *The Island Churches of the South Pacific* (Maryknoll, N.Y.: Orbis Books, 1982), p. 4.

[3] Ibid, p. 2.

[4] Ibid, p. 4.

[5] See Sione Latekefu, *Church-State Relations in Tonga* (Canberra: Australian National University Press, 1978).

[6] See A. Harold Wood, *Overseas Missions of the Australian Methodist Church*, vol. 2 (Melbourne: Aldersgate Press, 1978), p. 9.

[7] See R. A. Derrick, *A History of Fiji* (Suva: Government Printery, 1946).

[8] A. Ali, "The Indians of Fiji," *Economic and Political Weekly* 8:36 (8 September 1973).

[9] Known as the "Salisbury Dispatch," this document is often used to underscore Indian claims to equality in Fiji.

[10] For a study of this process see J. Narayan, *The Political Economy of Independent Fiji* (Suva: South Pacific Review Press, 1985); E. K. Fisk, *The Political Economy of Independent Fiji* (Canberra: Australian National University Press, 1970); and R. F. Watters, *Koro: Economic Development and Social Change in Fiji* (Melbourne: Oxford University Press, 1969).

[11] See D. T. Lloyd, *Land Policy in Fiji* (Cambridge: Cambridge University Press, 1982); see also, O. H. K. Spate, *The Fiji People* (Suva, Fiji: Government Printery, 1959).

[12] See K. L. Gillian, *Fiji's Indian Immigrants* (Melbourne: Oxford University Press, 1962); V. Naida, *The Violence of Indenture* (Suva, Fiji: University of South Pacific, 1980); B. Lal, *Girmityas* (Canberra: Journal of Pacific History, 1983); N. C. Mayer, *Indians in Fiji* (London: Oxford University Press, 1963).

[13] Ralph R. Premdas, "Fiji: Communal Conflict in the South Pacific," *Caribbean Affairs* 4:1 (1978), pp. 22-49.

[14] See *Diya* [Journal of the Indian Division of the Methodist Church of Fiji] (August 1977), p. 77; see also, Wood, vol. 3.

[15] E. Dean and S. Ritova, *Rabuka: No Other Way* (Suva, Fiji: Oceania Printers, 1988), p. 11. (Cited hereafter as *Rabuka*.)

[16] *Rabuka*, p. 27.

[17] Ibid.

[18] In advancing this argument, Rabuka relied heavily on a similar interpretation found in Sakiasi Butadroka's Fijian Nationalist Party. See Ralph R. Premdas, "Constitutional Challenge: Nationalist Politics in Fiji," *Pacific Perspective* 9: 2 (1980), pp. 30-44.

[19] See R. T. Robertson and A. Tomanison, *Fiji: Shattered Coups* (Canberra: Pluto Press, 1981); Ralph Premdas, "The Anatomy of a Revolution," *Pacifica* 1:1 (1989).

[20] See "Fiji Coups: Church Statements," *Pacific Journal of Theology* 2:1 (January 1989):38-39.

[21] See "Father Rouse Leaves," *Contact: Fiji's Catholic Newspaper* (30 April 1989), p. 1; M. Turaga, "Church Packed at Father Rouse's Final Celebration," *Contact*, p. 4; M. Turaga, "Archbishop: Tension, a Sign of Growth," *Contact*, p. 1.

[22] See "Fiji Coups: Church Statements," pp. 39-40.

[23] Personal interview with Archbishop Mataca in Suva, Fiji, 10 September 1988.

[24] Rev. Mataca, "To the Catholic Community of Fiji and Rotuma: A Pastoral Challenge," 22 May 1987, p. 1.

[25] M. Lasaro, quoted in J. Balawanilotu, "The Church and I," *Pacific Islands Monthly* (September 1989), p. 16.

[26] "Fiji Council of Churches' Statement on the Sunday Decree, March 11, 1988," *Pacific Journal of Theology* 2:1 (1989):46-47.

[27] Lasaro, quoted in Balawanilotu, p. 16.

[28] C. W. Forman, *The Voice of Many Waters* (Suva, Fiji: Lotu Pasifika Productions, 1986), p. 1. For a general work on the PCC see Charles W. Forman, *The Island Churches of the South Pacific* (Maryknoll, N.Y.: Orbis Books, 1982), p. 1.

[29] Forman, *The Voice of Many Waters*, p. 3.

[30] See *Report of the Fourth Assembly*, 3-15 May 1981, Nuku'alofa Tonga (Suva, Fiji: Lotu Pasifika Productions, 1981).

[31] "Fiji Coups: Church Statements," *Pacific Journal of Theology* 2:1 (1989):43 (statement by the PCC).

[32] Ibid., p. 44.

[33] *Rabuka*, p. 33.

[34] Ibid., p. 126.

[35] See Ralph R. Premdas, "Fiji: Elections and Communal Conflict in the First Military Coup," *Ethnic Studies Report* 5:2 (July 1987).

[36] *Rabuka*, p. 34.

[37] See S. Durutalo, *The Paramountcy of Fijian Interest and the Politicisation of Ethnicity* (Suva, Fiji: South Pacific Forum Press, 1986).

[38] See Peter France, *The Charter of the Land: Custom and Colonisation in Fiji* (Melbourne: Oxford University Press, 1969); Durutalo.

[39] Ibid.

[40] "Fiji Coups: Church Statements," p. 43.

[41] Ibid., p. 44.

[42] Ibid., p. 46.

[43] Ibid., p. 47.

[44] Ibid.

8

The Palestinian Center for Rapprochement between People

CATHERINE PECK

The key to lasting peace in the Middle East is reconciliation between Israelis and Palestinians in the Holy Land. The majority of Israelis are Jewish, and the majority of Palestinians are Muslim. What, therefore, does the local Christian church have to offer this conflict? Palestinian Christians in the West Bank town of Beit Sahour believe that by opening a dialogue between Palestinians and Israelis, they are laying the groundwork for future coexistence between Arab and Jew. They do not imagine that their efforts at bringing the enemies together will end the hostilities. "Peacemaking is for the politicians," they say. But once peace comes, there will need to be a framework in place within which people can find common ground. "Coexistence," says Ghassan Andoni, director of the Palestinian Center for Rapprochement between People (PCR), "can only occur between equals." Much of the work of the center, therefore, focuses on facilitating activities that allow Palestinians and Israelis to work together for justice.

Ghassan Andoni, along with a board which includes thirteen Christians and one Muslim, officially established the Rapprochement Center in 1990 under the auspices of the Mennonite Central Committee (MCC). But the work of the center started two years earlier when the community of Beit Sahour began inviting groups of Israelis to their town for discussions, worship, and meal-sharing in order to break down the stereotypes between the two peoples. Their activities attracted the attention of the Israeli military, and the principal activists were constantly harassed and repeatedly imprisoned during the two years before MCC provided an umbrella under which they could work with less fear of reprisal. To understand the radical nature of their early activities, some background on the contemporary situation is necessary.

The *Intifada*

Dialogue of the sort Ghassan and his colleagues envisioned would never have been possible before December 9, 1987, which marks the beginning of the

Palestinian uprising against the twenty-year-old Israeli occupation of the West Bank. Before that day, the relationship between Israelis and Palestinians was one of the strong dominating the weak. From 1967 to 1987 Israelis had come to count on relatively little opposition from the rank-and-file Arab populace as the Israeli government expropriated land, levied taxes, limited freedom of movement, and forced the Palestinian people to live under a spirit-deadening military rule. Suddenly, after a series of deadly clashes between Israeli civilians and Arabs in the Gaza Strip, Palestinians everywhere engaged in a spontaneous resistance movement that became known as the *intifada*, the "shaking off."

The Western media invariably characterized the *intifada* as a violent movement. Scenes of murderous-looking Palestinian men and boys throwing stones at soldiers and civilians filled North American television screens and newspapers. In fact, however, especially during the first two years, the hothouse atmosphere of the *intifada* forced the flowering of many creative nonviolent activities.

Three nonviolent ways the Palestinians chose to shake off Israel were to refuse to buy Israeli goods, to participate in worker strikes, and to refuse to pay taxes. Over twenty years Palestinians had become economically dependent on Israel. With much of their farmland expropriated for use by Israel, Palestinian men went to work for Israeli construction companies and farmers while Palestinian women worked as domestics in Israeli homes. Their formerly agricultural economy quickly became a cash economy, and the flow of cash depended on Israel.

Two features of this arrangement became particularly galling to Palestinians. One was that most of their goods and produce could not be sold in Israel, while Israeli goods flooded the Palestinian markets. The boycott of Israeli products was, therefore, effective both as a symbolic nonviolent move and as an economic blow to the Israelis.

The second thorn in the side of the occupied Arabs was that Palestinian laborers paid higher income-tax than did their Israeli counterparts, yet their tax money went primarily to support Israel's infrastructure while the West Bank received proportionately few services. During the *intifada* general strikes and work stoppages hampered the construction and agricultural industries in Israel, while tax refusal threatened the Israeli economy and enraged the government.

There was violence, to be sure. Palestinians threw stones at Israeli settlers driving to and from their new homes built on confiscated Palestinian land. The message was, You are not welcome here. Soldiers became constant targets of Palestinian anger and frustration, and acts of violence against them were certainly a feature of the *intifada*. But the most effective "shaking off" of Israel was accomplished by the strikes, the boycotts, and the general refusal of Palestinians to allow Israel to continue the occupation unchallenged.

The predominantly Christian town of Beit Sahour embraced the *intifada* absolutely. Lying directly to the east of Bethlehem, Beit Sahour counts among its ten thousand residents many of the olive-wood carvers, mother-of-pearl workers, and other craftsmen who depend on the tourist trade for their liveli-hood. Before the *intifada* the craftsmen of Beit Sahour were heavily taxed on their wares, and they became leaders in the tax revolt. Therefore, the people were especially hard-hit by Israeli "tax raids" during which they saw their machines and tools confiscated or destroyed, leaving them with no means of financial support. In addition, as tourism dropped off during the *intifada*, family incomes were drastically reduced. The military government frequently pun-ished the tax resisters by placing the entire town under curfew for weeks at a time, forbidding the people to leave their houses to work, to go to church, or even to shop for food.

In the face of these privations, Ghassan and a small band of colleagues began the community group that would ultimately become the core of the Rapprochement Center. The group was originally formed not to promote dia-logue but to "sustain the *intifada* and to help the people of Beit Sahour withstand the hardships." Members were instrumental in organizing the people to help one another. They began "victory gardens," established dairy coopera-tives which made it possible to avoid buying Israeli milk, began home-schooling cooperatives when the Israelis closed their schools, and invented many other ways to endure.

Israel's response to the *intifada* contributed to its turning violent. When villagers started chicken cooperatives, for example, the occupying govern-ment frequently cited them for running an establishment without a permit and confiscated their chickens. Permits, however, were almost impossible to ob-tain. Such activity led Palestinians to the kind of despair which later expressed itself in violence. Early in 1989, then Defense Minister Yitzak Rabin ordered the Israeli Defense Force (IDF) to "break the bones" of anyone found partici-pating in the *intifada*. Shopkeepers refusing to open their stores were dragged into streets and beaten. Those who refused to pay taxes had the tools of their trades destroyed or their shops sealed, and they were arrested and beaten. IDF soldiers caught children suspected of throwing stones and did, indeed, break their arms and legs, leaving them on their mothers' doorsteps.

The *intifada* ushered in a period of separation between Arabs and Jews. Legitimate fear developed on the part of Israelis who previously had shopped, eaten out, and strolled about Arab towns such as Beit Sahour, which is only a few minutes drive from Jerusalem. After the start of the *intifada* it became unthinkable for Jews casually to enter a Palestinian town. The yellow license plates on their cars marked them as Israelis (Palestinian cars have blue plates), and they could expect to be stoned or worse if they ventured into Palestinian neighborhoods.

There are those Israelis who speak nostalgically about the time before the *intifada* when they enjoyed congenial relations with Arabs. They blame a few inciters for starting the uprising and refuse to believe that the majority of people wanted it. "Their" Arabs were peace loving and wanted to compromise and be friends with Israelis. The point they missed, and had been missing for twenty years, according to Ghassan Andoni, was that the compromises they had witnessed were all one-sided. They were the compromises that weak people are always forced to make in order to survive in a world imposed on them by the strong.

According to the Palestinians, there was little genuine interaction between Israelis and Palestinians because, as Ghassan puts it, "The sheep and the wolf cannot coexist. On the grassroots level, it can only be harmful to take a powerful man and a less powerful man and pretend there is reconciliation."

As the Palestinians regained their dignity in relation to the Israelis, what had passed for coexistence was revealed as an illusion. What Rapprochement activists saw with stunning acuity was that the *intifada* offered an opportunity for the growth of genuine relationships between "real" Arabs and Jews. Now, ironically, at the height of the *intifada*, dialogue was possible.

"When the *intifada* started, a lot of Israelis discovered Palestinians for the first time," explains Ghassan. "The *intifada* made grassroots dialogue possible because we could speak with the Israelis as equals."

Indeed, the *intifada* marked an epiphany for some Israelis who had been "waiting for something to happen," according to Judith Green, an Israeli archeologist on staff at Hebrew University. One of the original group of Israelis who began to dialogue with the Beit Sahour group, Judith came to Israel from the United States in 1973 because she saw that Israel was entering an important period in Jewish history, and she and her husband wanted to be a part of it. They were politically liberal Americans who had naively expected to find normal relations between Arabs and Israelis. They were initially surprised to find few opportunities to meet Palestinians. But with a family to raise and jobs to find, Judith and her husband found, like most Israelis, that in their day-to-day lives they could entirely exclude the Palestinians and their problems.

Judith's political awakening began during the 1982 war with Lebanon, in which her husband served as a member of the Israeli reserves. After the massacres at the Sabra and Shatilla refugee camps in Beirut, Judith, like many Israelis, began thinking critically and became more politically active. She has since learned that Sabra and Shatilla marked a turning point for some Palestinians, also.

For the first time they [Palestinians] saw Israelis demonstrating against the government on behalf of Palestinian refugees, and Ghassan and others had begun to think in terms of meeting some of those demonstrators. But in 1982, there still were no organized activities in the West Bank with which we could connect. Not until the *intifada*. Ironically, it needed the spark of violence to open communication.

Until the *intifada* we did not know that the Palestinians in the Occupied Territories were being harassed and brutally oppressed and had been since 1967. We did not hear of any resistance to the occupation, so we assumed it was experienced by them as benign. When we began the dialogues, one of the first things we learned was that they had been scared to act, and that most resistance was covered up by our government. It was an eye-opener to hear the Palestinian version of what's happened in the twentieth century; to see people who have lived through the same things we have lived through, but who experienced those events very differently.

The Beginning of Dialogue

In 1988, when the Beit Sahour community group began to explore the possibility of a new kind of relationship with Israelis, Judith Green and ten other Israelis met with ten Palestinians in Ghassan Andoni's home.

"It wasn't easy," Ghassan recalls. "The first meetings were very tough. We did not try to be polite or keep the conversation at a comfortable level. The point was not to reach consensus, because change does not mean people change their basic beliefs. People change their attitudes; people change their stereotypes. But usually their basic beliefs remain the same."

Judith Green agrees, and she avers that in a real dialogue, people's ability and willingness to retain their integrity is essential.

> Some dialogue groups are gestures, but in order to form a group that lasts, you need tension. If the participants just want to commiserate with the opposite group, then there is no point in having a dialogue. After a while you run out of things to say.
>
> When we started, we were concerned to have serious Jews, observant Jews; people who were Zionists, not radical peace-people on the margin of Israeli society. Many immigrants were involved, as were Holocaust survivors—people who really represented the Jewish and Israeli voice.
>
> We respected the Palestinians and they respected us because we all saw the commitment on both sides to our own perspectives. Together it was a terrific group. People thought deeply about the situation. They also had great humor. And so, although it was intense, we recognized right away that these were people who, under normal circumstances, would have been our friends.

After several meetings, the combined group decided to launch a series of public actions. The first was to invite Jews in Israel to come to Beit Sahour not as occupiers, but as guests. "As occupiers you are not welcome," read the invitation. "But as guests the people will receive you in their homes."

Almost one hundred Israelis came to Beit Sahour December 18, 1988, a Sunday afternoon. The army, having heard of the plan, decided to stop it. The military governor declared Beit Sahour a closed military zone and sealed off the town by sending armed soldiers to guard all major roads. Following a circuitous mountain back-road, the determined Israelis, along with members of the press, made their way into Beit Sahour. A large gathering formed at a local church, and there were speeches from representatives of both groups urging reconciliation.

"That was a small beginning," recalls Ghassan.

It was a small signal. But the effect was tremendous. When the first soldier finally discovered us and saw hundreds of Palestinians and a hundred Israelis with *kippas* on their heads, he went crazy. He went mad. He started jumping! Then he brought others, and the orders were that the Israelis should be evacuated. They began recording license plates of Israeli cars to frighten our guests and to put them on a list. But the people stayed through the afternoon, and we had talks with one another.

The second public action was even more radical than the first. In April 1989 Beit Sahour had already experienced its share of retaliation from the IDF for its participation in the *intifada*. When Rabin intensified the army's power by ordering the breaking of bones, the community group proposed a unique response. "We decided to send to the Israelis another invitation," recalls Ghassan. "This time we asked, 'Why don't we break bread together instead of breaking bones?'"

Twenty-five religious Jewish families from Jerusalem accepted Beit Sahour's offer to come and spend Friday night and all day Saturday—the Jewish Shabbat—worshiping and sharing meals and living space with Palestinians. Again, the visitors had to sneak into town to avoid being turned back by the army. After they arrived, each Israeli family joined a Palestinian family. The guests lit the Shabbat candles in a place allocated for their prayers. Then everyone prepared the joint supper. The Israelis had brought kosher food while the Beit Sahour families provided salads and soft drinks. It had taken some persuasion to convince the Palestinians, who are famous for their hospitality, to allow guests to bring their own food. While the kids played together in the playground, adults enjoyed a meal and dialogue together.

On the following morning hundreds of Palestinians walked into town to join the gathering in the Shepherds' Field. They listened as Palestinians and Israelis talked of peace. At the end of the meeting, the entire group marched through the streets for a meeting with the mayor at the municipal building. And there the march was stopped by the Israeli army.

The commanding officer told the crowd that Beit Sahour was a closed military zone and ordered all Israelis to leave immediately.

"We can't leave, officer," replied one of the Jewish guests. "It is Shabbat."

The officer told them, "Mr. Rabin personally ordered us to get you out of the town."

The guest replied, "God ordered us personally not to travel on Shabbat."

Then an army officer told one of the guests, Knesset member Ran Cohen, that he had reliable information that Palestinians were planning to kill him and his family.

"What you do not know," Cohen replied, "is that I and my family spent the last night sleeping here in Beit Sahour. Honestly, I have never felt more secure in my life than last night."

"In the dispute between God's orders and Rabin's orders," reads one report, "God won."

"Those early activities were 100 percent positive," says Judith Green.

They were magical events. We were hopeful and felt we were in the vanguard of tremendous change. A border had opened. You know, living in Jerusalem is claustrophobic. It is impossible to drive in almost any direction without coming quickly to a border you cannot safely cross. To realize suddenly that it was possible to have contact with the societies around us was a thrilling revelation. We were breaking many taboos. It was a supposedly life-threatening act to go into the West Bank. The idea of going with children and having a Jewish Sabbath really brought us together. It was even illegal for Jews to stay overnight in the West Bank.

We were touched by the fact that it wasn't the members of the dialogue group who hosted us. A whole neighborhood invited us. They were taking an enormous risk. We had thought we had twenty friends in Beit Sahour, but 500 people showed up at the church.

Rapprochement

To guarantee that the activities would be positive experiences, during each Israeli visit to Beit Sahour the organizers needed to ensure that there would be no violence. To that end they enlisted the aid of young people in protecting the yellow-plated Israeli cars. With such creative planning, the small community group involved almost the whole town in the process of reconciliation. The importance of such inclusive involvement cannot be overstated in a land where factionalism is the norm on both sides of the Green Line. Ghassan sees several ways in which bringing the community along in realizing the vision of rapprochement helped the whole town.

If a community is ignorant of what each part is doing, it usually becomes very conservative. Our community is highly educated about the issues. Here, there is a level of trust. When we plan an activity, we don't go into closed rooms and make decisions. The Rapprochement Center is not separate from Beit Sahour because it involves activists from different political and religious parties. In Beit Sahour, nobody can ignore the fact that the work is common work.

Ghassan is most gratified with the knowledge that the actions of the Rapprochement Center helped to minimize the casualties in Beit Sahour during the *intifada*.

We made Beit Sahour a place where we always have foreigners, report-
ers and Israelis. The army is more hesitant to fire on us. Unfortunately
we have had five people killed by Israelis. But if we had not been active,
I assume we would have lost, as other places on the West Bank did, 30
or 40 people. And Beit Sahour was a hot place during the *intifada*. It
was not a quiet town. It could have been a disaster.

Our work increased the people's sense of power—that they are not
alone in the struggle. And our work also diffused the amount of fundamentalist activity, because usually fundamentalism comes out of a feeling
of being alone, surrounded and powerless. People actually started being
more active, but in a positive, non-violent way. They started acting as a
community in resistance, willing to suffer more and stand more. But
they didn't go desperate or wild.

This last point raises again the question of what Christians have to offer
the conflict. When one speaks of fundamentalism in the Middle East, one
almost always means the Islamist movement, which tends to separate Muslims from the rest of the world and to solve problems of oppression with
extreme, deadly violence.

The Islamist movement should be put into proper perspective in relation to
the *intifada*. Fundamentalism among Palestinians gained adherents as the
intifada dragged on, causing people to lose hope for a change in their condition. But at no time could it be said that a majority of Palestinians—Muslim
or Christian—embraced fundamentalist principles. Most Palestinians participated in the *intifada* as a political, not a religious movement.

Certainly the Christian influence in Beit Sahour offered an ameliorating
alternative to fundamentalist extremism. Ghassan describes Beit Sahour as
"the last Christian town," a reference to the fact that all other major Christian
centers in the West Bank, including Bethlehem, have lost so many Christians
to emigration that they now record a majority Muslim population. At the turn
of the century, Palestine's Christians comprised 30 to 40 percent of the over-
all population. Now that figure stands at less than 3 percent.

Ayman Abu Zulour, a twenty-six-year-old member of the Rapprochement
Center, describes the predicament of West Bank Christian Palestinians:

Christians have no claims here. We are no longer even allowed to enter
Jerusalem to pray. Tourists come from thousands of miles away to see
Jerusalem and Nazareth, but I and my family are forbidden by the Israe-
lis to enter those holy cities. Muslims claim the land, and Jews claim the
land. We have no claims. Yet the whole country represents Christianity.
Wherever you go in this land, it is holy for Christians.

The church doesn't want to be involved in politics, but wasn't Jesus
killed for political reasons? And we are being killed for political reasons. Sometimes I feel that the Church has forgotten Palestinian
Christians. Nobody cares about us. The concept of the church has been

changed to the church as a museum which people come and visit. People pay tribute to old stones. But we are the living stones.

While the Rapprochement Center explicitly defines itself as a nonreligious organization—a matter of prudence in such a religiously diverse region— Ghassan explains the role Christian philosophy has played in its formation.

What is the essence of rapprochement? Rapprochement is inclusiveness as opposed to exclusiveness. And rapprochement is finally reconciliation. For me this is a personal belief as well as a historical argument. Judaism put an emphasis on the idea of God/Man communication. Christianity shifted this into a horizontal relationship. You have communication with God through your neighbor. You work for the benefit of everybody. You love people and you help them.

Islam has come closer to Judaism on the question of exclusivity. What counts is the relationship of Man to God. Islam says you give privilege to the Muslims. Christianity is the essence of reconciliation when it asks: "How is it possible to bring people together?"

I do believe that the reason the idea of rapprochement emerged in Beit Sahour is that exclusiveness has never been a part of our psychology. We don't think of a Christian as privileged above others.

Ghassan, a lecturer in physics at Bir Zeit University, did not come naturally or easily to his philosophy of reconciliation. "I have never been a passive man," he said during an interview. "I have been active. Do you want my background?"

I was a radical freedom fighter. I was in Lebanon fighting against the Philangists and Israelis. In 1976, during the civil war, I was there. I am a militant; a radical nationalist. I have spent at least four years in the Israeli prisons.

I began to change during the war. I saw . . . I saw things that I never believed I would see. What does it mean when people believe only in weapons and fighting—when that becomes a tradition of life? Then, the noble cause just vanishes, and you only see people killing each other with brutality. You forget all about those beliefs and ideologies you are fighting for. There is nothing called "homeland." There is nothing called "noble cause." You end up with this reality: a gun and an enemy.

But being a freedom fighter and liberating your people is much more complicated than that. You need to bring the human dimension to the whole struggle. If you don't there is nothing noble in what you do.

I didn't stop resisting the occupation. I never said, even now, that my people have no right to fight. What I said is, "Look, bring this human dimension to the struggle, and see how it develops. Just bring it." I never deceive people and tell them that this is the solution. But I am convinced that there is no way you can be a freedom fighter without human obligations.

I am still a freedom fighter. I still dream of Jaffa, my lost paradise. But I have changed my methodology. My project is inclusive. From my point of view, I am much more radical than many Palestinians. I disagree with the idea that the victim has no moral obligation. Sometimes moral obligation limits your effectiveness, your efficiency. But you have to live with that. If you don't then I doubt that you can discriminate between the victim and the victimizer. Both will look alike. With the work of the Rapprochement Center, I am satisfied that we can be effective and still maintain the moral element.

Activities of the Center

While public activities continue—including an annual Christmas Eve candlelight procession which attracts eight thousand participants—the heart of the Rapprochement Center beats in the ongoing, biweekly dialogue. Every other Thursday night between ten and twenty Israelis travel to Beit Sahour by bus, and there they meet with an equal number of Palestinians to discuss issues relating to the conflict. There is usually one Israeli and one Palestinian facilitator, and the ground rule is that participants may say anything they want on any subject. Although there are a few "core" members on both sides who always attend, attempts are made each week to bring new people into the dialogue. Tourists who have read or heard about the Center frequently find their way to the small room set aside for the dialogue, and it is often filled to capacity with forty or fifty people. The conversation is in English, the language common to all comers.

Adults of all ages attend the dialogue. The core members are generally middle aged. Students from Hebrew University are often in attendance, and many of the regular Palestinian participants study at Bethlehem University. Almost every Palestinian man in the room has spent time in Israeli prisons, usually without being charged with any crime. Almost every Israeli has served in the army. Though the Israelis are most likely to be members of the political left-wing—supporters of the peace process—none would controvert the principles of Zionism, which demand an Israeli state at all costs. Although the Palestinians are now committed to finding common ground with the Jews, most, especially the young men, will admit to having participated in violent activities during the *intifada*.

The dialogues are usually, as Ghassan describes them, "hot." Resolution and agreement are rare. But all sides of any argument are heard, and heard well. No one leaves claiming not to understand the motives for recalcitrance on either side. While there might be anger and finger-pointing admonitions, there is also an underlying trust generated by the years of interaction the long-term participants have enjoyed.

The dialogue held in late March 1995 represents a typical evening in many ways. The topic raised by an Israeli participant was, "What do you think the situation will be in the year 2010?" The question divided the group into optimists and pessimists, and on that particular night, many people were in a pessimistic frame of mind.

At that juncture in the peace negotiations, it had become apparent that very little had changed for the Palestinians, and they were beginning to suffer from the oppression that characterized life before and during the *intifada*. In spite of an enormous legal effort to stop them, the Israelis had just confiscated a tree-covered mountain that had previously been part of Beit Sahour, and construction of Jewish homes was about to begin. Since March of 1993 Palestinians had not been allowed into Jerusalem without a permit, and permits had become impossible to obtain. During the week before this dialogue, the Arab bus on which Ghassan was traveling was boarded at a checkpoint by soldiers with dogs. The dogs went up and down the aisles sniffing every horrified passenger. Anger over such degradations showed itself in the Palestinian responses.

The Israeli participants were equally disgruntled. The dialogue took place only a few weeks after the latest in a series of suicide bus-bombings that had claimed the lives of Israeli soldiers and civilians. Since the beginning of 1995 a score of Israelis had been killed by Palestinian extremists. Given this state of affairs, it took only a few minutes for passions to flare.

One Israeli declared himself an optimist but said that peace would be impossible until the terrorism stopped. He raised the question of the Israeli settlements in the West Bank—the large housing developments built for Jews on confiscated Palestinian land—and said that the government was powerless to unsettle the settlements as long as terror continued. Then he called upon the Palestinians, and particularly upon Yassir Arafat, to control terrorists. "It is in the best interests of your internal prospects," he concluded, "to get rid of this internal opposition."

He was immediately countered by a Palestinian speaker who asked in a voice wavering with emotion,

What have we gained from this peace process until now as Palestinians? And what have we lost? We lost many things. I am sixty years old and I cannot now go to Jerusalem to pray. The headmaster of a school was killed in a free zone in Gaza by settlers when he drove by in his car. What is this? Is this a peace? Arafat must stop Hamas. But how? The people are angry, and he hasn't the means.

Another Palestinian weighed in at this point, responding to the first Israeli speaker.

My impression of your thesis is that terrorism is the evil and that's that. But I disagree. With occupation there is resistance. They go together. There is no way you can hold Palestinians responsible for resistance, while you don't hold Israelis responsible for continuing the occupation. If you want to continue the occupation, you should expect the continuation of resistance. Like it or not, this is the equation.

Another Israeli pointed out that the Palestinians who signed the Oslo peace accords had agreed to the conditions, had agreed to stop the terror. To which a Palestinian replied,

I'll be frank with you. Hamas is not the problem. The problem is now that Hamas enjoys a great popular support. And there you should look deep and see why. Palestinians do not hate Jews genetically. And I think we agree upon this. Certain Palestinians are supporting the ones who fight against the occupation in the same way the Jews supported the ones who fought against the British, sometimes with militant ways. No nation is better than another.

We have evil among us. It is my guess that we can control it. It's more problematic on your side.

To this last remark, an Israeli who had not yet spoken took offense.

I think it's a mistake to say it's worse on one side. When you do that you imply that evil has always been in us, and it's grown to large proportions. That's a mistake. It's important for Palestinians to see our side—that the evil is not something genetic. I try to understand that the evil on the Palestinian side comes from the oppression. You need to understand where our extremists come from. I think that's the only way any of us will get over it. Try to understand it.

Trust in Conditions of Uncertainty

Understanding is a pearl of great price in the Holy Land. In a place where every word has political implications, those who seek to understand the other side risk being misunderstood by their own people. Jews who criticize the Israeli government are publicly vilified. Palestinians who consort with Israelis risk being labeled collaborators in their communities. "That is why," Ghassan admonishes, "to be a peacemaker, you need the soul of a fighter."

The Israelis and Palestinians who meet at the Rapprochement Center to seek understanding are people of courage and compassion. After an hour of dialogue, even one as emotionally charged as the evening of March 23, they conclude with tea and laughter. They worry about the need to get something done, not just to talk, and someone always reminds the group that talking is the doorway to action. The foreigners all say they will remember this night after they've forgotten the holy sites they've visited. Some Israelis, for whom this is the first dialogue, are quiet.

Judith Green says:

Some people close up during the dialogue, and you know they are confronting their high ideals. Before the *intifada* started and revealed the nature of the occupation to us, we had not had our values confronted or tested. We had won all the wars, after all. Now, for some Jews, recognizing the truth is just too painful. Many people, even left-leaning Israelis, fall by the wayside quickly.

Theoretically the dialogue is the best way to test these values. On a human level, the experience is almost always positive; but on a personal level, it is very challenging. You lose your sense of balance for a while.

For those with the courage to continue working with the Rapprochement Center, the dialogue has provided a way to maintain their equilibrium through the dizzying and dangerous era of the *intifada*. Looking back on those years, and ahead to the still uncertain future, Ghassan Andoni and Judith Green reflect on the impact of the Rapprochement Center.

"We know our impact is limited," says Ghassan.

There is not a way a local center like ours will change the region or the world. But we believe we can make a small contribution to change. In the past seven years, we have managed to get thousands of people here from Israel. With each one we begin human communication, and no one is immune from that. Even if one comes here intent on convincing himself of something else, finally he gets the dose. Even if he is highly ideological, let him come. Let him deliver his message and close his eyes. But can he close all his senses in front of forty people? Even if he hears a small story and thinks at night about it, that's significant.

Judith sees that, in the long term, groups like the Rapprochement Center have had an impact on public opinion.

Right now, for example, Israel is confiscating land from Arabs in Jerusalem, and there is a big international cry of outrage over this. But the government has been confiscating land for years. Before, no one was interested in the problems Arabs faced when their land was confiscated. Now, suddenly, it is an issue. I do believe the outcry is the result of years of education on the part of people like us. Before, we collected information, but no one would listen. Now that people are asking questions, we are prepared to answer them. The period of hypnosis that we went through from '67 to '87 is at least over. At least there is a dynamic conflict. The whole place has become a tinder-box, but that is much better than hypnosis.

When we started this dialogue, we thought there would be a revolution, that things would happen quickly. Now we're much more cynical and unsure. We are still such a minority. If public opinion decides in favor of war, we lose. Also on the Palestinian side, the forces for peace may lose.

But even if that happens, we can say we did all we could; we can say we put our hearts into it.

9

A Dialogue on Reconciliation in Belgrade

The Report of a Participant

JIM FOREST

An "Ecumenical Dialogue on Reconciliation" occurred in Belgrade for several days in February 1996. The most poignant moment was, perhaps, the confessional statement of Father Mato Zovkić, a priest now living in Croatia but soon to return to Sarajevo, where he is vicar general of the Roman Catholic diocese. He was taking issue with his friend and fellow Roman Catholic the archbishop of Belgrade, Franc Perko, who earlier in the day had attributed the crimes committed in the wars in former Yugoslavia to atheists. Pulling a blue rosary from his pocket, Father Zovkić said that he had met Catholics who boasted of murdering Muslims and destroying Muslim towns while wearing rosaries around their necks. "Whatever we say about them, they regarded themselves as devout Catholics, not atheists. We Catholics cannot say we had nothing to do with the terrible things they did." Zovkić did not "find enough courage" in religious leaders to be "prophetic in confronting their failures."

Taking the First Step: Dissonant Voices

All three religious communities in Bosnia, Croatia, and Serbia have members who committed appalling war crimes in the past five years and who regard themselves not only as defenders of their nation but of their faith as well. No doubt they have met nationalist pastors who blessed their wartime activities. But few religious leaders have yet been willing to acknowledge that their own religious community did too little, was too cautious, or may have helped stir nationalist passions that resulted in crimes against neighbors.

The meeting in Belgrade may yet prove to have been a significant step within the Christian community, helping to heal the wounds created by war in the Balkans. The event was sponsored by the Theological Faculty of the Serbian Orthodox Church and the Geneva-based Conference of European Churches.

Sixty church delegates took part, half of them from Serbia, Croatia, Bosnia, and Slovenia, the other half from the rest of Europe and North America.

The meeting was opened by Patriarch Pavle, eighty-one years old, head of the Serbian Orthodox Church since 1991, a modest monk well known for his readiness to meet with anyone who seeks him out and for his preference for travel by tram and bus. In his brief address he called for the reconstruction of destroyed homes, churches, and mosques and prayed for hatred to be extinguished by "truthful forgiveness." He stressed our duty as coworkers of God not to abide by narrow political or factional criteria, but to see that the church in any nation must raise that nation to the stature of the people of God. "If [the church] deviates from that direction . . . it ceases to be that which it should be: the church of the Living God." Referring to the debate within European churches about whether or not the churches of former Yugoslavia have acted as they should during the war, he concluded that any church in the Christian family must be "judged by people of goodwill, and ultimately and unmistakably by God."

For many people the simple fact of being present at such a dialogue was hard work. Father Vladimir Vukasinović, assistant professor of liturgics at the Theological Faculty in Belgrade, told me he had been far too upset to say a single word during the first workshop in which he participated. All he could think of were his grandparents, all four of whom were murdered during the Second World War. "The Muslims killed my mother's parents. The Croats killed my father's parents. They have tried to kill us Serbs three times in this century and many times before that. And they will keep trying. It is dreaming to think in another way." Yet I could see him struggling hard to do so.

The next day Father Vladimir took an active part in group dialogue, objecting to the idea that when large numbers of people are involved in a communal act like war, no one bears individual responsibility for participation:

> There is no such thing as collective sin, all sins are personal. Even when groups commit sin, still each person involved is committing a personal sin. In war the first sin is to kill another, the second sin is to refuse to be a free person. Similarly we never relate simply to a group, only to concrete persons. There is no Mr. Everyone, there are only persons with names, only Peter and Paul. The first step in reconciliation is to make contact with an actual person.

"Reconciliation is possible," he continued, "but it cannot come from a thousand hours of political debate. It cannot come from Tito's way, imposed from above. It can only come from repentance."

One of the observers at the conference was Dragan Dragojlović, minister of religions in the Serbian government and a poet by avocation. Apparently he is an Orthodox Christian, as he crossed himself in the Orthodox manner when entering the chapel of the Theological Faculty. He saw the wars in former Yugoslavia as more religious in character than religious leaders want to admit: "Not that many combatants were devout believers, but they made little if any distinction between national and religious identity, nor did their religious communities encourage them to make such a distinction."

"So, is our war a religious war?" asked Father Anastasije Raketa, a young Orthodox priest from a destroyed village in Bosnia. "Yes—and no," he said. "Religion is not itself the origin of the war, but the instrument of war. The key to the solution is in collective responsibility not only of the nations that fought each other but of the world community." He recalled growing up in Bosnia with not only Orthodox but also Croat and Muslim friends.

> But suddenly winds blew from the north, south, east and west, and everything was destroyed, and not only neighbor killing neighbor. I knew personally Serbs who were killed by American bombs—one small house suddenly gone with all the people who had lived in it. Could they be guilty of anything? So we must think of collective responsibility and collective repentance. We have to find our own guilt and not simply accuse other people. As long as we search for the guilty, there will be no peace and there will be no reconciliation.

Professor Dimitar Kirov, of the Theological Faculty in Belgrade, said that the recent history of Yugoslavia had much to do with the war, including the suppression of all religious education. "The system imposed was not atheist so much as anti-theist. But a vacuum cannot exist in the life of real persons. If you are nothing, then you see your neighbor as a nothing."

By contrast, for Father Vladimir the recent events had little to do with the Tito era. "This war is the continuation of World War II. It isn't helpful to blame the Communists, except to note that Tito would not allow any process of actual reconciliation."

Mother Maria Rule, an Orthodox nun from England who lived for eleven years in Serbia, pointed out that it is not only the effects of the last two wars we have to think about to understand the Serbians. "Here I have encountered a different way of consciousness," she said. "The Serbs have never gone more than fifty to seventy years without an oppressor. This is their primary experience." The result is the Serbian tendency "to put people first in frames. First so-and-so is a Muslim, only afterward is he a man with a big heart. First a label, then a person."

Admitting Former Crimes

Among topics that emerged repeatedly in both group and private conversations was the harm caused when evils committed in the past are not admitted or are minimized, when there is no sign of repentance or effort made to seek forgiveness. No one knows exactly how many Serbs were killed by Croats during the last world war, when Croatia became an independent fascist state obsessed with racial purity. The usual estimate of people murdered by the Croatian Ustache is 600,000, chiefly Serbs, but also Jews, gypsies, and others who were regarded as racially inferior or as political criminals. Regarding the Serbs, the slogan of Croatia's head of state, Ante Pavelić, was "one-third killed, one-third converted [to Catholicism], one-third expelled." For Serbs, the name of the largest Croatian concentration camp, Jasenovac, is as infamous as Auschwitz is to the Jews—the difference being that not only Jews but everyone knows about Auschwitz, while only Serbians know about Jasenovac.

In the half century since the war ended, both the German government and the churches of Germany have in numerous ways acknowledged the crimes committed in the Hitler years, many times asked forgiveness, and sought to compensate survivors. But the Croatian Catholic Church has remained silent, neither acknowledging the genocide that happened (in which Catholic clergy often played an active part) nor seeking forgiveness. When Croatia again became an independent state, it chose as its symbol a red-and-white chessboard design almost identical to the one used during the time of fascism. Still more ominous, its head of state, Franjo Tudjman, is the author of a book in which he sought to minimize the number of Serbs killed (he estimated sixty thousand victims). It was the kind of "study" that neo-nazis published about the Holocaust. Now Croatia plans a memorial at Jasenovac, not to the people murdered at the camp but to Croatian soldiers who died in the war. "In this way they want to hide the crimes," said a Serbian layman at the conference.

> But there is not one Serbian family that does not have members who died at Jasenovac or similar places in those years, and every day we remember what happened to them. To Americans such events may seem in the distant past, but to us they are very fresh and painful. Even today if the Catholic bishops of Croatia were to admit what happened and express their sorrow, it would do much to change the way we relate to each other. What we feel instead is that we are still regarded as an inferior people whose disappearance would be no loss to the human race, people whom it is not a sin to kill.

We heard much less about the war crimes Serbians have committed against Croats and Muslims in the past five years and the fact that it is not only the Croatian Catholic Church which is infected by nationalism but also the Serbian Orthodox Church. "Our problem," said one Orthodox priest, "is that many of us, when we make the sign of the cross, might as well be saying, 'In the name of the Father, the Son, and Saint Sava.' This is what easily happens whenever a church becomes the sole guardian of national identity. We are experts on the sins committed against our nation, yet we try to forget the sins our people have committed against others."

"I am thinking about what churches, not just individuals, can contribute to reconciliation," said Heinz Ruegger, secretary of the Federation of Swiss Protestant Churches. "As long as there is nobody who takes responsibility, we cannot solve it. Consider Germany and World War II and those people who, after the war, were able to take responsibility upon themselves even though they were not immediately responsible for the crimes that were committed. The impact of their action was immense."

Bishop Ignjatije, a young member of the Serbian hierarchy and a professor at the Theological Faculty, pointed out that the church had no "authoritative influence" in shaping national policies. Still, he didn't regard the church as blameless.

> We [in the church] did not manage to differentiate a common stand for the church. The tendency was to escape into an abstract space that really did not mean too much. Reality was different. People wanted something concrete from the church. We were asked to take a principled stand and give a principled viewpoint. Such a thing may be possible in the west but it is very difficult in our situation.

He felt that in both the East and the West there is a wrong perception about the Kingdom of God, on the one side too caught up in history, on the other too detached. The Western side tries to create the Kingdom of God by its own efforts, while the Orthodox side has the tendency passively to await the gift of the Kingdom, identifying eschatology with history. A synthesis is needed. "The truth lies in communal life," he said. "Communion with the other person has primary value"—including those who want to follow the historical process and those who await the coming Kingdom of God.

Because of the Orthodox tendency to be passive in its response to history, "we [Serbian Orthodox] may have seemed biased in the eyes of the West, yet at least we always made a clear distinction between what we in the church were doing and what the [political] authorities were doing." He added, "I can't understand why the civilized world does not understand that in a conflict there is not only one guilty party." Nonetheless, he regretted that the church had made "some compromises which did not help either the church or the people. Some of us have the idea that we don't need anyone around us, that all around us are our enemies. Our children are taught in school that the other person is the enemy."

Jean Fischer, general secretary of the Conference of European Churches, expressed the worry that, unless religious leaders take a lead in expressing repentance for specific crimes committed on their own side, the cycle of violence and counter-violence will simply go on and the Dayton Agreements will become one more item of failure in the history books. He recalled that the French did not make fine distinctions about Germans after the war. "The French considered all Germans—all—as Nazis. It has taken fifty years to get over this. We should do what we can to prevent this happening to other peoples so that they are not regarded as collectively guilty." He went on to speak of the collective guilt of many countries for the war in the Balkans. "It wasn't just the peoples within the borders. Where did the weapons come from? In which factories were the land mines made?"

The Power of Symbols

Since most people are influenced not so much by rational thinking as by significant symbolic gestures, Jean Fischer raised the question how an entire people can be rescued out of a state of general antagonism toward another group. "What gestures can religious leaders offer that can help ordinary people see beyond antagonism?"

He suggested that one area of possible ecumenical work to overcome division would be a joint effort to help find the eight thousand people who are listed as disappeared—many will probably be found in mass graves—and to provide a religious burial according to the traditions of the victim's family. Many families simply don't know what happened to particular persons and still nurse the hope that a missing person may be found alive.

Bishop Henrik Svenungsson of the Church of Sweden noted that many local pastors look back to times when Catholics, Orthodox, and Muslims lived together peaceably and still long for such times to return. "We are not at the zero point. Also we must not think the process of reconciliation isn't already under way. Many people are doing work to heal social wounds. One thing the churches can do is to offer strong support to those already doing reconciliation work at the local level."

The problem of the mass media was a recurrent topic. There was a consensus that the world press has normally presented a one-sided, dangerously out-of-balance picture of events in Serbia, Croatia, and Bosnia-Herzegovina so that the Western world was presented with the impression that overwhelming guilt for the war and its crimes belonged to the Serbs, with the Croatians a distant second, and the government of Bosnia-Herzegovina nothing more than a victim. Bogdan Lubardić, assistant professor of philosophy at the Theological Faculty, spoke of the "virtual reality" the mass media have created. "What can we do about media domination? It is spiritual deceit on a global scale." Others may have felt that while the media often distorted the reality, they did prevent many massive crimes from remaining a secret.

The reality of the war was brought out vividly by a visit during the conference to a local hospital where many people seriously wounded in the war (some as combatants, others simply bystanders who stepped on a land mine) are being fitted with artificial limbs and learning to use them. It was in some ways an inspiring visit—one could see the progress patients were making in dealing with personal catastrophe. But the hospital is understaffed, underequipped, and has no program for follow-up work once patients leave. All the patients are missing at least part of one limb, and many are far more severely handicapped. The emotional and spiritual struggle is just as hard as the physical. Attempted suicides are not unusual. In most cases the patients have lost not only part of their bodies but their life partners. Often close relatives and friends have been killed. Many have lost their homes. Now they must enter into an economy in which even the able-bodied have a difficult time surviving. Jelena, a young nurse several of us talked with, said she often falls asleep crying.

Common Resolutions

Dr. John Taylor, staff member of the Conference of European Churches and the main organizer of the Ecumenical Dialogue, was confident that despite painful moments and the disagreements that were expressed, the dialogue had been constructive. "Reconciliation is a process, not something you can make. It is something that can only be done step by step."

If the conference had a single theological stress, it was on the Holy Trinity and the love that binds the three Divine Persons into perfect oneness—a model of diversity in unity with profound implications in social life. We were reminded of the teaching of St. Sergius of Radonezh, "Contemplation of the Holy Trinity destroys all enmity."

Actions for Reconciliation

The following are extracts from a text approved unanimously by the Ecumenical Dialogue for Reconciliation at its final plenary meeting in Belgrade on February 22:

> Christian faith gives energy and vision to Christians to work with their neighbors of other faiths or world-views, to heal the divisions and hatreds which have been forged from the past. In the countries of the former Yugoslavia in the last five years alone, millions have been driven from their homes, hundreds of thousands have been killed, and thousands have disappeared and may be found dead, unburied or in collective graves. Without repentance and compassionate action in response to these tragedies, reconciliation is an empty word.

> The participants committed themselves and called on their churches, international organizations and neighbors, to undertake and support reconciling actions, which include:
> • Restoring homes to the displaced, ideally in their original regions, and providing pastoral care
> • Searching for the missing, ensuring a decent burial for the dead, and caring for the bereaved

- Helping rebuild the economy with special attention to restoring self-confidence, and providing job opportunities for women and those disabled by war
- Reaching out to youth deprived and traumatized by war
- Repairing or rebuilding destroyed places of worship, whether of one's own community or of one's neighbor
- Promoting multicultural education (including religious curricula), inter-religious dialogue and common prayerful witness for peace
- Encouraging religious media not to contribute, but to counteract, the one-sided misrepresentation of complex situations which is so characteristic of much mass media coverage of Balkan events and which propagates fear and hatred
- Offering the services of international or local religious leaders to help monitor elections
- Continuing ecumenical and interreligious dialogues, in particular including the rich contribution that women make to reconciliation
- Contributing experiences and visions of reconciliation in the countries of the former Yugoslavia to the Second European Ecumenical Assembly at Graz in 1997 on the theme of "Reconciliation: Gift of God and Source of New Life."

Although the vast majority of people long for peace, specific steps to achieve reconciliation can be difficult and controversial. Some of the most courageous and effective actions that Christians and their neighbors can undertake begin at the local level, but these can be a powerful challenge to national and international leaders. Christian clergy and laity can be among those who help lead the way to reestablishing community. They can set an example through public confession of past failures and public criticisms of specific violations of human rights.

Churches can play a vital role in the creation of democratic social structures, being vigilant in defense of social justice and ready to challenge political and military leaders when necessary.

10

Reconciliation and the Churches in Northern Ireland

MICHAEL HURLEY, S.J.

The Churches are very much part of the solution—rather than part of the problem—in Ireland today.

—*The Irish News*[1]

The occasion for this editorial was a visit by a delegation from the Presbyterian Church in Ireland to the Forum for Peace and Reconciliation in Dublin to make a submission on behalf of their Church and Government Committee. The visit was highly significant. The Forum, which held its inaugural meeting on October 28, 1994, was established by the Dublin government "to consult on and examine ways in which lasting peace, stability and reconciliation can be established by agreement among all the people of Ireland." It was "especially anxious that the voices of members of both the Unionist and Nationalist traditions as well as of others, be heard." Unionists, however, especially the main Unionist political parties, have been conspicuous more by their absence than their presence.

The Presbyterian Church in Ireland is not to be confused with Dr. Paisley's Free Presbyterian Church, which is Presbyterian in name only. On the other hand, although it does include a large number of members who are outstanding in every way—in particular The Very Rev. John Dunlop, a former moderator—and although it is in no sense "The Unionist party at prayer," its membership is in fact mostly Northern, mostly Unionist and mostly un- and anti-ecumenical: in 1979 it suspended and in 1980 it terminated its membership of the World Council of Churches; in 1990 it declined to join the new Council of Churches for Great Britain and Ireland, of which the Roman Catholic Church in England and Wales did become a member. An *official* submission from this church is, therefore, in the words of *The Irish News*, "an important ground-breaking development," all the more so as (according to this newspaper) it urged a "growing togetherness" among all the people of Ireland, Catholic and Protestant, North and South. The submission stated: "We yearn for a new kind of society in Ireland, marked by co-operation, mutual affirmation, honour and respect, in which all are winners. . . . We must work with models of co-operation, and not with models of domination or assimilation."[2]

Many other facts, as this essay hopes to indicate, corroborate the judgment of *The Irish News* that "the Churches are very much part of the solution—rather than part of the problem—in Ireland today." But was it always so, and what is the problem? According to *The Irish News*: "It has often been wrongly suggested that tensions between the two communities in Northern Ireland stem from religion rather than politics." This is a restatement of what has been a traditional Nationalist, Catholic viewpoint and, though it plunges us in medias res, some consideration of it will be of help to begin with.

Nobody denies that Northern Ireland is a political and also an economic and cultural problem.[3] The island is territorially, politically divided. According to the Unionist story the twenty-six counties of the South seceded from the United Kingdom some seventy-five years ago. According to the Nationalist story the Northern Unionists refused to be included in the Home Rule Bill passed at Westminster in 1913 and succeeded eventually in securing a separate existence for the six counties in the northeast of the country.

So Ireland is partitioned; there are two political jurisdictions. One, with its headquarters in Dublin, comprises twenty-six of the thirty-two counties; it is a republic and largely (91 percent) Roman Catholic in population. In its Constitution the Dublin jurisdiction lays claim to the six counties of the North; it looks forward to a united Ireland, to the abolition of the border dividing the country politically. The vast majority of the people in the South are now Nationalists but, with the growing apart of the two jurisdictions especially since World War II, their nationalism has become more notional than real, more a patriotic aspiration than a political goal.

The other jurisdiction, with its headquarters in Belfast, comprises the remaining six counties, where some 60 percent of the population is Protestant. It is part of the United Kingdom of Great Britain and Northern Ireland. Until 1972 it had its own parliament at Stormont but is now governed by direct rule from Westminster. It rejects the constitutional claim of the South and its majority is determined to maintain the union with Britain. But there is also a large minority in the North, some 40 percent, who are Nationalists, most of them being Roman Catholic.[4]

As the last twenty-five years, indeed as the whole history of Northern Ireland has shown, some Nationalists and Unionists do not hesitate to resort to violence and bloodshed to further their ends. Between 1968 and 1994 nearly thirty-five hundred people were killed. But happily the violence is now over.[5] The IRA (Irish Republican Army), the Nationalist para-militaries, declared a ceasefire that began on September 1, 1994, and their Unionist counterparts, the CLMC (Combined Loyalist Military Command), followed suit on October 14. At the time of this writing the Dublin and Westminster governments have published "A New Framework for Agreement: A Shared Understanding between the British and Irish Governments to Assist Discussion and Negotiation Involving the Northern Ireland Parties." The matter at issue is: How is Northern Ireland to be governed? And how, in consequence, are its economic, social, and cultural problems to be solved? An answer satisfactory or acceptable to all interests will take years rather than months to emerge. In the words of former prime minister Dr. Garret FitzGerald, architect of the Anglo-Irish Agreement of 1985, the way forward will be "long, tortuous and thorny."[6]

But is Northern Ireland not also a religious problem? Is it wrong to suggest that the tensions between the two communities stem, if not "from religion rather than politics," at least from religion as well as politics?

Unbelievable as it always sounds to outsiders, the church in Ireland is *not* partitioned. There may be two political jurisdictions, but there are not two ecclesiastical jurisdictions. The church in Ireland is not territorially divided. Each of the main churches is a united, all-Ireland, thirty-two county organization, as was the whole country up to some seventy years ago, and the primatial see for both Anglicans and Catholics is in Armagh in Northern Ireland. The history of the churches goes back centuries and bears witness to the way things were before the political border was created earlier this century. So it is that there are Anglican and Roman Catholic dioceses, Methodist districts, and Presbyterian presbyteries that are partly in the South, partly in the North, which straddle the political border because they predate it. So it is that in ecclesiastical affairs and circles there is no controversy as to whether a certain city is to be called Derry (as in Nationalist parlance) or Londonderry (as in Unionist parlance). For both Anglicans and Roman Catholics it is now, as always, the diocese of Derry, and for Presbyterians too it is now, as always, the Presbytery and Synod of Derry. It may be noted, however, that, unlike the church, the Jewish community in Ireland did reorganize itself and become "partitioned" in 1919. An Irish chief rabbinate was set up in Dublin, whereas Belfast and the North continued to be under the jurisdiction of London. The traditional contacts between Southern and Northern Jews, however, have been maintained; in the main all would be Orthodox.

Precisely because it is not itself partitioned, the church in Ireland has been a unifying factor, if not within Northern Ireland, at least between North and South, and to that extent it has always been part of the solution to the conflict. The coincidence in the North of political and religious loyalties, however, does give the conflict a religious dimension. This is especially true in the Unionist experience and has been put beyond question by the work of, among others, sociologists John Hickey and Steve Bruce, both of whom lived and taught in Northern Ireland.

In *Religion and the Northern Ireland Problem*, John Hickey, one-time senior lecturer in sociology at the University of Ulster in Coleraine, underlined the "deep core of fear, suspicion, and hostility" prevalent among Northern Unionists and concluded that "politics in the North is not politics exploiting religion. . . . It is more a question of religion inspiring politics than of politics making use of religion."[7] Bruce, formerly at the Queen's University of Belfast and now professor at Aberdeen, published *God Save Ulster* in 1985 and *The*

Edge of the Union in 1994. He too stresses the religious character, the anti-Catholicism of classical Unionism:

> Why be a unionist? To avoid being part of a united Ireland. What is wrong with a united Ireland? It would be a Catholic country. If you do not want to be a Catholic, what are you? A Protestant. If we understand that sequence, we can understand the political success of Ian Paisley and the role of evangelicalism in the thinking of Ulster Protestants.[8]

The anti-Catholicism of Dr. Paisley doesn't hesitate to unchurch the Roman Catholic Church and to include in the hymnbook of his own church such provocative language as the following:

> Our Fathers knew thee, Rome of old,
> And evil is thy fame;
> Thy fond embrace, the galling chain;
> Thy kiss, the blazing flame.
>
> Thy sentence dread is now pronounced,
> Soon shalt thou pass away.
> O soon shall earth have rest and peace—
> Good Lord, haste Thou that day.[9]

Northern Ireland Unionism, however, does not in general depend on such an extreme form of anti-Catholicism. What is more typical of Northern Unionists is a fear that their civil and religious rights and liberties and their economic standard of living would be in danger under the domination of the Roman Catholic Church as they perceive the Republic of Ireland to be. As a distinguished English Methodist who had lived for many years in Belfast put it:

> [The Northern Ireland Protestant] is not afraid that if he lives there [in the Republic of Ireland] he would be unable to practise his religion; but he is afraid that he would be obliged to live a great part of his life according to the pattern laid down by someone else's religion. . . . The philosophy of "No Surrender," "not an inch" is kept alive through fear [of Rome]; and I say again, it is religious fear, which only the Churches can exorcise. . . . Unfortunately the result of such fear is not only to rule out the reunion of the country; it also produces in the popular mind a less justifiable resistance to any form of shared government in Northern Ireland.[10]

Contrary to what is often believed, this "religious fear," the anti-Catholicism of Northern Ireland Unionism, its fear of Rome, is a middle-class as well as a "working-class" phenomenon. If this is less obvious it is only because the middle classes everywhere are usually more sophisticated, more inhibited in expressing themselves. It may also be noted in passing that two new forms of unionism have just begun to emerge: a) a secular unionism, which wants to have little or nothing to do with religion or church; and b) a unionism that is ecumenical in its Protestantism and studiously eschews anti-Romanism. Neither form has as yet acquired much, if any, political influence.[11]

The "new kind of society" for which the Irish Presbyterian delegation "yearns" in its submission to the Dublin *Forum* tells us all too clearly, if implicitly, how things have been, what kind of society has up to now prevailed in Northern Ireland. Instead of togetherness and cooperation, politico-religious segregation has been the order of the day: separate churches, separate schools, separate teacher-training colleges, separate hospitals, separate newspapers, separate sporting activities, separate clubs, separate neighborhoods.

The Northern Nationalist Catholic minority deeply resented and resisted the partition of the country and as far as possible withheld cooperation. Only very few, for instance, ever joined the police force (the Royal Ulster Constabulary). Indeed, by equipping themselves with their own separate social infrastructure, they can be said to have formed a kind of "state within a state." On the other hand, the Unionist Protestant majority has been characterized by a curious amalgam of superiority and insecurity. The Unionists have tended, in the words of a recent history, to regard the Nationalists "as a hostile 'fifth column,' deserving only of second-class citizenship."[12] To retain control they used their power unfairly, especially in the sphere of local government where only ratepayers had a vote, and so brought about the emergence in the late 1960s of the Civil Rights Association to protest against Unionist injustices, such as discrimination in the allocation of publicly provided housing.

Although most of the Nationalists' grievances have been redressed, it has to be admitted that the violence of the last few decades—what we euphemistically call "the troubles"— has in some ways only worsened the apartheid in Northern Ireland and so postponed at least the full achievement of the Nationalists' political aspirations. The people are now further apart than before, not only psychologically but also geographically. Because of the reversal of their fortunes, the Unionist/Protestant community has become alienated from Britain; because of the mutual killings, trust and confidence between the communities within Northern Ireland has suffered; because of the resulting fear, and therefore for reasons of security, mixed neighborhoods have shown a sharp decrease in number. According to the (Methodist) superintendent of the Belfast Central Mission, the city is "more segregated than ever before with up to 80 percent of people living in segregated areas."[13] And "this pattern has been replicated in other towns throughout Northern Ireland, most of which now have clearly defined areas in which the minority population—of Catholics in the east and of Protestants in the west—cluster together for mutual support and a feeling of safety."[14]

This, however, is far from being the whole truth. Ceasefires have taken place and almost miraculously have held for the best part of a whole year now. After a quarter of a century there is optimism as well as hope that a political settlement will be reached in due course. For this achievement the churches can take much of the credit; instead of being simply part of the problem they have become a significant part of the solution.

If one of the major factors in the sad, tragic history of Northern Ireland has been the coincidence of political and church affiliation, of Catholics with nationalism and Protestants with unionism, then two events stand out in my memory as particularly significant, heralding the liberation of the churches from their political captivity and the coming of peace.

The first of these events was the installation of Bishop Cahal Daly in Belfast in October 1982 as Bishop of Down and Connor. In the course of his address on this occasion he stated:

> Mutual recognition in each community of the complete legitimacy and legality, the equal dignity and rights, of the other community, with its own self-defined identity, its own sense of loyalty, its own aspiration, so long as these are peacefully held and peacefully promoted is a Christian task to which we are all called at this time.[15]

This new vision in which nationalism and unionism are no longer mutually exclusive came to find expression two years later in chapters four and five of the *Report* of the New Ireland Forum established by the Dublin government in 1983; it is at the present time struggling to become a political reality. Then Bishop, now Cardinal Cahal Daly has been outstanding in encouraging the fresh political thinking and the ecumenical initiatives that reconciliation and peace require.

The second event was the demonstration against the Anglo-Irish Agreement that took place at the Belfast City Hall in November 1985. The Anglo-Irish Agreement, signed on November 15 of that year by the British and Irish governments, established an Inter-Governmental Conference to deal on a regular basis with political matters affecting Northern Ireland. This involvement of "a foreign power," even if only on a consultative basis, in the administration of Northern Ireland was anathema to Unionists for whom Dublin rule was Rome rule. In his fury Dr. Paisley did not hesitate the Sunday afterward to lead his congregation at the Martyrs Memorial Church in the following prayer:

> O God, in wrath take vengeance upon this wicked, treacherous lying woman [Margaret Thatcher, British Prime Minister]; take vengeance upon her, O Lord, and grant that we shall see a demonstration of thy power.[16]

The protest marches that were organized to object to the Anglo-Irish Agreement and which converged on the City Hall in Belfast on November 23, 1985, drew a crowd of over 100,000 people. It was all meant as a reminder of, indeed as a kind of reenactment of the signing of the Solemn League and Covenant against Home Rule on Ulster Day, September 28, 1912. The November 1985 demonstration was similar in intent, in inspiration, and in size to that of September 1912, but with one immensely significant difference. The 1912 signing of the Covenant in various centers throughout the North was a religious, ecclesiastical, Protestant event; it was preceded by church services, took place in church halls, and was led by church ministers. In Belfast the list of signatories was headed by the two great political leaders, Sir Edward Carson and Lord Londonderry, but immediately after them came the moderator of the Presbyterian General Assembly, the bishop of Down, Connor, and Dromore, the dean of Belfast, the general secretary of the Presbyterian church, the president of the Methodist Conference, and the ex-chairman of the Congregational Union.[17] In 1985, however, the Church of Ireland and the other Protestant leaders, apart of course from Dr. Paisley, were conspicuous no longer by their presence but rather by their absence.

How this sea change came about is told by two well-known and highly regarded Methodists, Eric Gallagher and Stanley Worrall, in their joint work *Christians in Ulster 1968-1980*. Here they give an honest, sober appraisal of the role of the churches during the first half of the present "troubles." Their concluding chapter is entitled "Churches on Trial." The record of the churches they find to be "not wholly a negative one." On the credit side they emphasize ecumenical developments.

> The main thrust of the Churches' contribution has taken the form of greatly enhanced ecumenical collaboration at a time of increasing polarization between the communities at the secular level. In the sixties it seemed for a time as if the suspicion and hostility that divided Catholic and Protestant in the social and political spheres might be subsiding in the light of common interests. The resurgence of violence that followed the demands of the civil rights movement put an end to that, and revived the antagonism of the past. Nevertheless during the 1970s the organized Churches achieved considerable innovations and development in their relationships. There have been setbacks and disappointments in the ecumenical field, but they must not be allowed to obscure the fact that there is now more contact, more mutual respect and understanding, between the Churches than at any earlier period of Irish history. How far this will develop is very uncertain at the time of writing.[18]

It was the outbreak of the "troubles" that spurred or rather shamed the churches into official contact for the first time. The groundwork of course had been done; the foundations had been laid in the early 1960s. The Irish Council of Churches goes back as far as 1923, but not until Vatican II did its members, the various Protestant churches, have much if any contact with the Roman Catholic Church. With Vatican II, however, interchurch meetings of many sorts had begun to take place that, though not yet official, were mostly held with the knowledge and blessing of church authorities. When the crisis came, official contacts, though still controversial and arousing fierce opposition in some quarters, were sufficiently acceptable to become a practical reality.

So a small Joint Group on Social Questions was set up in 1970 and, among other things, appointed a number of working parties, one of which produced in 1976 the important report *Violence in Ireland*. The work of the Joint Group led to the establishment in 1973 of the Ballymascanlon meetings (named for the place where they were held), and these in turn, after some reorganization led in 1984 to the formation of the so-called Irish Inter-Church Meeting (IICM). This is composed of representatives of the Irish Episcopal Conference of the Roman Catholic Church and of the member churches of the Irish Council of Churches and meets approximately every eighteen months. It has set up a Department of Social Issues and a Department of Theological Questions. The former established a Working Party on Sectarianism, which produced a very forthright, challenging Report in 1993. The latter wrote a document on "Freedom, Justice and Responsibility in Ireland Today" for submission to the IICM session of November 1995.

On the debit side, Gallagher and Worrall admit that "it is in the translation of this general will towards reconciliation, which they have effectively fostered, into practical steps that would be socially and politically effective that the Churches have so far failed."[19] That, however, was in 1981. It is only since then that much of what they record has come to fruition, that, for example, the Ballymascanlon meetings have been consolidated and developed into IICM and managed to retain the ecumenically lukewarm Presbyterian Church in Ireland as a member—but without yet becoming a really dynamic force. Again it is only since 1981 that many other ecumenical initiatives (taking courage from the example of the Corrymeela Community and the Rostrevor Christian Renewal Centre and the Irish School of Ecumenics, which already existed) have got under way and succeeded, although mostly unofficially, in exerting a very considerable influence. These new ventures include, for example, the ECONI (Evangelical Contribution on Northern Ireland) group, the Inter-Church Group on Faith and Politics, the Cornerstone Community, the Columbanus Community of Reconciliation, Youth Link:NI (Inter-church Youth Agency), the Armagh Clergy Fellowship, and many others. Deserving of special mention is the fact that before the ceasefires a number of individual church people (notably the Redemptorist priest Alex Reid and the Presbyterian minister Roy Magee) were outstanding in initiating and maintaining contact with para-military groups and acting as intermediaries between them and political and government representatives.[20] Fourteen years later *The Irish Times* of Dublin, echoing the views of *The Irish News* of Belfast, has been able to state:

> One of the profoundest changes in the political climate in the North in recent years has come from the concerted effort by the churches, among their members as well as between themselves, to further the cause of reconciliation.[21]

The occasion for this editorial was the submission of the Church of Ireland to the Forum for Peace and Reconciliation in Dublin and in particular the efforts by its primate, Archbishop Robin Eames, to encourage more positive thinking among Unionists and to remind us all about the fears of each other that still subsist in both communities and which seriously jeopardize our renewed efforts at reconciliation.[22] The new interest in and appreciation of the churches' ministry of ecumenism and reconciliation is a complex phenomenon. It is not simply that the churches have become less self-sufficient, more humble, more cooperative, more ecumenical. It is also because recent events in former Yugoslavia and elsewhere have brought in their train the realization that Northern Ireland is no monstrous anachronism, that religion is indeed more potent—for good and ill—than much secular thinking, especially Marxist, was able previously to recognize.

Although togetherness is the official Northern Ireland policy of both British and Irish governments at present, togetherness is not the only solution in conflict situations. In *Northern Ireland: The Choice*, Boyle and Hadden have reminded us that "one of the fundamental choices that arises in most conflicts of this kind is between separation or sharing."[23] And with their eyes on Belgium and Switzerland they devote one of their chapters to "Structures for Separation." If, however, government policy is to succeed in Northern Ireland, a great deal now depends on the churches. Their role is still paramount. Indeed, a survey by The Centre for the Study of Conflict of the University of Ulster on *The Churches and Inter-Community Relationships* could in 1991 still conclude:

> The Churches in Northern Ireland are the oldest indigenous social institutions in the land and they are communities of people where values are passed on, friends are made, community is experienced and times of supreme personal and societal importance—baptism, first communion, marriage and burials—are shared. Even for those, mainly Protestant, who no longer maintain any active link to a Church or to belief, the Churches are pervasively present and important. Identity remains most accurately gauged by denomination. Friendship, marriage, residence and school remain stubbornly loyal to religious barriers.[24]

In these circumstances the challenge facing the churches to overcome segregation and sectarianism and to renew their ministry of reconciliation in accordance with the spirit and suggestions of the IICM report on sectarianism is indeed a daunting one. It is a challenge that, at the time of writing, the success of the peace process (the ceasefires in particular) seems to be giving the churches a new confidence to accept.[25] We are no longer hoping against hope but hoping with hope, hoping indeed with the hope that does not disappoint (cf. Rom 5:5).

Notes

[1] Editorial, *The Irish News*, March 24, 1995.
[2] Submission, reported in the *Forum* [Dublin].

[3] For what follows see Jonathan Bardon, *A History of Ulster* (Belfast, 1992); Oliver P. Rafferty, *Catholicism in Ulster 1603-1983* (Dublin, 1994).

[4] According to Kevin Boyle and Tom Hadden (*Northern Ireland: The Choice* [Penguin, 1994], p. 31), "it is clear that the proportion of Catholics in Northern Ireland has increased from a figure of at least 33 percent in 1971 (31.4 per cent stated + some unstated) to a figure of at least 40 percent in 1991 (38.4 per cent stated + some unstated)." This rate of increase is unlikely to be maintained in the next decades. According to the demographer Paul Compton, writing in 1985, "the likelihood of an eventual Roman Catholic majority, despite superficial appearances to the contrary, is now receding and is more remote than seemed possible a decade or so ago" (see "An Evaluation of the Changing Religious Composition of the Population of Northern Ireland," *The Economic and Social Review* 16:3 [1985]:201-24). There is still a perception among some that Catholics may well outnumber Protestants in the foreseeable future, and this aggravates Unionist/Protestant fears (see *A Citizens' Enquiry: The Opsahl Report on Northern Ireland*, ed. Andy Pollak [Belfast, 1993], pp. 38-43). Paul Compton once again rejects this prognosis in his recent *Demographic Review of Northern Ireland 1995* (Belfast, Northern Ireland Economic Council, 1995), considering it to be "a gross exaggeration of the real speed of change" (p. 241). He concludes his summary of the projection scenarios as follows: "What we can be certain of, however, is that the numerical gap between ODs [other denominations] and Catholics will continue to narrow, possibly eventually leading to [a] situation of rough numerical equivalence with neither group in a decisive majority" (p. 227). "Extrapolating current birth and death rates by denomination"—but excluding other factors such as migration—"produces a Catholic majority in around the year 2030" (p. 226).

[5] N.B. that this article was written during the summer of 1995. [Editor]

[6] *The Tablet*, March 18, 1995.

[7] John Hickey, *Religion and the Northern Ireland Problem* (Dublin, 1984), pp. 122, 167.

[8] Steve Bruce, *The Edge of the Union* (Oxford University Press, 1994), p. 29.

[9] Dennis Cooke, "Evangelicalism and Reconciliation," *Reconciliation in Religion and Society*, ed. Michael Hurley (Belfast, 1994), p. 136.

[10] Stanley Worrall, *Conference on the Role of the Churches in British-Irish Relationships, Dublin, 26-27 November 1985* (Dublin, 1986), pp. 36-37.

[11] The former form of unionism I associate with Dr. Christopher McGimpsey, who stated at the New Ireland Forum in 1984 that Unionism is "a particular political ideology," adding "I would like to see that ideology not exclusive but general so that anyone of any religious persuasion could join it." The latter I associate with ECONI (Evangelical Contribution to Northern Ireland, c/o 12 Wellington Place, Belfast BT1 6GE), which has published *For God and His Glory Alone* (1992) and other materials.

[12] Eamon Phoenix, *Northern Nationalism* (Belfast, 1994), p. 399; cf. also, Rafferty, p. 221.

[13] Quoted in *The Irish News*, March 24, 1995.

[14] Boyle and Hadden, p. 7.

[15] "Commemorative Publication," printed after the installation by *The Irish News*, p. 10.

[16] Quoted by Paul Bew and Gordon Gillespie, *Northern Ireland: A Chronology of the Troubles 1968-1993* (Dublin, 1993), p. 189.

[17] *The Ulster Covenant, A Pictorial History of the 1912 Home Rule Crisis*, ed. Gordon Lucy (Banbridge: The Ulster Society, 1989), p. 29.

[18] Eric Gallagher and Stanley Worrall, *Christians in Ulster 1968-1980* (Oxford University Press, 1982), pp. 207, 211. Dr. Stanley Worrall was an English Methodist layman

who lived for many years in Northern Ireland, working mainly in the field of education as principal of Methodist College, Belfast. Rev. Dr. Eric Gallagher is a former president of the Methodist Church in Ireland. A book of essays in his honor was published in 1994 by The Methodist College Belfast (*Esteem*, ed. T. W. Mulryne and W. J. McAllister).

[19] Ibid., p. 198.

[20] Cf. John McMaster, *An Inter-Church Directory for Northern Ireland* (Belfast, 1994); Andy Pollak, "Let Us Praise Unknown Priests," *Intercom* (Dublin) (December-January 1995):26-27; John Hume, "In Praise of Peace Priests," *Link-Up* (Dublin) (December 1994):18-20.

[21] *The Irish News* [Belfast], May 16,1995.

[22] In his presidential address to the General Synod of the Church of Ireland, Archbishop Eames stated: "Let us be frank about it. Fear of each other lies at the root of our problems. We have failed to trust each other" (*The Belfast Telegraph*, May 16, 1995).

[23] Boyle and Hadden, p. 2.

[24] The Centre for the Study of Conflict of the University of Ulster, *The Churches and Inter-Community Relationships* (Coleraine, 1991), p. 111. The survey was conducted by Duncan Morrow.

[25] Some of the evidence for this confidence I find in the publication in 1995 of three books: the first, in order of appearance, by Roman Catholic Rev. Brian Lennon, S.J., *After the Ceasefires: Catholics and the Future of Northern Ireland* (Dublin: The Columba Press); the second, by Anglican (Church of Ireland), Rev. Timothy Kinahan, *Where Do We Go from Here? Protestants and the Future of Northern Ireland* (Dublin, The Columba Press); the third, by the Presbyterian former moderator Very Rev. John Dunlop, *A Precarious Belonging: Presbyterians and the Conflict in Ireland* (Belfast: Blackstaff Press). All three books are full of encouragement. My own emphasis this past year has been on the neglected, as I see it, role of forgiveness in the churches' understanding and practice of their ministry of reconciliation (see *The Jurist* [The Catholic University of America, Washington, D.C.] (Spring 1996).

11

The Role of the Churches
in Polish-German Reconciliation

GREGORY BAUM

The Polish-German Treaties of Reconciliation of 1990/1991 settling definitively the common border and creating good-neighborly relations between
the two countries were an extraordinary achievement, a source of joy for the
two countries and the whole of Europe. Reconciliation between former enemies *is* possible.

Historical Background

The Poles had every reason to be afraid of Germany. In the Middle Ages the
Knights of the Teutonic Order had with great brutality moved eastward along
the Baltic Sea to colonize and christianize the lands of the Slavs. In the eighteenth and nineteenth centuries Prussia collaborated with Austria and Russia
to extinguish Poland's national identity and divide the country into three parts.
The incorporation of these parts into the three powerful monarchies was le-
gitimated by the deceitful myth that the Poles were stupid, incompetent, and
unable to take care of themselves. In 1919, after World War I, Poland was
again allowed to become a sovereign nation. In 1939 Hitler's Germany invaded Poland with the intention to conquer its army, liquidate the Polish state,
murder its leaders and intellectuals, humiliate the Catholic church, and re-
duce the people to obedient agricultural servants of the German Reich. Prior
to his attack Hitler had made a nonaggression pact with Stalin, in which the
German dictator approved of Stalin's plan to integrate sections of Eastern
Poland into the Soviet Union. After the conquest Hitler decided to build on
Polish territory the death camps in which six million Jews and millions of
Poles and members of other nations were systematically murdered. Twice
German armies overran Poland with destruction—in their treacherous attack
on Russia and again in their desperate retreat. Poland lost a quarter of its
population.

There were further reasons Poles had every right to be afraid of Germany. In August 1945 the victorious Allies meeting at Potsdam, decided to redefine the political map of Eastern Europe. The Potsdam Conference ceded to the Soviet Union the sections of Eastern Poland that Stalin, with Hitler's approval, had claimed before the war, which meant that the Poles in these sections had to leave their properties and move westward. The Potsdam Conference also decided that to compensate Poland for the loss of its eastern territories, it would be given territories in the west that had belonged to Germany (Silesia, Pomerania, and part of East Prussia); the new border between Poland and Germany would be the north-south line along two rivers, the Oder and the Neisse. The Oder-Neisse border was to be made definitive at a future peace treaty. The Potsdam Conference agreed on the need to remove the German populations or parts thereof living in the new Poland (and Czechoslovakia and Hungary), stipulating that this transfer be carried out in an orderly and humane manner.

Many Germans had already fled the eastern parts, afraid of the arrival of the victorious Russian troops. The remaining Germans, the great majority, experienced the expulsion by the Poles not as an orderly and humane affair but as a chaotic and brutal one. The Germans were forced to leave their farms and their property without compensation. A remnant of Germans stayed in the new Poland. The greater part of the several million Germans expelled from Eastern Europe settled in what came to be the Federal Republic of Germany (West Germany); because of their strong anti-communist feeling, they avoided settling in what was to become communist East Germany. With enormous dedication and energy and the help of the Marshall Plan, West Germany was able to rebuild its cities, recover its industrial strength, and create a success-ful, Western-style democratic society. In the process it was able to offer some compensation to the Germans expelled from the new Poland and succeeded to a remarkable degree in integrating them into the national life and the economy. Still, the Germans expelled from the new Poland were not reconciled to the loss of their lands. They insisted that the expulsion of innocent people from their home is against international law. They called their situation an injustice that called for redress. Since the Potsdam Conference had not defined the Oder-Neisse border as definitive, they united in powerful organizations and vehemently opposed any conversation of Germans and the German govern-ment with Poles that might encourage Poland to think the present border was acceptable. The strong anti-communism of those expelled, encouraged by the Cold War, strengthened their determination to make no concessions to Po-land. They were outraged in 1950 when communist East Germany signed an agreement with Poland that recognized as definitive the Oder-Neisse line. In the same year they produced a charter document that spelled out their human rights, including *"das Recht auf Heimat,"* the right to the homeland.[1] While West Germany had sought and achieved a formal reconciliation with France, its western neighbor, reconciliation with Poland became a taboo subject in Germany. The government did not dare to touch it.

It is not surprising that the Poles, now settled within their newly created borders, lived in fear; they were made to believe that Germany would eventually reclaim its former territories. While Britain, France, America, and other Western nations had already accepted the Oder-Neisse border as definitive, the German government was unwilling to do so. All the German government promised was that it would never reclaim the formerly German lands with violence.

In this situation the churches broke the ice. They produced public documents that offered a historical framework for understanding the present conflict, removed the taboo from discussing the issue of the German-Polish border, and provoked an ethical debate in Germany involving all levels of society. The impact of these Christian documents on public opinion freed the government to take the first significant steps in the direction of German-Polish reconciliation. Even secular observers who have no particular Christian sympathies have recognized the role of the churches in initiating the process of reconciliation that, many years later, produced the German-Polish Treaties of 1990/1991.[2]

To tell the story of the churches in detail demands an entire book, a book that has not yet been written. To write this chapter I have available to me two large volumes. The first, *Feinde werden Freunde*, is a collection of forty articles dealing with various aspects of the process of reconciliation, including pieces on the contributions made by the German Protestant Church, the correspondence of the Polish Catholic bishops with their German colleagues, and the Bensberger Kreis, a circle of German Catholic intellectuals. The second volume, *Bonn-Warschau: 1945-1991*, is a collection of the important documents related to the process of reconciliation, beginning with the communique of the Potsdam Conference right through to the two Treaties of Reconciliation on the Oder-Neisse border and the neighborly cooperation and exchange between Germany and Poland, signed by the two governments in 1990 and 1991. This volume includes the documents, speeches, and letters of Protestant and Catholic Christians related to the process of reconciliation.

To tell the Christian story here I shall, leaving out many details, report consecutively on three important events: i) the publication of the controversial *Ostdenkschrift* by the German Protestant Church in 1965, which got the ball rolling; ii) the letter of the Polish Catholic bishops to the German Catholic episcopate and the latter's response; and iii) the *Polen-Memorandum* of the Bensberger Kreis, a circle of German Catholic intellectuals unhappy over the reticence of the German Catholic bishops.

My special interest in this article is theological. I am persuaded by Robert Schreiter's proposal that reconciliation between peoples or groups burdened by past hostilities demands that, through a spiritual conversion of mind and heart, they learn to acknowledge their past, recognize the wounds received and the wounds inflicted, retell the stories that define their identity, and discover themselves as participants in the same history jointly responsible for their common future.[3] Reconciliation is the work of the Holy Spirit. We shall see in the following the efforts made by German and Polish Christians to open themselves to this process, ask one another for forgiveness, and attempt to rethink and redefine their history.

The *Ostdenkschrift*

Because in the 1960s several Protestant groups had published memoranda on the moral claims of the exiled Germans arriving at different conclusions, the German Protestant Church (EKD) decided to appoint a commission to study the issue in the light of Protestant social ethics. The commission's report, "On the Situation of the Exiled and the Relation of the German People to Their Eastern Neighbours," was so controversial that it was not adopted or recommended but only "received" by the EKD. The report was published on 1 October 1965. In German the document is usually referred to as *Ostdenkschrift*, literally translated as "Writing Memorializing the East." I shall call it the Memorial Report.[4]

When read today the Memorial Report is a modest document. The main part is a set of detailed legal considerations designed to demonstrate the problematic character of the legal arguments used by the organizations of those expelled and their charter document to demand the return of their lands and the nonrecognition of the Oder-Neisse line. The two crucial legal questions are whether Polish sovereignty over the formerly German territories is legitimate and whether the expulsion of the Germans from their home is a violation of international law and thus demands appropriate redress. In dealing with these questions the Memorial Report reveals great respect for the suffering inflicted on those expelled and a deeply felt appreciation that for all Germans the loss of Silesia, Pomerania, and East Prussia was like the amputation of an arm.

Still, when the Potsdam Conference honored Stalin's wish, approved by Hitler in 1939, to integrate Poland's eastern territories into the Soviet Union, Churchill and Roosevelt and not only Stalin recognized that in compensation for this loss, Poland had to be given full administrative power over the German lands lying west of Poland up to the Oder-Neisse line. While this administrative power is not equivalent to sovereignty in the full sense, the legitimacy of Polish rule over these parts has since been recognized internationally, in the east and the west, so that it has become highly questionable whether Polish sovereignty can still be challenged.

The appeal of the charter of those expelled to international law is also uncertain, and this for several reasons. Since international law gives expression to humanity's evolving social conscience, its formulations are usually ethical imperatives rather than strictly defined laws. Because there is no agency that can enforce them, their application is left to the individual states. Added to this is the difficulty that the international laws affirming the rights of peoples to self-determination are of recent origin, formulated after World War II, to protect the anti-colonial struggles of peoples in Africa and other parts. The expulsion of the German population was indeed a grave violation of justice and is seen as such by civilization's age-old ethical tradition, but this fact alone is not an adequate basis for an appeal to international law. From a legal point of view, the Memorial Report concludes, the appeal to international law is uncertain.

Yet there are other considerations of justice that deserve attention. The Memorial Report insists that it would be quite unjust to put the blame for the expulsion on the people themselves, as if the Germans living in the eastern parts of Germany were more guilty for Hitler's war of aggression than the Germans living further west. Nor is it justified to accuse them of harboring hatred or seeking vengeance. Their appeal is to justice.

At the same time there is also the issue of justice to Poles. The Memorial Report recognizes the vulnerability of the Polish people, pushed without consultation from their eastern lands and driven into the formerly German lands of the west. Poles live in fear that their newly designated homeland will be challenged and again be taken away from them. Justice demands that they receive the guarantee that will allow them to live in peace and security. Second, the right to the homeland on which the expelled Germans rightly insist now, twenty years after 1945, also applies to the Poles who have settled in Silesia, Pomerania, and East Prussia, who have worked there, built up the land destroyed by war, brought forth and educated their children there and presently look upon these territories as their Polish home. In fact, since the expelled Germans have for the most part found a new home in West Germany, justice assigns greater weight to the Polish right to the homeland.

The Memorial Report's conclusion is quite modest, even if it appeared explosive in the West Germany of the sixties. From a purely legal point of view, there is no hope of resolving the present stalemate. An appeal to justice is not sufficient. The Memorial Report summons the German people to turn to the perspective of Protestant theological ethics, which recognizes claims to justice and justification only if they are accompanied by repentance and compassion. Germany needs a new approach to the Polish question. The Memorial Report remains aloof from the strictly political sphere, which, it claims, is not the church's business. For this reason it does not recommend that Germany acknowledge the Oder-Neisse line or that it withdraw its title to its former territories. The report's intention is to revitalize the ethical culture of West Germany. While addressing itself directly to those expelled, the report invites all Germans to remember their recent past, adopt an attitude of humility, and enter upon a new ethical debate. The report wants to promote a widely held public opinion suspicious of self-justification and willing to accept God's judgment on German history. Only a change of attitude on the part of all West Germans will free the government to initiate negotiations with Poland.

German and Polish observers of the slow process of reconciliation look back upon the Protestant Memorial Report, however modest its conclusion, as a breakthrough event that started the transformation of West Germany's consciousness. Yet, at the time, West Germany's reaction to the report was rather negative. The loudest voices belonged to those who expressed outrage and repudiated the report's conclusions. An organization of those expelled produced a counter-report to promote its own point of view. Still, members of the German government reacted positively to the report and used its message and the subsequent debate to legitimate taking initiating steps toward German-Polish negotiations.

A Digression

The hesitant way in which West Germany's Protestant Church (EKD) approached the national question and the issue of the German-Polish border was startlingly different from the bold approach taken by the Protestant Church of East Germany at the same time.[5] In West Germany the national question, the partition of Germany after the war, was an issue even more taboo than the Oder-Neisse border question. West Germany did not accept as definitive the imposed division and hence refused to acknowledge East Germany (the German Democratic Republic) as a sovereign state. West Germans spoke of the other Germany simply as the eastern zone. The West German attitude was hardened by the Cold War, which aligned communist East Germany with the hated Soviet Union. Even the open-minded Memorial Report shied away from saying with all clarity that Germany, having started the war and having inflicted death and misery upon countless millions, had to bow in repentance before God's judgment and accept the conditions imposed on it by the victors. The report only hinted at this when it asked the German people, without giving all the reasons, to bow before God's judgment. To suggest that the Germans ought to accept the partition of their country was taboo in West Germany.

The Protestant Church in East Germany saw the German question quite differently. From the sixties on, the church wanted to prove to the communist government that it was neither an agent of the Western powers nor an ideological defender of capitalism, but a community with a mission to proclaim and practice the gospel in the socialist society to which it belonged. For pastoral reasons the Protestant Church accepted East Germany's political reality. The East German Church distanced itself from the German Protestant Church (EKD) of the West and created its own East German Church Federation, which was both loyal to its country, the German Democratic Republic, and boldly critical of the communist government. To persuade its members to give up the nostalgic dream of returning to a past that no longer existed and help them pastorally to act as Christians in their new society, the church repeatedly reminded the people that Germany, as bearer of an evil philosophy, had started the war, invaded and conquered its neighbors, organized the extermination of the Jews, and in addition brought suffering and death to millions upon millions of Europeans. Because of this past, the church continued, Christians must recognize God's judgment in the defeat of the German Reich and humbly accept as God's punishment the division of their country and the creation of two sovereign German nations, east and west. Since the important church leaders in East Germany had been, prior to the war, members of the Confessing Church and were thus keenly aware that the German Protestant Church as a whole had not resisted National Socialism, they believed that Protestants had a special reason for repentance and for accepting without resentment or bitterness the events that had created socialist East Germany. The church was not hindered from preaching this radical message because East Germany itself defined its collective identity by focusing on Hitler's criminal war and on the rescue from fascism and the gift of distinct nationhood thanks to the Soviet Union. The East German communists—and the East German Protestant Church—were troubled by West Germany's resistance to exploring and confronting its own fascist past.

The Letter of the Polish Catholic Bishops[6]

In 1965, during the last session of Vatican Council II, the thirty-six Polish bishops present in Rome discussed among themselves whether to send a letter to the German bishops initiating a process of reconciliation. The Polish bishops shared Polish fears in regard to Germany. The Vatican itself had not yet fully accepted as definitive the Oder-Neisse border, and for this reason had not redefined the ecclesiastical boundaries of the German dioceses affected by the new border. The Polish bishops attributed the Vatican's reluctance to normalize the existing situation to pressure exerted by the German bishops. Should we, the Polish bishops asked themselves, address the German bishops and take the risk of being rebuffed? A cool reply from the German bishops would only increase Poland's feeling of insecurity. While for spiritual reasons several Polish bishops—most vocal among them Bishop Kominec—were most eager for reconciliation, the more cautious bishops, including Cardinal Wyszynski, feared that such a letter would be interpreted by the Polish people as a concession to the enemy and by Poland's communist government as an irresponsible entry into international politics. On the other hand, since the Polish church suffered under the control of the atheist government, it was important for her to strengthen her bonds with the western churches. According to Hansjacob Stehle, journalist and friend of Bishop Kominec, it was the text of the Protestant *Ostdenkschrift*, shown to the Polish bishops a week before its publication, that convinced the Polish bishops of the openness found among German Protestants and prompted their decision to send the letter to their German colleagues.[7]

The letter is a remarkable document. Since the Polish bishops were preparing for the celebration of the millennium of Christianity in their country (1966), they invited the German bishops to attend the ceremonies. They used the first part of the letter to offer their understanding of Polish history.

Soon after the foundation of the church and the nation by the baptism of Duke Mieszko I in 966, Pope Silvester II created several Polish dioceses, some of which, centuries later, became German-speaking. The letter refers to other historical events, suggesting that the formerly German territories recently settled by Poles had been originally Polish and hence were not assigned to Poland by an arbitrary decree of the Potsdam Conference. Poles were returning to their own.

The bishops went on to show that in the Middle Ages the relations between Poles and Germans were on the whole excellent, that Germans made important contributions to the creation of Polish culture, and that some Germans remained in Poland and became Polish-speaking. A symbol of this spiritual friendship is Saint Hedwig (Jadwiga), venerated by Poles as the great benefactress of their country. She was a German princess married to a Polish sovereign, a pious and generous woman who learned the Polish language to become a helper among the ordinary people. After 1200, the letter continued, Poland brought forth its own saints. The glorious list of Polish saints is long, reaching to the present with Father Maximilian Kolbe, who, as a prisoner in a German concentration camp, offered his life to save the life of a co-prisoner, a married man with children.[8]

In the next section the letter told the story of German aggression beginning with the medieval Teutonic Knights, who invaded the Slavic north along the Baltic Sea and forced the local populations with fire and sword to be converted to Christianity. These knights created Prussia, out of which, centuries later, came the cruel and ambitious men who destroyed the reputation of the Germans in Polish lands: the kings of Prussia, Bismarck, and eventually Hitler. The Poles regard Frederick II, also called the Great, as the sovereign most responsible for initiating the thrice-repeated division of Poland at the end of the eighteenth century, the division which lasted until the end of World War I. After a brief resurrection of the Polish nation, Hitler arrived intent upon destroying the country altogether. Here the letter recounted in detail the human cruelty and the damage inflicted by the Germans on the Polish people, murdering a quarter of its population, including a third of its priests, and setting up death camps on Polish lands killing, in addition to Poles, millions of Jews and members of other nations. The letter then recounted the poverty and discouragement of the Poles after the war, their cities and their lands destroyed, deprived of the eastern regions by the Soviet Union and pushed into new western territories by the Potsdam Conference. Since then the Poles have struggled hard to survive and recover.

The letter recognized that many Germans also suffered under the Nazi regime, that some Germans resisted the dictatorship and lost their lives, that a few courageous priests and bishops spoke out against the government, and that eventually the entire Catholic church was suspected by Hitler as a subversive force. These are the reasons, the Polish bishops wrote, they now addressed the German bishops with so much confidence.

At the end the letter dared to touch the "hot iron," the controversial issue, the definitive character of the Oder-Neisse line. With a gesture of openness the Polish bishops recognized the pain suffered by Germany after the war. They acknowledged "that the new Polish-German border is for Germany an extremely bitter fruit of the war of mass destruction, accompanied as it was, following the decree of the Allies, by the suffering of millions of refugees and exiles." The Polish bishops sympathized with those expelled. The letter explained that for Poland the new border along the Oder-Neisse line was not an issue of territorial expansion or an expression of political ambition; it was rather an issue of life or death, "*eine Existenzfrage.*" After the westward move of the eastern border, there was simply no space for the Polish population in the narrow corridor granted to Poland under German rule. Without the lands assigned to it as compensation, the Polish people could not survive.

Despite the hostilities of the past and today's as yet unresolved conflicts, the Polish bishops said to their German brothers: "Let us try to forget, no polemics, no Cold War; instead the beginning of dialogue." The letter then asked the German bishops to deliver thanks and greetings to their Protestant brothers who also sought a solution for the present problem—a hint revealing the Polish appreciation of the *Ostdenkschrift.* Then the Polish bishops added "in the most Christian and at the same time truly human spirit . . . we grant forgiveness and we ask for forgiveness."[9]

Why did the Polish bishops ask for forgiveness? The letter suggests that they regretted the ruthless way in which the Poles had handled the transfer of the Germans to the west and deplored the hostility against Germans and all things German still harbored by the Polish population. In asking for forgiveness, the bishops took a spiritual step: they opened themselves to the story of "the other" and tried to integrate that story into the account of their own story, the story of the Polish people.

This letter cost the Polish bishops dearly. Wide circles in Poland, not only the government but also Catholic groups, were outraged by the bishops' "disloyalty" to their fatherland. How could they ask for forgiveness! In doing so, they seemed to imply that Poles had committed an injustice and should now be willing to renegotiate the border—a suggestion that greatly threatened Poland's national security.

Even the reply of the German bishops was disappointing. Their letter was respectful and warm.[10] It sounded positive. The German bishops expressed their gratitude for the initiative taken by their Polish colleagues; they readily acknowledged with great sorrow the horrors committed by Germany under Hitler's rule; they too wished to forget and asked to be forgiven. But then they added that if the expelled Germans demand their "*Recht zur Heimat,*" they do this— with a few exceptions—not in a spirit of aggression or revenge, but rather because they think that the lands and homes they lost were rightly and legally theirs. Those exiled are aware, the letter added, that the young generation of Poles brought up in the lands assigned to their fathers also look upon these regions as

their home. As had the German Protestant Church, the German Catholic bishops refrained from directly touching the issue of the border. Yet they did not go
as far as the EKD in admitting the weakness of the legal arguments. Nor did
they call upon the German people, as the Memorial Report did, to rethink their
position from a Christian perspective of repentance and compassion.[11]

The Polish bishops decided to interpret the reply of the German bishops in
a positive way. They were grateful that the dialogue had begun and a year
later welcomed the German bishops who came to Poland for the celebration
of the millennium. Only in 1970 did Cardinal Wyszynski admit, in a letter
addressed to Cardinal Döpfner,[12] how disappointed the Polish bishops had
been by the cool reply of the German episcopate, especially since German
Protestants with fewer links to Poland were so much more generous.

Why did the Polish cardinal write this letter in 1970? Negotiations between
Germany and Poland, strongly supported by Germany's Social Democratic
government, had in 1970 arrived at a Trade Agreement between the two countries that was subsequently severely criticized in Germany, especially by
members of the Christian Democratic Party. According to these German critics, the Trade Agreement could be read as a formal recognition of the
Oder-Neisse border. Since there was so much Christian opposition to the agreement, Cardinal Wyszynski believed that a reconciling message from Germany's
Catholic bishops who had expressed their solidarity with Poland would be
helpful. In his letter to Döpfner, Wyszynchski revealed the disappointment
over the German bishops' reply in 1965 and suggested that a new moment had
arrived when an expression of solidarity on their part would hasten the reconciliation between the two peoples.

In his reply Cardinal Döpfner gave three reasons why even now he was not
ready to make a public statement on the Oder-Neisse line.[13] First, it was not
the task of the church to take positions on concrete political issues; second,
the reserve on the part of the church and the Christian Democratic Party persuaded the millions of those expelled in Germany to remain loyal to these
institutions and thus prevented them from becoming a radical, right-wing
movement calling for violence and revenge; and third, the more supportive
attitude of Protestants was related to their theology of Germany's "collective
guilt," while Catholics believe that guilt is personal, depending on each person's
free participation in an evil enterprise. The space I have does not allow me to
comment on these arguments. In his reply Döpfner makes no mention whatever
of the *Polen-Memorandum*—with which Wyszynski was well acquainted—published in 1968 by a circle of German Catholics offering strong support for justice
to Poland.

Before we turn to this interesting circle, I wish to say a word about Boleslaw
Kominek, archbishop of Wroclaw/Breslau, the ardent advocate of reconciliation among the Polish bishops and the author of the first draft of a letter sent
to the German bishops. An article by Hansjacob Stehle, journalist and
Kominek's friend, records the early initiatives taken by the archbishop to foster the spirit of reconciliation in the Polish church and his public disagreement

with bishops, including Cardinal Wyszynski, who harbored suspicion and fear.[14] Eventually, at the end of Vatican Council II, Kominek was able to draw the Polish bishops, including the cardinal, with him.

In the material available to me, this is the only case-study of a person deeply committed to initiating Polish-German reconciliation. Kominek was born into a Polish family residing in Upper Silesia, still German at the time. He grew up as a loyal Pole participating in German culture. At home he was punished when he spoke German, and at school when he spoke Polish. To him this non-communication between two cultures seemed irrational. In the years after the war, while firmly supporting the Oder-Neisse border as a loyal Pole, he was the first ecclesiastic to express his sorrow over the suffering inflicted on the Germans chased out of their lands. He remained in touch with the German priests and bishops who had been his friends. In promoting Polish-German reconciliation he was motivated by deeply engaging personal experiences.

It would not surprise me if behind every collective effort at reconciliation stand certain highly motivated personalities whose spiritual conviction has been created through important personal experiences. There are men and women whose lives have made them bridge-builders. I suspect that there must have been such personalities in the Protestant commission that produced the *Ostdenkschrift* and the Catholic circle of intellectuals that produced the *Polen-Memorandum*. To explore this would be valuable research.

The *Polen-Memorandum*[15]

In 1966, following the invitation of Walter Dirks, Catholic editor of the critical *Frankfurter Hefte*, a group of Catholic intellectuals met in the town of Bensberg to take a public position on German-Polish reconciliation. They called themselves the Bensberger Kreis. They were unhappy with the cautious reticence of the Catholic bishops; and while they greatly admired the Protestant *Ostdenkschrift*, they felt that it did not go far enough in calling upon Germans and their government to accept as definitive the Oder-Neisse border. In the document published by them in 1968, the so-called *Polen-Memorandum*, they complained that the German government offered a confusing double-message when it told the Poles that Germany would never use violence to regain its lost territories and then added that it was unwilling to renounce its legal claim on them. Many Germans were greatly offended by the *Memorandum*. A Catholic organization of expelled Germans refuted the proposed arguments in a publication of its own. Nor were the Catholic bishops pleased with the Bensberger Kreis. Yet the *Memorandum* made an important contribution to the slowly evolving process of German-Polish reconciliation; significant for this chapter is that in addition to its ethical reflections on the political order, the *Memorandum* provided important elements of a theology of reconciliation.

Reading the *Memorandum*'s first section I detect the influence of Johann-Baptist Metz's political theology. Metz was actually a member of the

Bensberger Kreis. With other well-known theologians, including Karl Rahner and Joseph Ratzinger, Metz's name appears on the list of the one hundred and sixty Catholic intellectuals who signed the *Memorandum*. The purpose of Metz's political theology was to "de-privatize" the gospel, that is to say, to uncover its meaning and power for contemporary society.

Christian hope, according to the *Memorandum*, is not a personal matter. The message of Jesus provoked the opposition of the religious and secular authorities because they realized that his gospel of peace and justice had world-transforming power. It follows that faith, hope, and love summon the church to exercise a world-transforming mission in the society to which it belongs. A test for this mission in Germany, says the *Memorandum*, is reconciliation with Poland. Christians may not abide by the taboos defined by the establishment. Christians must free themselves from the hostile images and ideologies mediated by the dominant culture and, in reliance on the Holy Spirit, take the first step.

The immediate task is to analyze the burdened history of recent German-Polish relations. In doing so we must be conscious that the perpetrators of evil deeds forget the past more quickly than do their victims. For the victims the deeds remain present. Since the crimes committed must not be forgotten, the *Memorandum* recalls again Hitler's invasion of Poland in 1939, his intention to enslave the Polish people, the organization of the Holocaust on Polish territory, the confiscation of Polish lands in the east by Soviet Russia with Hitler's approval, and the devastation of Poland by the German army. In 1945, after the victory, the Potsdam Conference recognized the new Polish-Russian border; assigned to Poland the western, formerly German territories up to the Oder-Neisse line; and approved of the expulsion of the German population from the new Poland and other parts of Eastern Europe. While all of Germany suffered from the loss of Silesia, Pomerania, and East Prussia, the greatest burden was borne by those expelled, who lost their home, their lands, and their cultural identity; when resettled in the west, they experienced economic privation and social discrimination—even though they were not more "guilty" than any other Germans. The expulsion was an unjust deed.

Calculating and comparing the accounts of guilt does not normally help the process of reconciliation between two nations. In the present case, it does not work at all. The crimes committed in the name of Germany were aimed at the total destruction of a civilization, aided by coldly planned and efficiently executed terror, producing endless tragic consequences that did not stop with the war. These consequences included the post-war expulsion of Germans from Eastern Europe. The German crimes were so massive, the *Memorandum* argues, that any effort at weighing the respective accounts of Polish and German suffering simply breaks down. The Memorial Report had hinted at this when it asked the German people to bow before God's justice. The *Memorandum* chose to be blunt and specific.

Even weighing the respective burdens of German-Polish history prior to the war does not serve a useful purpose. The *Memorandum* makes the important point that what is indispensable is that Polish and German historians co-operate in producing a common, mutually acceptable historical account of German-Polish interaction throughout the centuries. Such a cooperative scholarly effort will take years. The *Memorandum* hints that the somewhat mythical history of the Polish nation given in the letter of the Polish bishops will not do. Nor will the efforts of Poles who try to legitimate their presence in Silesia, Pomerania, and East Prussia by showing that these parts were Polish prior to the fourteenth century. Since Poland's legitimate title to these parts was created by the Potsdam Conference, Polish historians may well afford to look in a more open way at the complexity of German-Polish history. German historians must also redo their research. In their histories they have often failed to acknowledge the Poles as a people, preferring to look upon the regions east of Germany as sparsely populated territories open for German settlement. Modern methods of historical research accompanied by an ongoing conversation between Germans and Poles will enable historians to produce a common story of the past, acceptable to both peoples.

The *Memorandum* recommends the appointment of a joint commission with the task of examining and, if need be, correcting the history books used in the schools and universities of both countries—after the model of the official French-German School Commission created to promote reconciliation between France and Germany. After the Trade Agreement of 1970, a Polish-German School Commission was in fact established.[16]

The *Memorandum* makes a great effort to think about the present non-communication from the Polish point of view. Following the line of thought of the Polish bishops, the *Memorandum* recognizes that the formerly German territories are an essential condition for the viability of the Polish nation. Without these territories, Poland would not have enough land space to settle its population. Yet Poland finds itself facing a Germany that is unwilling to guarantee its western border and, worse, that has been i) helped by America to become a wealthy industrial nation, ii) remilitarized by America, and iii) made a launching ground for nuclear weapons. In this critical situation, the *Memorandum* concludes, Germany must act to deliver the Poles from their fears.

The *Memorandum* shares with the Memorial Report the opinion that the legal arguments based on international law for reclaiming the lost territories are uncertain. Yet the *Memorandum* becomes more specific. A country that starts a war takes the risk of losing it and then being obliged to make reparations, reparations that may include the loss of territory. For this reason Germany must willingly assume the liability (*Haftbarkeit*) for Poland's destruction during the war and honor the conditions of peace necessary for Poland's present survival. As they reflect on Hitler's evil and insane project of domination, Germans will learn to accept the loss of their eastern territories; even those expelled, while victims of injustice, will learn to accept their difficult lot. They have every right to be angry, but their anger should be directed against Hitler, not against the Allies or the Poles.

With other German theologians, the *Memorandum* distinguishes between guilt (*Schuld*) and liability (*Haftbarkeit*). Even if it were possible to accuse the German generation of the Hitler years of "guilt" or willing participation in evil deeds, it is impossible to regard the Germans of the sixties, over half of whom were born after 1930, as guilty of Hitler's monumental crimes. Yet a people—in this case, the German people—is "liable" for the damage done by its country, meaning obliged in justice to assume responsibility for this damage and make appropriate reparations. The distinction between guilt and liability is important in all efforts of collective reconciliation. Why? Because one reason many serious people oppose these efforts is that they refuse to regard themselves as guilty for actions undertaken before they were born. Guilty they are not—this is quite true. But this does not mean that they are thereby free of all legal obligations. They assume a certain guilt only when they refuse to accept their liability.

In the final section the *Memorandum* outlines the steps that Germans should take to promote reconciliation and friendship with Poland. I have already mentioned the recognition of the Oder-Neisse border and the elaboration of a common, mutually acceptable history. What is demanded of Germans is a transformation of their cultural consciousness, a repentance of their false sense of superiority, a turning away from the stereotyped images of the Poles, a sorrowing over their tradition of aggression and conquest, and a new commitment to peace—one which includes resisting American pressure to rearm. The *Memorandum* leaves it to Polish advocates of reconciliation to articulate for their own people what changes of mind and heart are necessary if they want to move toward reconciliation with Germany. Reconciliation is a spiritual process on both sides.

Many Germans, as I mentioned above, were outraged by the *Memorandum*. Yet the response of the Polish bishops and many Polish intellectuals was very positive. To increase the credibility of the Bensberger Kreis in Germany, the members had appointed as their spokesmen intellectuals from among those expelled. These men were now invited to Poland, honored in public receptions by churches and universities, and looked upon by many Poles as concrete symbols of Germany's willingness to move toward reconciliation. The German government, at that time under Chancellor Willy Brandt and his Social Democratic Party, welcomed the *Memorandum* because it promoted the ethical debate in German public life initiated by the Protestant Memorial Report. Two years later, in 1970, Brandt's government negotiated a Trade Agreement with Poland as a first step toward normalizing the relations between the two countries. The Agreement was accepted by the German Parliament only because the Christian Democratic Party, then the opposition, was internally divided on the issue and hence abstained from voting in the House. In the same year, on his visit to the Polish capital, during a ceremony before the ruins of the Warsaw ghetto, Willy Brandt, overwhelmed by emotion, fell on his knees. The photograph published in the newspaper gave another impetus to the ethical debate in Germany. Gradually, as the two governments continued negotiations, the two peoples became ready for the Treaties of Reconciliation of 1990/1991.

Notes

[1] See *Bonn-Warschau: 1945–1991—Analyse und Dokumente*, ed. Hans-Adolf Jacobsen and Mieczyslaw Tomala (Köln: Verlag Wissenschaft und Politik, 1992), pp. 73-74.

[2] For secular politicians and intellectuals who have recognized the important role played by the churches, see *Bonn-Warschau*, the articles by Mieczyslaw Tomala (pp. 10, 13) and Hans-Adolf Jacobsen (pp. 35, 36); *Feinde werden Freunde*, ed. Freidbert Pflüger and Winfried Lipscher (Bonn: Bouvier Verlag, 1993), the contributions by Rita Süssmuth (p. 2), Friedbert Pflüger (pp. 12-13), Willy Brandt (p. 57), and Rainer Barzel (p. 61).

[3] Robert Schreiter, *Reconciliation: Mission and Ministry in a Changing Social Order* (Maryknoll, N.Y.: Orbis Books, 1992), pp. 36-40.

[4] For major excerpts of the *Ostdenkschrift*, see *Bonn-Warschau*, pp. 125-35. For commentaries, see in *Feinde werden Freunde*, the essays by Helmut Hild (pp. 90-102) and Josef Homeyer (pp. 254-58).

[5] See Gregory Baum, *The Church for Others: Protestant Theology in Communist East Germany* (Grand Rapids, Mich.: Eerdmans, 1996).

[6] For the text of the letter, see *Bonn-Warschau*, pp. 135-42.

[7] *Feinde werden Freunde*, p. 79.

[8] In this context the Polish bishops made a theological statement that shows how far removed they were from the modern Catholic consciousness in the West. "Our people," they wrote, "honors its saints and regards them as the most noble fruit a Christian country can produce" (*Bonn-Warschau*, p. 139). Compare this with the statement found in the pastoral letters of the American and Canadian bishops, that Christians evaluate a society in accordance with the way it treats its poor and vulnerable members.

[9] *Bonn-Warschau*, p. 142.

[10] For the text, see *Bonn-Warschau*, pp. 142-45.

[11] To my knowledge the debate among the German bishops that preceded their reply has as yet not been researched.

[12] For the text, see *Bonn-Warschau*, pp. 209-10.

[13] For the text, see *Bonn-Warschau*, pp. 211-14.

[14] *Feinde werden Freunde*, pp. 74-89.

[15] For major excerpts, see *Bonn-Warschau*, pp. 170-82. For commentary, see Manfred Seidler's essay in *Feinde werden Freunde*, pp. 103-12.

[16] See Wladyslaw Markiewicz's article on the German-Polish School Commission in *Feinde werden Freunde*, pp. 182-92.

12

Testimonies of Atonement

A German Protestant Movement Aktion Sühnezeichen Friedensdienste (ASF)

ANDREA KOCH AND BRIGITTE SCHEIGER

In 1958 a group of Christians who had been active in the Protestant resistance during the Nazi period founded a volunteer organization with the purpose of confronting the crimes committed by the Nazi movement and enacting gestures of atonement for the sins of Germany during World War II. They called it Aktion Sühnezeichen, which means literally "Action Signs of Atonement." A few years later, they added the word *Friedensdienste*—in English, "Services for Peace." In North America the movement is known as Action Reconciliation Service for Peace.

During the Synod of the German Protestant Church held in 1958, Lothar Kreyssig announced the foundation of this organization, read a statement entitled "Appeal for Peace" that explained its purpose, and asked the members of the Synod for their support. Over half of them signed the appeal. Lothar Kreyssig was well known to them. He had been an active member of the Confessing Church and had courageously resisted the Nazi policy of killing the handicapped. In 1958 he was a member of the governing board of the German Protestant Church.

These sentences are taken from the "Appeal for Peace":

We Germans began World War II and for this reason alone, more than the other participants, are we guilty of bringing immeasurable suffering to humankind. Germans have murdered millions of Jews in an outrageous rebellion against God. Those of us, who did not want this annihilation, did not do enough to prevent it. For this reason, we are still not at peace. We have not been truly reconciled with God. . . . We therefore ask all peoples who have suffered violence at our hands to allow us to perform good deeds in their countries . . . and in doing so communicate symbols of reconciliation. Let us begin in Poland, Russia and Israel, whose people we have perhaps hurt the most.

For several reasons Aktion Sühnezeichen (AS) started its volunteer program in other countries than those mentioned in the "Appeal for Peace." Apart from the fact that the end of the fifties was the height of the Cold War, it was still too soon for some of the countries named to respond positively to the request, the wounds of the recent past being still too deep. In the early years, starting in 1959, young volunteers helped to build a social academy in Rotterdam (the Netherlands), a church and a home for the handicapped in Norway, a synagogue in Villeurbanne (France), a kindergarten in Skopje (Yugoslavia), an irrigation plant on the Island of Crete (Greece), and an international meeting center in the ruined cathedral of Coventry (Great Britain).

The 1958 Synod of the German Protestant Church was still attended by the Protestant Church of the German Democratic Republic, also known as communist East Germany. So Aktion Sühnezeichen was founded as an all-German organization. Sending young volunteers from both West and East Germany was seen as an inherent part of the program. Several young East Germans volunteered to work in Norway and the Netherlands. When the East German government decided to interrupt relations between East and West Germans, Aktion Sühnezeichen repeatedly applied for special permission to continue sending East German volunteers to countries of the West. Yet the East German government rejected the applications in 1959. The reason it gave was that Aktion Sühnezeichen was not a project that helped the country to reach its goals. After this, projects in which volunteers from the two Germanies participated became impossible, and Aktion Sühnezeichen became divided into a Western and an Eastern branch.

In East Germany the work continued after 1962 by helping rebuild three churches in the East German town of Madgeburg which had been destroyed during the war. Out of this developed an extensive summer camp program, bringing together young people from Poland, the former USSR, Hungary, and Romania.

In West Germany, AS continued its work with a long-term volunteer program involving a growing number of young men and women. In 1968, when AS added to its name the word *Friedensdienste*, it came to be known as ASF. From the end of the sixties on, social peace-services took the place of construction work. Supporting and working with people in various social projects, with survivors of the Holocaust and with minorities suffering discrimination, as well as involvement in peace and Holocaust education became the principal engagements of the volunteer program.

In 1991, after the reunification of Germany, ASF again became a single organization. Today, more than twenty-five summer camps are organized in ten European countries with four hundred participants yearly. The summer camp volunteers work on Jewish cemeteries and memorial sites of former concentration camps, and in a variety of social organizations. At this time, one hundred and fifty long-term volunteers, most of them between the ages of nineteen and twenty-five, are active in eleven countries: Belgium, France, Great Britain, Israel, the Netherlands, Norway, Poland, the Czech Republic, the United States, the Commonwealth of Independent States (CIS), and Germany. These young men and women commit themselves for a period of eighteen months of service. Conscientious objectors have the government's permission to fulfill their obligation of national civil service as volunteer workers in ASF.

The organization presently is active in the following areas:

• Long- and short-term volunteer service in Israel, the United States, and Western and Eastern Europe.

• Educational work, together with survivors of the Holocaust, at memorial centers of former concentration camps, in institutes, and in museums.

• Confronting German history, challenging right-wing extremism and antisemitism, lobbying for the recognition of "forgotten" victims of the Nazi oppression, and participating in peace groups and initiatives.

Projects Past and Present in Two Countries

Given the vast program of ASF, we have decided to focus on the work in two countries, the Netherlands and the United States. The work in the Netherlands is particularly interesting because the first volunteers of ASF were invited into this country and because thirty-five years of service in the same country allow us to see how the volunteer work has changed over this period. The work in the United States has been chosen because of its particular interest to the North American readership of this book. We have decided not to offer a detailed account of the programs in these two countries, but rather to quote from letters and reports written by participants in these programs, that is to say, by our partners, the volunteers, with whom we are working. We think of this chapter as providing testimonies offered by members of ASF.

ASF in the Netherlands

The first invitation to a country occupied by the German army came from the Netherlands through Dutch Christians who had been in close contact with members of the German Protestant resistance during the Nazi period. In Ouddorp, a small village on a Dutch island, Goerree-Overflakkee, a holiday home for workers' families from Rotterdam was to be built. In April 1959 a group of (West) German volunteers started to work there. A project of this kind was not a matter of course at a time when the war was still so fresh in the minds of the Dutch population. The German occupiers had destroyed the dikes in this region in February and March of 1944, hoping to prevent an invasion from the Allies. Extended areas had been inundated. In the coastal regions, about 400,000 Dutch had been forced to leave their farms and villages. Seen in this light, it is not surprising that the local population was reserved and skeptical at the beginning of the project—and some friction did occur in the daily life and work. Yet the ability of many of the Dutch to transcend their feelings made possible the first steps in getting to know one another. "A very special sign of friendly hospitality was the patient and sensible help of the mayor and the architect, both men who had suffered under German concentration camp detention during the war," reported the newsletter of Aktion Sühnezeichen on 26 June 1959.

This was apparently a good start. Further groups of young German men and women followed the first example. In 1961 a youth center in Friesland was built. In Rotterdam, a city which had been destroyed by German bombs in the first days of the German occupation, an International Social Academy was built mainly by German volunteers. It was given as a present to the city. This was the biggest construction project undertaken by Aktion Sühnezeichen; it was also the last one. From the late sixties on the volunteers started to work in social services: working with underprivileged groups in urban neighborhoods, the handicapped, groups wrestling against racism, initiatives helping refugees and centers promoting Holocaust-education, peace, and third-world development.

Rosenstock-Huessy House
The Rosenstock-Huessy House in Haarlem is the project in the Netherlands with the longest tradition of cooperation with ASF. Rosenstock-Huessy House was founded by a small group of people influenced by Rosenstock-Huessy's humanistic and universalistic philosophy. Since 1972 eighteen young Germans have spent their voluntary service there. This living and working community set two main goals. One was to live in a community where people who experienced a crisis in their lives and/or were in need of psychiatric help could live for a year or so in order to find themselves again and be able to live on their own. The other goal was working on crucial questions for humanity on the brink of the third millennium. To further this goal, the House allowed various philosophical and political groups, among them ASF, to make use of its rooms.

In 1991 Wim Leeman, a Dutchman, one of the founders and long-term inhabitants of the Rosenstock-Huessy House, wrote the following account of his experiences with ASF volunteers:

When our living-community started in the fall of 1970 with the acquisition of a very large, old and run-down house it urgently needed help and support. We especially needed young enthusiastic people who wanted to volunteer a part of their life in order to help us. Aktion Sühnezeichen Friedensdienste and its volunteers were already known to us through the construction of the academy in Rotterdam. We asked for a volunteer and had a lot of luck. The first volunteer was not only very nice, but he had also finished his studies in electro-technology. With the help of local students, Edmund Hartmann laid down the electrical wiring and installation in the whole house, many kilometers of wire. Yet above that he learned an excellent Dutch, built up close friendships and is until this day a very welcome guest in our house. He started a long row of volunteers.

This was the time when the volunteers were greatly influenced by the student movement of the late sixties. Everything having to do with power and authority was being questioned. Especially parents, the fathers and mothers of this generation, were called to account for their doings. It was understandable and justifiable that the young people took a critical stand against the war generation. Yet this confrontation did not usually result in a clash between two generations. What clashed were two world views. We discovered that because of the reigning ideologies, during a war people fight their adversaries without knowing them. One fights imaginary people, with images of the enemy that Heinz, Gérard and Mahomet have to fill. Yet in reality, Heinz, Gérard and Mahomet do not fit these ideological images.

This has been the most important lesson for many volunteers and their host organizations. They discovered that only a real encounter with the living Heinz, Gérard and Mahomet gives them the chance to free themselves from lies and caricatures they have inherited. In this concrete human experience lies the importance of ASF and other voluntary organizations. They break through the false images about each other and take the risk of growing and changing together.

Eugen Rosenstock-Huessy formulated this philosophy of life in a few words, *Respondeo, etsi mutabor*: I answer even if I change because of this. We, the Dutch, learned how many young Germans wrestle with their past, and at the same time we also became aware of the dark side of our own history, for example our colonial presence in Indonesia. Discovering your past became a joint process involving the "messengers of God" who had been "visiting" us for twenty years and ourselves, the Dutch, who had stayed at home. We recognized that there are always new ways of crossing boundaries from one people to another. We can be born as a German or as a Dutch person, as a man or a woman, as educated or uneducated, young or old, but when we cling to our given self-understanding, we block off future energies and power. Women and men who choose to leave their country for one year or longer open themselves to the energy of crossing borders. In this way the volunteers of ASF become bearers of light in the darkness that has fallen upon the human race. Thank you, Aktion Sühnezeichen (of the past) und Friedensdienste (of the future), for influencing our age so that the present becomes possible.

ASF in the United States

At the foundation of Aktion Sühnezeichen, when the "Appeal for Peace" was made, it was not envisaged that AS would send volunteers to work in projects in the USA. Yet in 1968 the traditional peace churches of the United States—the Quakers, the Mennonites, the Brethren—and friends within the United Church of Christ (UCC) and the Presbyterian Church asked ASF to send German volunteers to the United States. These churches had sent many volunteers to work in refugee camps and settlements for "displaced persons" (survivors of concentration camps and forced labor camps) in regions of Europe afflicted by the consequences of World War II. These North American churches now invited German volunteers to the United States so that the volunteer peace services would not remain a one-way-street. The first ASF-volunteer placements in the United States were at camps for children from poor neighborhoods, camps of migrant workers, community centers in the urban ghettos, halfway houses, and Indian reservations.

Three months after the ASF volunteers had started working in the United States, Don Sneider, the training director of the Brethren Voluntary Service (BVS), wrote to the ASF office in Berlin:

> Hundreds of conscientious objectors were sent to Germany in the days of "reconstruction," and they are still volunteering today. It would be promising if it could be a reciprocal venture. The idea of reconciliation is so important in these days. The Christian message of reconciliation and the demonstration of good will and compassion must be heard in these days of hate and destruction.

In 1968 six ASF volunteers were placed in the United States; in 1969 another fourteen volunteers came and worked in projects sponsored by UCC and BVS. Starting in 1970 volunteers were also placed through the Mennonites and started to work in Canada. By the end of 1973 fifty ASF volunteers were active in the United States and Canada. They worked in a broad range of organizations, a third of which were not affiliated with the peace churches. In order to meet the demands of a growing number of volunteers, ASF opened an office and installed a staff person to coordinate the ASF program in North America in 1974.

Given ASF's mission, it was clear from the beginning of the work in North America that it would be very important to reach out to the Jewish community. Many Jews had escaped from Europe after 1933 or immigrated after 1945 to North America. It took almost ten years to build up a relationship of trust that would enable a German volunteer to work in a Jewish organization. The first volunteer was placed at the Anti-Defamation League in New York City in 1980. In 1984 the first volunteer started working at Project Ezra, serving the Jewish elderly on the Lower East Side in Manhattan. (Project Ezra will be described in more detail later on.)

Presently ASF volunteers are placed in the United States in four main areas:

1. Holocaust education and work within the Jewish community: working at Facing History and Ourselves in Boston, Holocaust Center of Greater Pittsburgh, the Jewish Council on Urban Affairs in Chicago, the United States Holocaust Memorial Museum in Washington, and with Jewish elderly in two home-care projects as well as in two nursing homes.

2. Social services: working with the homeless, the handicapped, battered women, disadvantaged children and youth, people with AIDS, the elderly, and the mentally ill in Chicago, New York, Boston, Cleveland, and in two communities in the countryside of Massachusetts.

3. Community organizing: volunteering in poor neighborhoods in larger cities, mostly in the Midwest.

4. Peace education: undertaking disarmament, nonviolent conflict resolution, and solidarity work with the Third World, especially Central America. Since 1968 more than six hundred ASF volunteers have worked in these areas and presently about twenty-five volunteers are active in the United States.

In the rest of this chapter two particular projects will be highlighted: community organizing at the National Training and Information Center in Chicago, and Project Ezra in the Jewish community. Community organizing projects are of particular importance to the American ASF program, because our volunteers learn there a form of political and social activism that is not widely known in Germany. In these projects the volunteers encounter not only the problems of poverty and social deprivation in the United States but also become acquainted with democratic, grassroots-based, problem-solving ideas and practices. Project Ezra is the ASF project in the Jewish community with the longest history of cooperation, revealing the progress made over the years.

Community Organizing

Shel Trapp, the director of the National Training and Information Center (NTIC) in Chicago, wrote a letter to ASF in 1992 that contained the following sentences:

> For many years NTIC has had many volunteers from your organization. We have always been pleased with their commitment and ability to assist us in organizing in low income neighborhoods. In a real sense they make a bigger contribution to the growing awareness of our whole world as one big neighborhood, in which we all have to learn to live together and celebrate our diversity. It is very important that the fine work of your organization not only continue, but expand. For as your volunteers work in our communities, the perceptions of our residents about people from other countries are shattered and our people begin to understand that we all share a common responsibility for world peace. I also feel that the skills that NTIC can impart to the volunteers will pay dividends back in Germany when the volunteers return home to work for social change in their country.

Volunteer Alex Pöter wrote the following about his experiences at NTIC in 1993:

As a community organizer the biggest challenge for me is how to make use of my personal capabilities. There are theoretical concepts and rules for community organizing, yet the practical realization—which includes for example, the ability to communicate these strategies and techniques to others—is mainly dependent on using one's own personal powers. This calls for psychological insight into people's culture, a high degree of flexibility, the capacity to judge a situation unemotionally, the talent to communicate with simplicity and clarity, the readiness to adopt a politically and religiously neutral stance when working with a community, a willingness to engage in conflict, a high amount of psychological stress endurance, the capacity to encourage people, and an unlimited trust in the success of the work as a community organizer. Another challenge for me is the fact that as a white German speaking broken English I work in a community where the majority are Mexicans and Puerto Ricans, about half of whom speak only Spanish, and where the minority is made up of Asians, African-Americans and Europeans. Yet when I sit in the living-room with Maryann, Trudy, James, Bonnifacius, Brenda, Frederico and all the rest and am invited to dinner, and we tell each other about our personal lives, or I play with the children or listen to their stories about their homeland, I realize that even if I am only twenty-one years old, white, German, and speaking broken English, I am respected, and they really appreciate my work.

Even though organizing means working 50 to 60 hours a week, including weekends, and I often feel overworked and stressed, and even though work and private life become almost inseparable and I realize that most people have no idea what a community organizer does or what kind of abilities he or she has to have for this work, I continue to be obsessed with the spirit of organizing. I have been an agent for social change in several areas. Never has my work as an activist been so near the grassroots, never have I been so closely connected to the goal of the change, and never have the results of my work been so real and visible. For me community organizing is the best living example of grassroots democracy. I now know why some people make great sacrifices for this practical philosophy and are willing to pay every imaginable price just to make a small, but real and tangible contribution to social change.

Project Ezra
We wish to introduce Project Ezra by citing the words of co-director, Misha Avramoff:

I personally encountered Action Reconciliation in 1982 at a speaking engagement I had in Washington, D.C. A woman approached me, introduced herself, and acquainted me with the ethos of Action. She wanted a relationship with a Jewish group working with a population in need, who could use a German, non-Jewish volunteer who would be involved in their work and "bear witness" to the past. I knew that our elderly were not ready emotionally for such a step. We work with the Jewish elderly in need on the Lower Eastside of New York. We have some survivors, but most were raised in this country, worked as waiters and heavy machine operators and saw their families in Europe perish in the Holocaust.

We at Ezra decided to begin a relationship with Action Reconciliation for two reasons. The primary reason remains valid to this day. According to Jewish sources, we cannot turn away a person who wants to do *tshuvah*. *Tshuvah* is a word for turning to the past to confront it. It is an act that acknowledges guilt: an individual is symbolically confronting the guilt of his nation and willing to build a future based on an honest confrontation with the years between 1933 and 1945. The new Germany has to be more forceful about acknowledging its past; these volunteers from Action Reconciliation are a beacon.

The second reason we were eager to begin a relationship is because our intuition tells us that people, once they get to know one another as human beings, begin to shed the baggage of the past and form a relationship based on this human contact and present circumstances. There were obstacles. Some of our elders told us they would refuse to see a "German." Our first wonderful volunteer came to Project Ezra in 1984. At group functions and within a few months, barriers began to fall down. Before six months had elapsed, Tim began to work one on one with our elders, including our survivors.

Our Ezraites from Action Reconciliation have been hard-working and incredibly interesting to our elders who always marvel at these blond, blue eyed (not all!) young people with strong German accents whose grandparents fifty years ago were the perpetrators of the final solution. These volunteers go to the city projects and tenements and visit and give solace to the very old and very frail. We had the privilege of working with the most sensitive and committed of the young generation of Germany today. They are indeed the pride of a new Germany.

We have had eleven productive years together. We will be saying goodbye to our current co-worker and friend, Christian Kirchner, and we expect to welcome our next volunteer with open arms. There is a former volunteer back in Germany now who is working in trying to create awareness among the young. He is wearing a mezuzah I gave him as a reminder that we all have to come to grips with the past in order to build a better future.

And we wish to share with you the experiences of two ASF volunteers, Tim Gehrke and Christian Kirchner, the first volunteer and the latest volunteer working for Project Ezra. Tim Gehrke wrote in his report in 1985:

Since all the old people that I visited needed help very urgently, the distrust that they had because I was German lost its importance for them. However, every day I felt the fact that I was a German, that I belonged to a people whose ancestors had killed six million of their people. In the beginning this was painful for me, with time I began to accept it more and more as a part of every day life. If I was introduced to someone or if a conversation developed in the elevator while I was working, due to my British school English, usually the following dialogue occurred: "Oh, arc you British?" "No, I am German." "You mean from Germany?" "Yeah, from Germany." Pause and embarrassment on the other side. . . . "But you are Jewish?" "No, I am not Jewish." Now either my counterpart ends the conversation abruptly by turning away or he/she shows more interest. If the latter is the case, I have to explain my work for the nth time during the 18 months. In the end I could recite the history and founding of ASF, its goals and aims, as well as my own interests and aims in my sleep. Those who listened were interested, surprised and sometimes even enthusiastic, but often there also stayed a perceptible distrust.

A great number of the old people I dealt with had been directly affected by the Holocaust. I remember one experience during the first weeks of my work at Project Ezra that demonstrated very clearly to me as well as to my colleagues at Ezra how explosive my work was for the old people. I was asked to fetch some medicine for an old woman and bring it to her home at great speed. I was told that the matter was urgent, that no one else had the time to take care of it, and that under no circumstances should I tell her that I was German since her whole family had been murdered in German concentration camps. I went there, fighting on the way with a strong identity problem—what should I say, if she asked me where I came from? When I brought her the medicine, it was as I had expected: she asked, and I murmured something about being "European." I felt so bad about saying this that I immediately added the truth. The old woman began to cry and told me amid tears about her family, who had been completely killed by the Nazis. She couldn't understand what I wanted from her. Again I told her why I was working for Project Ezra and which German organization had sent me. This couldn't still her pain, I couldn't dry her tears and didn't want to, but we parted by shaking hands.

Back home, in the Federal Republic of Germany, I had witnessed for over twenty years the will power with which the generation of my parents and grandparents had tried to make forgotten what had happened in Nazi-Germany. Now, here in New York I was confronted on a daily basis with this part of German history. The Holocaust became present-day reality. In effect I brought this woman her medicine because she didn't have a family any more, had no one who could have done this for her. I experienced many elderly, who started crying when they heard that I was a German,—again and again I heard awful stories recalling the cruelty and pain inflicted upon their families.

When I asked Sarah, a German Jew who had immigrated to the USA in 1950, about Germany and wanted to hear where she was born and had lived, her answer was Bergen Belsen. That was seemingly foremost in Sarah's memory. When Sarah and I got to know each other better and I visited her once at her home, she suggested in her broken English, which actually consisted of more German than English words, that we could talk in German. She said two sentences in German, stopped in her tracks, her eyes were suddenly filled with fear, and we continued talking in English. I thought I saw in her eyes the fear of her memories.

The distrust against Germans and Germany I not only encountered in the older generation of Jews. Often I met Jews of my age, who, if they would travel with an Interrail ticket through Europe, would not travel through Germany and who could not see themselves ever visiting my home country. Through the many encounters I had with them in conversations that went deeper than the usual "small talk" I realized where this distrust came from. They couldn't trust, because their mothers and fathers, their grandparents and for thousands of years the generations before, had been persecuted and murdered without a reason, only for being what they were, Jewish. I realized that they were inescapably linked with the history of their people, with the history of persecution and genocide, exactly as I am linked with the history of my people, the history of exploiters and mass-murderers during the period of Nazi-Germany.

When I applied for this work I only had a vague idea as to just how much I was linked to my history. I did not realize how much I still had to learn. This learning took place during my eighteen months at Ezra.

There was the conversation with Leah, one of my colleagues, who asked me why I was really doing this work in the Jewish community, why I felt responsible, and if it had anything to do with what my parents had done during the Nazi era. I answered, no, that my parents had been too young, that they couldn't have been even potentially guilty. I told her how difficult it was, especially in one's own family, to do research on this part of German history, that I had once asked my grandmother about her life during this period and had only got the answer that she hadn't known about anything. I also told Leah that I knew this wasn't the truth, even though I didn't think that my grandmother was a liar. She had probably already started on the first day after the capitulation of the Third Reich to tell herself that she hadn't known about anything. Leah then said, while lost in her thoughts and more as a realization for herself rather than a remark made to me, "It must be hard for young Germans to love their parents or grandparents." I was shocked. Yes, it was probably this truth, only partially realized, that motivated me to go abroad and do this service. It seemed to me that German life was lacking in love, the love of one's own country, one's tradition and one's own family. I felt that life in Germany was sad.

It is difficult to love all of that, after one has heard of the atrocities Germans inflicted upon others. The question must be asked, Who were these Germans? What Germans were involved in these crimes? Who approved of them and who resisted them? The fear that their own parents or grandparents were among those implicated in these crimes has kept many Germans from asking these questions. If one overcame the fear of a painful truth, one would probably not get a satisfactory answer. Had the parents been a part of the resistance, one certainly would have heard about it. In this situation, many must have listened to lies. For one cannot expect that the person by whom one is loved and whom one loves in return would risk this mutual love by answering for example that, yes, he or she also spit on Jews on the street and threw stones through their windows or even was a guard at a concentration camp. Or shot innocent French hostages or burned down Russian villages.

I had been conscious of the fact that it was difficult for me to develop a German identity. This had to do not only with information gained from history books, but also with something very private, even intimate, which I clearly recognized only because of Leah's remarks. I can't and don't want to learn from so many of the generations before me. Yet in the one and a half years abroad I learned a lot: from the elderly and from children about Jewish culture and religion, about the USA, about New York, how wealth and poverty can exist so close to each other, . . . and about what was a few thousand kilometers away, Germany and German history, about my origin and about myself.

Ten years later Christian Kirchner wrote this:

On my first visit to one client, her first question was. "Are you hungry? Then make yourself something to eat. I'll show you where everything is, so that you can just help yourself in the future." I think all ASF volunteers who have been with her were asked to eat something. Often the subject of the Holocaust comes up, how they feel now that a German sits at their table drinking coffee with them or helping them with their everyday things. One woman answered: "God bless the German kids, and we are happy to have you here." Another said: "It is good that you haven't forgotten us and what happened then." When I get answers like these I am very pleased, since they show me again how important are peace services such as this one.

This is all that Christian Kirchner mentions about the confrontation with German history in his report on his work at Ezra. While Tim was forced to reflect very deeply on his own German identity and its relation to the crimes of the past, ten years later Christian does not seem to be challenged by the elderly in the Jewish home care service. This is most likely due to the fact that the elderly have gotten used to the presence of young German volunteers and to the positive experiences they have had with them.

The Ezra volunteers learned a lot about Jewish culture, religion, and history, something they would most likely not have learned with that intensity in their own country. But the elderly Jews and their children also learned something; thanks to the presence of the volunteers, they changed their mind about Germans. They now recognize that there are some young Germans who want to deal with their nation's past. While this is not reconciliation, it is a small step toward mutual recognition and a new way of confronting the past.

Concluding Remarks and Future Outlook

The period of long-term voluntary service organized by ASF is divided into phases of preparation, reflection, and evaluation. Through these the volunteers learn to look upon German history from a new perspective. They begin to recognize that the movement of democratization wrestling against Germany's authoritarian political structures and civic attitudes had been too weak to prevent the catastrophe of 1933. They come to understand the inescapable connection between the past and the present, in other words, the responsibility of each individual to strengthen civil society by defending the human rights of all.

While doing their service in the different parts of the world the volunteers try to assist in alleviating the current problems of their host countries. To do this they learn about these societies, their peoples, cultures and problems, and the solutions that are being sought. It is hoped that the volunteers will bring these insights back to Germany. It is not insignificant that small communities of ex-volunteers are growing in all parts of Germany, with a wide variety of learning experiences. It has been observed that many volunteers keep in close contact with their former host country, continue to learn from its experiences, and communicate new ideas and practices to their German environment.

Recently ASF has expanded its long-term volunteer program to Poland, the Czech Republic, and to the Commonwealth of Independent States, because the changes in Eastern Europe have radically altered the possibilities of sending volunteers into these countries. ASF finally has the opportunity to realize what the founders once envisioned: sending volunteers from all parts of Germany to work in countries that suffered under the Nazi regime—in both East and West. ASF has always been distinguished by the close contact it kept with the East and the West. The recent developments allow ASF to give a more concrete expression to its original philosophy.

Many of our project partners have asked ASF to send volunteers from their countries to work in Germany. As the United States-American peace churches did in 1968, ASF is planning to invite volunteers from the countries in which it works to come to Germany and work in anti-racism and refugee projects as well as in educational facilities on sites of former concentration camps in Germany. The historical focus of ASF will not be lost; rather, it will be enriched by the viewpoints of the international volunteers. In this way ASF wishes to contribute to a growing international network in these important fields of work. Due to financial limits ASF will start this new phase of its program on a small scale, inviting eight volunteers from four countries in East and West. Should this be fruitful, the program will be enlarged and will certainly change the scope of the work ASF is doing. We look forward to this challenge.

13

Understanding with New Hearts

A Protestant Church and the Aspirations of Quebec

A. H. HARRY OUSSOREN

Background

Quebec is Canada's largest province, with a surface area of approximately 1.5 million square kilometers. Its population of about 6.5 million, just over a quarter of Canada's entire population, is made up of 82 percent francophones, 12 percent anglophones, and about 5 percent allophones. Long inhabited by North America Native peoples, the land was officially claimed for the king of France by Jacques Cartier in 1534. It was not until 1608 that the village of Quebec was founded. The word *Quebec* is rooted in the Algonquian language and means "where the river narrows."

The colony grew very slowly. By 1666 only 3,418 settlers lived in New France. By 1760, when Britain conquered New France, only 10,000 French immigrants had arrived. Little immigration followed the conquest. By the Royal Proclamation of 1763 the British authorities initially sought to assimilate the people of New France into the dominant English colonial culture. By 1774 they had come to terms with the determination of the francophone population to retain its distinct identity. The Quebec Act of that year ensured the cooperation of the subjects by allowing them to continue their patterns of social, religious, legal, and cultural organization.

Various attempts to integrate Quebec into the political structures controlled by British authorities proved difficult and trying. In 1867 Quebec became a province within the Canadian confederation. Until 1950 the province was relatively isolated behind the walls of linguistic, cultural, and religious difference, dominated economically by English-speaking Montrealers. With the modernizing work of the "quiet revolution" of the 1960s and massive secularization, Quebec nationalism emerged as a powerful force claiming more recognition as a founding people and more control of its own affairs, including its economy.

Since that time, constitutional negotiations have been held with increasing regularity in order to clarify the nature of the relationship between Quebec and the rest of Canada. A referendum in 1980 gave Quebecois the opportunity to reject separation. Another referendum in October 1995 again asked Quebecois whether they wished to become a sovereign nation or remain part of the Canadian confederation. By the narrowest of margins (50.5 percent), voters defeated the Quebec government's quest for sovereignty. To the great embarrassment of most supporters, Quebec's Parti Quebecois Premier Jacques Parizeau attributed the defeat to "money and the ethnic vote," feeding the fears of Quebec allophones. Soon afterward Parizeau was replaced by Lucien Bouchard, a former Conservative federal cabinet member and the charismatic leader of the secessionist movement. The defeat left sovereignists disappointed and federalists stunned at the near break-up of the nation and the fear that Quebec sovereignty was now just a matter of time.

Subsequent events revealed great fatigue in the entire Canadian populace with the never-ending issue of sovereignty. While skirmishing continued between the federal and Quebec governments, there was general readiness to put the independence question on hold so that urgent economic issues, especially Quebec's very high unemployment rate, could receive governmental attention.

Is The United Church of Canada an English-speaking Church?

The "Quebec issue" surfaced quickly in the first session of the 34th General Council of The United Church of Canada meeting on August 14, 1994. Barely had the five hundred commissioners (delegates) and guests finished singing the national anthem, "O Canada," when several participants protested English-only lyrics provided on overhead screens (ROP 1992, p. 71).[1] Insensitivity to the French-speaking membership of the church and to Canada's official bilingualism policy was unacceptable, complained the exasperated voices.

The incident was especially ironic given that the council was gathered at the University campus in Fredericton, the capital of Canada's only formally bilingual province, New Brunswick.

Symptomatic of the United Church's linguistic profile, the English lyrics had been assumed to suffice. In an overwhelmingly English-speaking church of about 800,000 members, francophones with twelve little churches and about 400 members are virtually invisible. Overlooking this tiny minority is easy, official church policy notwithstanding.

Official bilingualism should be visible in the life of the church, the General Council of 1982 had declared in approving a report entitled "The Church Whole." The crest of the church, as well as "all documents, books, booklets, posters, brochures, etc. published under church auspices [should] have the name of the denomination imprinted in both French and English." National church units should assess annually the advisability of translating key documents into

French (ROP 1982, p. 411). Resources for French-language training and cross-cultural orientation were made available for its ministry personnel, on the assumption that "appreciation of the Quebec socio-cultural reality and that of French-speaking areas in general is critical if the ministry and mission of The United Church of Canada is to be whole" (ROP 1982, p. 409).

The "O Canada" incident indicated how far the United Church itself still had to travel before arriving at bilingual wholeness. The intervention also served as a foretaste of other concerns these persistent voices would raise in the council. Both linguistic groups need to be taken seriously, they would argue, if the church wishes to truly be The United Church *of Canada* in its entirety, and not just of anglophone Canada.

Few commissioners in Fredericton expected the 34th General Council to make a significant contribution to the church's history of what was usually called "French-English relations." In spite of political developments in the context, the preparatory materials contained little to indicate that the Canada-Quebec issue was a matter of burning concern in the church.

Previous General Councils had requested and received high profile reports on the issue. In 1972 the Saskatoon General Council heard a report from the Special Commission on French-English Relations. This initiative of the 1971 General Council had been labeled a "very urgent matter" after the 1970 October Crisis (ROP 1971 p. 58f.). In this unusual moment of Canadian history, the kidnapping and murder of Quebec cabinet minister Pierre Laporte by Quebec nationalists had incited Prime Minister Pierre Trudeau to declare in force the draconian War Measures Act, suspending normal legal rights and giving police authority to take into custody hundreds of known Quebec activists.

In its report, the commission based its conclusions on three assumptions: "that the Church has a calling to be an instrument of reconciliation; that the real possibility of peaceful change is essential to a just society; and that violence in effecting or resisting change should be disavowed" (ROP 1972, p. 198). The council adopted the commission's statement that "a crucial factor in the shaping of future political structures must be the deliverance of French Canadians from any sense of subjection and that such deliverance requires an openness to a consideration of the present structures of Confederation" (ROP 1972, p. 199).

The commission's report did not, however, acknowledge the substantial role English-speaking Canadians, including members of The United Church of Canada, played in causing the majority population of Quebec to experience "subjection" and some to resort to violent means of change. For the United Church to identify itself as a potential "instrument of reconciliation" was both presumptuous and hypocritical, given its own history of participation in the domination of francophones in Quebec and beyond.

This point was not missed by two voices calling on the council to adopt a radically different approach from that offered by the commission. In a one-person minority report, Rhoda K. Hall (then of Saskatoon) pled for an end to official commissions with their pretentious statements to governments. Instead, she asked for a time of silence in the face of the evil and humiliation caused by the anglophone spirit of superiority, which had poisoned relations between francophones and anglophones since the beginning of the Canadian experiment (ROP 1972, p. 194). The plea fell on deaf ears and no action was taken on it.

The second voice, Ontario delegate Horst Rueger, took aim at a key recommendation of the commission, urging

> members of the United Church to recognize that Canadians may and do . . . reach strongly divergent conclusions regarding the optimum political future for Canada, and that this divergence of view demands respect and does not represent a moral failure on the part of either of two parties who may disagree (ROP 1972, p. 199).

He proposed a simpler, more heartfelt statement:

> We are concerned: we want to listen to your complaints! Where we have wronged you we seek your forgiveness. Let us sit together and work toward repairing the damage and together build a better future for our children.

The minutes of the council record cryptically that the amendment was lost (ROP 1972, p. 59). It took twenty years for the idea to gain acceptance by the General Council!

Reports to intervening General Councils concentrated on political and social circumstances complicating the Canadian puzzle. Little attention was paid to the church's own part in the problem. The 1980 General Council in Halifax affirmed basic values to be upheld in any conflictual situation:

> 1. Love Means Justice. We cannot truly love without doing justice. . . . The basic question always will be: do we have the social, political, and economic conditions which favor the widest justice (love) context possible?
>
> 2. Reconciliation. Our call is to reconcile, that is to do as Christ did: walking the way of conflict (cross), know that there must be a solution worked out in the context of a political process of which conflict is an essential element. Before the resurrection, there is a cross and care should be taken neither to avoid nor to deny this element.
>
> 3. Hope. The issues are complex but the resurrection teaches us that no stones are permanent. All of them can be turned aside—even the stones of prejudice, misunderstanding and political differences (ROP 1980, p. 149).

Still perched on a branch of moral superiority, the church felt authorized to proclaim the principles by which the solutions to the Canadian conundrum could be found. It continued to assume that it could be an agent of reconciliation in the Canadian dilemma without acknowledging its own substantial contribution to the impasse and its own need for conversion. In several French/English relations reports made to successive General Councils, there was no recognition that the church's understanding of the complex issue might be lacking.

The Church Itself Involved in the Problems of Canada

At the Fredericton General Council, however, persistent voices drew to the church's attention the fact that (in)justice is not just an "out there" issue. They made the council uncomfortably conscious that the church itself was deeply involved in the problems of the Canada-Quebec issue and blind to the inadequacy of its own knowledge in the matter. Fine words directed to others rang hollow when the church paid little attention to the francophones in its own midst and beyond. These strangers needed to be heard so that the church might discover its own part in Canada's problems and be freed to contribute toward real solutions.

This judgment was reinforced in the council's first session by a theme presentation entitled "There Is a River," by Douglas John Hall, professor of Christian Theology at McGill University in Montreal. Hall suggested that the church should "address to French Canada—an 'apology' comparable to its apology to the indigenous peoples."[2] The apology was a necessary step toward reconciliation, insisted Hall, because United Church people had "represented too uncritically the opinions—often, indeed, the foolish biases—of Anglosaxon Canadians; and we have not explored with sufficient consistency and imagination the resources of the Gospel for coming to terms with the reality of our 'two solitudes'" (ROP 1992, p. 71).

Heightening the council's awareness of the Canada-Quebec issue was the dramatic meeting of Canada's First Ministers in Charlottetown, Prince Edward Island, starting 18 August 1992. Canada's chief political leaders and representatives of Canada's First Nations would gather once again to attempt to solve Canada's ongoing constitutional problem, namely, to create the structural conditions that would enable Quebec to voluntarily participate within the Canadian constitutional framework.

A 1981 arrangement freeing Canada to amend its Constitution without the approval of the British government, and a new Canadian Constitution, had been imposed on Quebec by the federal government and nine provinces without the Quebec government's consent. A recent effort to solve the problem—The Meech Lake Accord of 1990, with its "distinct society" label to describe Quebec's unique role in the Canadian confederation—had failed to receive the required approval of all provincial governments. Charlottetown represented another emotional and publicity-charged attempt by Canada's political leaders to come up with a palatable solution to the thorny issue.

Anticipating the First Ministers' meeting, the General Council had agreed to interrupt its planned proceedings so that intercessory prayer could be offered at the time the First Ministers were convening. On the morning of 18 August, the sessional committee on "The Future of Canada" led the council in prayers for Canada, its peoples, and its political leaders. Offered by three members of the committee speaking in French, English, and Cree, the prayer included a specific plea for a united Canada. This plea no doubt reflected the hope of the vast majority of commissioners. Voices were quickly raised, however, to point out that some at the council did not share a vision of a united Canada and that to them the concept was objectionable. Subsequent printings of the prayer's text omitted the word *united*.

The sessional committee's draft report for the council's consideration reflected time-worn sentiments of support for a unified, officially bilingual Canada. The committee asked the council to reaffirm all Canada's diversity, commit itself to "preserve and strengthen our country within its current boundaries," and support "renewed federalism based on justice and dignity for all." The council was also urged to ask the Canadian government to recognize Quebec as a "distinct society" (à la Meech Lake), to enshrine "linguistic duality" in the Constitution, to promote the "development of . . . official language minorities," and to acknowledge the inherent rights of the first nations to aboriginal self-government (ROP 1992, pp. 120f.).

The reaction from some commissioners and visitors to the draft recommendations was quick and vocal. The persistent voices again objected to the appeal for renewed federalism, since some were actively engaged in a political process that might result in Quebec's formal separation from the Canadian confederation.

Some lamented the fact that the council (and the church) was again simply rehearsing its biases and prejudices. It was time for the church to recognize its ignorance and send a study team to Quebec to gain new information (ROP 1992, p. 123).

The sessional committee withdrew the draft report and decided to hold an open meeting that evening inviting all to share their views so that the committee could prepare a more adequate report for the council. In addition to the committee's thirty-three members, about twenty commissioners and visitors, primarily from Quebec, came to voice their opinions. A passionate affair, the meeting was an opportunity for deeply rooted prejudices to be challenged and strongly held convictions to be expressed.[3]

The sessional committee came away from this conversation moved to a new awareness that an innovative approach to the perennial "problem" needed to be proposed to the General Council. A formal statement, informed by the concerns of the visitors, was drafted for the council to consider (ROP 1992, pp. 121f.).

On August 20 commissioners approved the sessional committee's statement with one change. The statement's "hope for a unified Canada" was formally amended to "hope for Canada and its peoples." This reflected the growing feeling that expressions about unity should first be informed by "the hopes and aspirations of various social and political movements in Quebec." The council admitted it was "insufficiently representative of Canada's diversity," and the official constitutional process had not made the hopes of Quebecois plain to anglophones in the rest of Canada (ROP 1992, p. 124).[4]

A Mission Study Team of Church Leaders

The persistent voices had helped the council to acknowledge that there are some within The United Church of Canada and many beyond who do not share our hopes for a Canada based on renewed federalism and who pursue a political option that could result in the separation of Quebec from the rest of Canada and that the bases for their position are largely unknown to us (ROP 1992, p. 122).

The time had come, therefore, to listen to the other principal linguistic group in order to gain an understanding of its situation first hand. The council instructed its Sub-Executive, scheduled to meet in October, to create a task group with a two-part mandate to:

> gain understanding from and about the divergent social, political and religious movements in Quebec, and the hopes and aspirations of all Quebecois;
> report [its] findings, including implications in light of political developments, to appropriate units of the Church (ROP 1992, p. 122).

The former French/English relations officer of the church, Claire Doran, suggested that the task group be a "mission study team of church leaders"—a "blue-ribbon" group. This suggestion was accepted by General Secretary Howard Mills, who presented an implementation proposal to the Sub-Executive of the General Council meeting on 2 October 1992. It appointed a task group to administer the project and provide support to a "listening team" of church leaders to travel in Quebec for eight days to hear the concerns and hopes of mainstream Quebecois.

The Moderator's Listening Team to Quebec, as it became known, was led by the moderator of the United Church, The Rt. Rev. Stan McKay, of Beausejour, Manitoba, with the general secretary of the General Council, Rev. Dr. Howard M. Mills, of Toronto. Four other current members of the General Council Executive were included: The Rev. Dorothy Cunningham of Morin Heights, Quebec; Mrs. Louise Poudrette of Montreal, Quebec; Mr. R. Keith Snell of Swastika, Ontario; and The Rev. Ron Vincent of Fredericton, New Brunswick. A former moderator, well known for his record of involvement in social issues, The Very Rev. Dr. W. Clarke MacDonald of Toronto, was also appointed. Jacquelin Isenor, a diaconal ministry candidate from Calgary, completed the team as a youth member.

The team began its work on January 22, 1993, in Montreal. As part of its orientation to the task, team members reflected on the story of the Syrophoenician woman, who persisted in begging Jesus to heal her daughter (Mk 7:24-30). Their meditation confirmed the team in a "listening stance" born of humility and a desire to learn.

We went to Quebec with the General Council mandate to hear those who by-and-large have no voice in English-speaking Canada and who have not been heard adequately by people within the United Church. We spoke with people who were part of the mainstream movements in Quebec and able to articulate a vision of Quebec's future. We sought out people in various spheres of Quebec life known to have a commitment to the future of Quebec. Those who agreed to meet with the team received oral and written background information about the team and its mandate. Translation facilities were arranged. This preparatory work, we believe, was crucial to the success of our visit and the success of comparable efforts by others in the church (p. 10).[5]

Encountering Quebecois-es on their ground and seeing with their eyes was a significantly new departure for the United Church. Traveling in minivans, the team encountered an eclectic array of engaged Quebecois. They represented local French-speaking churches, both Roman Catholic and United Church; the Montaignais First Nations; labor and farm organizations; women's groups; university educators; and religious communities. A planned meeting with Claude Beland, leader of the powerful Quebec Cooperative movement, was canceled at Mr. Beland's initiative.

In March 1994 the team's report appeared in English with the title "Hearing Quebecois-es with New Hearts." A study guide was provided, setting the report into a context of quotations from submissions made by church members and congregations about the future of Canada after the Meech Lake debacle. The French-language edition of the report appeared in April without the study guide.[6]

The name given the report was an unambiguous clue about the impact the journey had had on the team. It signaled a transformation experienced by the team as it listened to Quebecois-es articulate their concerns and hopes: "We heard people who forced us to reassess our routine ways of looking at them" (p. 14). "In our listening we were surprised, enchanted, enlightened, humbled, and, in significant measure, moved to new understandings. We believe God spoke to us through the voices of the Quebecois-es we encountered" (p. 13).

The language of conversion and repentance is not used in the report. Nevertheless, the team clearly indicates that by attending to what Quebecois-es themselves said (as opposed to media reports, which too often distort reality) its way of seeing the majority population of Quebec was substantially altered.

This note of welcome enlightenment is replete in the report: "Throughout our sojourn in Quebec we felt that our views about Quebecois-es were being challenged and, in many cases, shattered. We were meeting for the first time Quebecois-es as they have become, as opposed to the Quebecois-es we thought we already knew and understood" (p. 14). "We were surprised at the depth with which Quebecois-es have pursued their cultural-political issues" (p. 16). "We were struck by the collective nature of this enterprise [of addressing foundational issues of Quebec society]" (p. 17). "We discovered 'a people'—the Quebec people—who have an identity that is much clearer than anything we anticipated" (p. 18).

Even the political goals of Quebecois were less straightforward than the team had assumed. "We heard Quebecois-es express their willingness to be 'within' a renewed Canada, but we also heard their readiness to 'go it alone' if the reality of Quebec cannot be accepted by the rest of Canada" (p. 21). "We sensed that Quebecois-es would welcome a partnership with a 'rest of Canada' which was clearer about its identity and more confident about its future as a 'nation' or as a community of 'peoples'" (p. 25).

As representatives of an overwhelmingly English-speaking church, the team had feared it might become scapegoats for the sins of the English-speaking majority within the church and in Canada. The team "had undertaken the trip with some trepidation, not knowing what to expect" (p. 14). "We were pleasantly surprised that no anger was directed at us, who represent a predominantly English-speaking institution" (p. 16). Instead, the team reported it was graciously and generously welcomed by Quebecois-es prepared to share confidently and energetically, without "demands," but "simply to report who they were and what conclusions they have reached after deep and passionate searching" (p. 14).

Fundamental differences notwithstanding, the team discovered it held much in common with Quebecois-es. Common human qualities and experiences were cited, as was fatigue with the perpetual constitutional process. But above all, they were united "as children of the same Creator" who share a "desire to have harmony and cooperation on the land mass we call 'Canada'" and "SHALOM for all the peoples of this land" (pp. 26f.).

The conclusions the team wanted the church to hear reflect the transformative nature of the encounter. "We believe that God is calling us and the entire church to a new awareness and appreciation of the majority people of Quebec and their emerging place in Canada" (p. 27). The basis of conversations between anglophones and francophones needs to become that of equals, insisted the team. If there is to be Canadian "unity," it needs to take seriously the "otherness" of Quebec. "Pseudo-unity with Quebec needs to be replaced with covenant relationship where these two peoples and the First Nations, with sensitivity to other ethnic and cultural communities, come together by the grace of God to commit themselves as equal partners to a shared future" (p. 28).

Reflecting its own experience, the team declared that apprehension and fear must be transcended in relationships between anglophones and francophones. Anglophones need to be given the ability "to really believe what Quebecois-es are saying about their future." A new way has to be discovered to help the peoples in Canada resolve the issues that have divided them (pp. 28f.).

Dramatic as the team's new discernment was, there is in the report no direct call for repentance and apology. Perhaps this can be attributed to the fact that the entire enterprise was already an admission by the church of its previously inadequate and presumptuous ways of dealing with the Canada-Quebec crisis. Perhaps the fact that interlocutors did not accuse the team or "demand" an apology but engaged instead in grace-filled human encounter permitted the team to defer the questions of guilt, repentance, apology, restitution, and forgiveness.

The team nonetheless did express the hope that the church might gain the ability "to perceive [Quebecois-es'] situation with their eyes and ears and hearts (as we have begun to do with women, indigenous peoples, gay and lesbian people and others)" (p. 28).

This conclusion is very significant. It points to the church's experience of learning that reconciliation is not a simple process to be promoted from a remote position of moral authority. On the contrary, it is a process the church must itself undertake.

The team reminds the church that as it had listened to women, Native people, and gays and lesbians about the evil effects of the church's own sexism, racism, and hetero-sexism and homophobia, it experienced the Word of God drawing it to a more faithful way on the road to reconciliation. With the team, the church discovered once again the gift of grace that comes from attending to the voices of those alienated by church attitudes and practices.

On behalf of the whole church, the General Council's Sub-Executive meeting on January 22, 1994, approved the team's recommendation, inviting units in the church to "study the Listening Team's report and consider how they might play an active and creative role in creating God's shalom in Canada" (p. 33). All United Church people were urged "in a spirit of humility . . . to learn more about Quebec and Quebecois-es—their past, their present, their future'" (p. 34). The report was distributed to all commissioners of the 34th General Council, and in a pastoral letter from the moderator congregations were invited to make use of the resource.

Evaluating the Report

The actions of the Fredericton General Council and the Moderator's Listening Team represent a redemptive moment in the difficult history of Canada's linguistic majorities. By attending carefully and respectfully to the thoughts and experiences of Quebec's francophones, the team modeled for all anglophones a "spirit of humility" seldom present in discussions on the Canada-Quebec issue. By identifying with humanity in the life, ministry, suffering and death of Jesus Christ, God models for all humanity the humbler way by which liberation from the captivity of sin is effected and reconciliation is gained (Phil 2). Mandated with the liberty of walking in the shoes of Quebecois and seeing reality through their eyes, the team lived the scriptural witness that a spirit of humility is indispensable if reconciliation is to become a possibility.

New covenant relationships in Canada require peoples "liberated from the power inherent in the image of the 'conquest' with its victorious majority and a conquered minority" (p. 23). The team found in Quebec a people already affirmed and confident in their particularity, who in many senses, if not constitutionally, could be described as *maîtres chez eux* (masters in their own house). Anglophones, on the other hand, still have a long way to go before the sense of being the victorious majority is overcome. This destructive self-image still pervades in the popular mind. But for anglophones to experience liberation from the image and other caricatures that distort Quebecois-es, they too will need to encounter Quebecois-es as they have become.

The action of the 34th General Council and the work of the Listening Team demonstrate that reconciliation comes not from lofty pronouncements but from the encounter of humble and respectful people intent on discovering others as they are, rather than as they are presumed to be. This is the stuff of which hearts are warmed, bridges built, and covenants made.

The Ambivalent Reaction

Quebecois-es aware of the process and report received the team's work as a sign of hope and reacted with admiration for this reconciling initiative by the United Church. In correspondence to the moderator, appreciation was expressed for the church's "openness and sense of dialogue," "for acting as the wise mediator," and for offering "English Canada as well as French Canada and Quebec a true 'projet de société.'" Roman Catholic officials asked for copies of the report. The Jesuit Centre for Faith and Justice in Montreal organized one of its "Relations" evening programs on the initiative as an experience of conversion.

This enthusiasm for the team's work was, however, not shared by United Church membership in Quebec. At the May 1994 annual meeting of the Montreal and Ottawa Conference (one of the thirteen regions of the United Church) resolutions critical of the report were received from at least seven local churches and two presbyteries. Strong language punctuated the debate. Words such as "imperialistic," "unfortunate," "paternalistic," "out-of-date," and "polarizing" were used to describe the team's process and report.

Two concerns appeared to dominate. First, the Listening Team had not "heard" the United Church's English-speaking membership in Quebec. The conference felt bypassed, notwithstanding the fact that the conference's delegates had suggested the initiative and its leaders had been apprised of developments throughout the process of implementing the General Council mandate. Although acknowledging that the conference had not presented the whole church with a vision for mission in the new realities of Quebec, some conference members complained inaccurately that the gap should not be filled by people coming from the moderator's office in Toronto but by people from within the conference.[7] Formally, the conference demanded a new study process and initiated its own Dialogue Quebec Committee to start the job.

The plaint assumed that to address the Quebec-Canada issue, the United Church should follow the typical French-English relations pattern of primarily looking through the eyes of its membership in Quebec. This, however, did not take into account two key factors. First, English-speaking members of the United Church had and have, as their impact on the 35th General Council demonstrated, direct access to the General Council and other structures of the church. The voices of Quebec's majority population, on the other hand, have no such entry into the church and are heard primarily through inadequate media filters. Second, it failed to recognize that the issue is one in which the entire church has a substantial stake, that is, the well-being of the nation. The Listening Team's membership had been carefully composed to reflect the church's national interest. One quarter of the team—an anglophone and a francophone— were leading members of the United Church in Quebec. The rest were chosen from other parts of the land.

A more substantial concern of conference members centered on the fact that the Listening Team had met primarily with Quebecois-es, that is, the majority population. Anglophones had hardly been consulted and no allophones had been heard. These groups, who together make up about 17 percent of the Quebec population, cannot be excluded, it was argued, because they are citizens of Quebec and integral contributors to Quebec society. By not "hearing" these groups, the team, it was charged, walked into the old trap of affirming ethnic nationalism and risked undermining "many of the positive advances that have been made in community-building in Quebec society" (ROP 1994, p. 540).

Hence the team report's affirmation that Quebecois-es are "a people" and the recommendation (not approved) that a new church policy be developed recognizing "'the peoplehood' of the majority population of Quebec and its right to negotiate as a people in relation to the other peoples of Canada" were pounced upon by a few extreme critics as racism that fatally flawed the work of the team.[8]

As a result, the conference formally asked the upcoming General Council to shelve the report. It also initiated and sought General Council assistance with its Dialogue Quebec Committee for a "more complete process of listening to all legitimate voices in Quebec" (ROP 1994, p. 540).

Meeting in August 1994 in Fergus, Ontario, the 35th General Council considered the conference's requests but did not rescind the Listening Team's recommendations as approved by the January Sub-Executive. In fact, the General Council expressed "thanks and deep appreciation to the members of the Moderator's Listening Team to Quebec for their commitment, work and the much needed challenge they have held out to all of us in the church to listen with new hearts."

However, two commissioners from Montreal and Ottawa Conference proposed and did gain approval for an amendment to label the report and study guide "a historical document." Their presumed intention was thereby to shelve the report, as had been done with another controversial document under consideration at the Victoria General Council of 1988. The intended significance of this amendment was not announced at Fergus, leading the General Council Executive meeting in November 1994 to state that it did "not regard the document 'Hearing Quebecois-es with New Hearts' as shelved." The executive committee also encouraged continued distribution of the report (Pastoral Letter of the Moderator, December 1994).

In reality, however the church's courageous step toward reconciliation between anglophones and francophones was seriously undermined. Breaking down barriers with francophones had surfaced reasons for alienation among the church's English-speaking members, not unlike the costly strife generated by the effort in the 1980s to seek reconciliation with its own homosexual minority. "Listening with new hearts" to the majority population of Quebec had been the transformative journey of a few, whose offer to share their experiences was hardly accepted by their English-speaking sisters and brothers. There was little will to press on if the result was to be renewed conflict within the church.

Also contributing to the lack of will to go further down the road of reconciliation with Quebec's majority population were the untimely deaths of both Howard Mills and Clarke MacDonald. The gap created by the loss of these influential and articulate members of the team was not filled.

Doubtless the team's report was flawed by its lack of precise definition of *peoplehood, nation, ethnicity,* and *citizenship.* This is an endlessly complex debate, whose stakes are clearly very high, as the former Yugoslavia has painfully demonstrated. In the more peaceful Canada-Quebec context, this lack of precision could perhaps be overlooked by the more magnanimous understanding that the report of the Listening Team was but the first step (as the November 1994 General Council Executive affirmed) on the part of a largely English-speaking Canadian church seeking faithfully in the light of the gospel to renew the hearts of its own people numbed into complacency and self-righteousness by far too many lofty statements of principle on the Canada-Quebec problem.

Reconciliation, after all, is an affair of the heart—the heart of God softening human hearts to live as the beloved children of God.

Notes

[1] ROP refers to the *Record of Proceedings* of the General Council issued by The United Church of Canada's General Council offices after each meeting of The United Church of Canada's national decision-making court; for example, ROP 1994 is the Record of Proceedings of the 34th General Council's meeting in 1994.

[2] In 1986 at Sudbury, Ontario, the General Council of the United Church formally apologized to Native peoples within the United Church.

[3] The author was the chair of the sessional committee and is drawing on personal recollection of the event.

[4] The statement reads:

The 34th General Council of The United Church of Canada prays for and declares its hope for Canada and its peoples, where Aboriginal peoples, Quebecois and other francophones, Metis, anglophones, and people of many other cultural heritages share this land together in peace and justice, with respect and appreciation for each other's history, culture, language, and other distinctive gifts—a sign of hope for the global family of nations.

We deeply believe that in God's reign, to which we are called, there can be no room for creating "enemy images"; we are sisters and brothers of the One creating, redeeming and sustaining God.

In light of the facts that the 34th General Council is insufficiently representative of Canada's diversity; the official constitutional process has not revealed to anglophone Canada the hopes and aspirations of various social and political movements in Quebec; the 34th General Council had before it a limited range of petitions dealing with this crucial issue, which requires the attention of all Canadians; therefore, the 34th General Council acknowledges that there are some within The United Church of Canada and many beyond, who do not share our hopes for a Canada based on renewed federalism, and who pursue a political option which could result in the separation of Quebec from the rest of Canada; and the basis of their position is largely unknown to us, and the 34th General Council calls upon all United Church members and adherents and all people of goodwill to respect the strongly held differences of opinion which characterize the constitutional process and debate.

[5] This and the following quotations are from "Hearing Quebecois-es with New Hearts: The Report of the Moderator's Listening Team to Quebec" (Toronto: The United Church of Canada, 1994).

[6] The author served on the task group backing up the team and served as editor for the final report of the listening team.

[7] Unpublished report on Montreal and Ottawa Conference Annual Meeting, 27-29 May 1994, to the General Council Secretaries, Toronto, by the General Council representative.

[8] Correspondence, June 20, 1994, to the author from Tom Edmonds, minister of Granby United Church. The video recording of the evening at the Centre de Justice et Foi in Montreal reveals another leading Quebec United Church minister expressing similar sentiments.

14

A First Nations Movement
in a Canadian Church

STANLEY McKAY AND JANET SILMAN

For Aboriginal people in Canada, overcoming injustice and moving to-
ward justice is an arduous and complex task. In the following
conversation, Stan McKay and Janet Silman recall the First Nations
movement in The United Church of Canada,¹ which has led to:
  • the denomination making an apology to Aboriginal peoples;
  • the formation of the All Native Circle Conference;
  • the development of indigenous programs of theological education.

JS: The development of the All Native Circle Conference can be seen as a
case study of how Aboriginal United Churches moved from white leadership
to having their own ministers and forming their own church courts.

SM: In 1979 I remember receiving a questionnaire on Native ministry sent
out from the national United Church to all Aboriginal churches and ministers.
A number of us responded with some anger and frustration. We were not going to answer yet another survey, yet another study. Out of that response came
the first-ever Native consultation. It was held in White Bear, Saskatchewan,
in the summer of 1980.

JS: I also received that letter from the Division of Mission in Canada² when
I was the minister at a First Nations community in Southern Manitoba. I recall
most clearly that two or three days into the consultation, somebody suggested
that the Aboriginal people meet together, with others meeting at the same
time if they wished. Some white people were upset about the suggestions,
while some thought it was a good idea.

SM: The only warm room was the one the Aboriginal people chose. (laughter)

JS: The basic point I remember from the all-Aboriginal meeting report was:
"We want you to teach us the politics of the United Church, how it is structured, and how it works, and we will teach you about our Native spirituality."

172

SM: That is about reconciliation. Behind that statement was: "We have something to give and you have something to share. There is a mutuality here." It was the beginning of a different mind-set from that of one-way giving, the old charity model.

JS: And a recognition that white culture needed something in the way of spirituality. The offer showed that Aboriginal people recognized a need on the part of the dominant white culture to learn about the Spirit, which was wisdom the Aboriginal people clearly had. The dominant church knew the politics, held the knowledge, practice of power, and control of church structures. The request was direct and to the point. It was asking for knowledge for the purpose of effecting change. White Bear was the beginning of momentous changes.

SM: At that time I went to Saskatchewan for some meetings about the formation of the Dr. Jessie Saulteaux Resource Center. The development of this Aboriginal learning center for ministry was happening at the same time.

JS: From the very beginning of the Aboriginal self-government process in the United Church, education for church leadership was recognized as being key. Remember Dr. Jessie Saulteaux's story of being at a church gathering? She thought she was going to be asked to speak, then was not. But she had a vision of little lights dancing over the people's heads, and she recognized the stars as young Aboriginal people rising up to be leaders in their own churches. It was the vision of Dr. Jessie and other Aboriginal church elders who "dreamed the dream" of indigenous church leadership arising. To me, I see the gospel pressing to emerge here, pressing to be incarnated in the people's own cultural identity. The good news cannot be proclaimed by a people who are denied their own voice, their own leadership. The development of a learning center run *by* Aboriginal people *for* Aboriginal people was a big step in giving the gospel the people's voice.

SM: All of those early consultations were focused on the development of Native leadership. In May 1982 a proposal was developed to hire a national person to coordinate the work. I was hired in that staff position in October of 1982. We had direct access to the national governing body of the United Church. That gaining of voice was an important process.

The national consultations initiated at White Bear had become an annual event. After a period of working through a lot of anger and healing of individual pain, by 1983 a clearer sense developed that this was a movement of people. The circle image then became very, very strong. An executive was planning the consultations every year, and the pattern developed of meeting in communities in every region through a cycle. Those were very powerful sharing times. The reason for strength and momentum, I believe, was that there was reconciliation through the various First Nations coming together. Reconciliation between the Mohawk and Ojibway involved the overcoming of old political separations, because people now had a common struggle within the church. Historic mistrusts began to be addressed.

Alberta Billy, a First Nations woman from Cape Mudge, British Columbia, was one of our representatives at General Council Executive (the highest court of The United Church of Canada).[3] The executive required written reports about two months before their meetings, to control what came before them. We always complied, until one report that Alberta Billy made. That was the *kairos* moment. She already had talked to me and the National Native Council about the elders being silenced and the church being responsible, in some ways, for the silence of the elders. First she gave the report that the council had worked on together. Then she put it down and said, "It is time you apologized to Native people." That totally blew the meeting away. No one was prepared. It was not new to the Native Council, but it was Alberta's decision to say then and there to the General Council Executive, "You need to apologize to us for the historic injustice."

We both knew it was not according to the rules. But the Executive also knew that this was not something to be simply discarded. The printed agenda was dropped and discussion started in the room. A couple of people wanted to apologize then at the meeting. However, a number of people realized that Alberta was not asking for an apology right there. It was suggested that we take it back to our National Native Council, where we would plan a process. That was the most exciting eighteen months in my five-year term as national staff. We had a year and a half before the next General Council, it being the best place to raise the question of the apology. We were blessed with eighteen months to prepare, and we began.

We developed a pamphlet that went out to all the congregations in the United Church informing them of the request for an apology from the church and inviting them to reflect on it. As we got near to the 1986 General Council, I remember the elders sitting together at the annual consultation. There was some trepidation as to what the church would do with this, but the elders knew by then that we must ask the church for an apology. There was no question about that.

Some of us had a deep fear about what it would mean if the church refused. But I have an image that will always stay with me around the request. The elders said, "We will have the drum group come." There was discussion about that. Then someone said, "What if the church doesn't apologize?" The elders' response was, "Well, it doesn't matter. We have to dance whether they apologize or not." That positive framework of being a people, whatever the church did, was for me the moment of a statement of liberation.

Our strategy was good. We met for about four days before General Council at our own location in Sudbury, Ontario. We would request the apology and then leave the room. We would not take part in General Council's reflection on the issue or be cross-examined about our purposes.

We requested the apology on the floor of General Council, then asked all First Nations commissioners to come with us as we left the room. We went down to the sacred fire where we waited and prayed for two hours. We had a ceremony of tobacco offerings at the sacred fire. Jim Dumont, a traditional teacher, led us in a ceremonial prayer. The strongest words in the prayers of the people that evening were, "There is nothing more that we can do than ask in a good way, and continue to pray for strength."

The evening had been overcast with light, drizzly rain. By the time we could see the commissioners walking down toward us, the moon was out. In the clear night there was a sense of things being well in the universe. The elders met with the moderator (the elected head of the United Church) in the teepee to hear what the moderator would say. The apology was made:

> Long before my people journeyed to this land, your people were here, and you received from your elders an understanding of creation, and of the mystery that surrounds us all that was deep and rich and to be treasured. We did not hear you when you shared your vision. In our zeal to tell you of the good news of Jesus Christ we were closed to the value of your spirituality. We confused Western ways and culture with the depth and breadth and length and height of the gospel of Christ. We imposed our civilization as a condition of accepting the gospel. We tried to make you be like us and in so doing we helped to destroy the vision that made you what you were. As a result, you, and we, are poorer, and the image of the Creator in us is twisted, blurred and we are not what we are meant by God to be. We ask you to forgive us and to walk together with us in the spirit of Christ so that our peoples may be blessed and God's creation healed.

The elders' response was, "We must go back and talk to the people," which had a great deal of wisdom. We danced with the drum. Everyone danced.

When the apology had been made, I remembered Jim Dumont having a questioning look in his eyes, wondering, does this really mean anything? In talking to him the day following, he was not sure. It might have some impact, but his reading was that the church was not going to change much. Yet he was interested enough that he was there.

JS: Jim's involvement with the apology speaks to me of reconciliation. That he would be involved—an Aboriginal person who went through theology, then left the church and recovered his traditional ways—suggests a spirit of reconciliation. To me that is a powerful symbol of wholeness overcoming alienation, a spirit of reconciliation bringing people into relationship, overcoming some of the divisive things done in the name of Christianity.

SM: It is interesting that several years later the tension among the people about traditional ceremonies reemerged. It started again to gnaw at some people in the All Native Circle Conference and continues to be there. But in that evening, there was no question about having a traditional teacher lead in the ceremonies. Jim's presence did embody a spirit of reconciliation.

United Church television produced a program around that time on Jim and Alf Dumont's reconciliation as brothers, one brother following the Christian way and one the traditional way. That night after the apology Alf went with

Jim back to the lodge for prayer. As I recall, they had not done that together before.

With the public apology made by the United Church, some of us felt that now we could take that home to our people. It was a sign that the church knew it had made a mistake in condemning our cultural ways. Those First Nations church people reluctant to look at Native spirituality, or wondering about the church's position on our traditions, now had some indication. Yet what the apology really means, even now, is not completely clear. But it did give momentum to the development of the Dr. Jessie Saulteaux Center. The apology strengthened the Native Council and was followed with the dream of an All Native Circle Conference.

At the same time as the apology process, we were discovering that the church had not given us all the information about how it worked politically, but we were leaning from our own experience. Those of us who went to General Council Executive twice a year could see that we were in a state of "suspended animation." We were not finding what we needed in the existing presbyteries. The conferences (larger regional courts of the United Church) that we sat in were largely irrelevant to us. We had the national council and the annual consultations but they had no impact on the political life of the church. Our occasional recommendations to General Council Executive or national church divisions were having no impact on the future of our own communities. With that analysis, the National Native Council could see that we had gone as far as we could in our informal process of council. If we were going to play an active part in the church, we would need to have our own structure, our own decision-making processes. This also was driven by the need for our own leadership. As in all self-government, we needed to try some things ourselves.

Keewatin Presbytery in Northern Manitoba and Northwestern Ontario already had gone through a process of development as the first all-Aboriginal United Church presbytery.[4] I remember being a part of the northern meeting when Keewatin decided to become a presbytery. It was not formalized right away, but to be tried for a year. At the end of the year, they decided: "This is complicated stuff. We cannot do this by ourselves." So they gave up. But one year later, after going back to the various surrounding presbyteries, they decided, "We can't take any more of this! The mistakes we were making were better than this garbage!" (laughter)

We began to see that, as Keewatin had decided, we had no choice. If we were going to have any self-determination, any sense of involvement, we had better do it ourselves. But the model was still wrong. We were still trying to be a presbytery exactly like all the other presbyteries. That is where the struggle really began to take shape.

When the national council saw what Keewatin was doing, Keewatin Presbytery became a model. The elders would come out for meetings, some not speaking any English. They would tell the other regions of the country, who had good command of English and some political knowledge, how they were the church. So Keewatin was a very clear message that, not only did we have to do this, but it did not matter what people assumed about our skills or capacity to organize our own church. Many elders from the north became symbols of that liberation.

About that time Christina Baker was ordained, the first woman from a Native village to be ordained in the United Church. A whole series of events were breaking the old cycle. Keewatin Presbytery was mainly dominated by male leaders, and to see Christina take her rightful place in that process and claim respect was a powerful sign.

That was basically the story. We then looked for a model that might be possible. I certainly did not have sufficient cultural insight to know what would work best, but the circle was well established. The circle is where everyone has a voice and everyone is respected and included, where decisions are made by consensus, wide-ranging discussion, and a wide-open agenda—all things that empower people.

JS: And the large annual gathering each summer now became known as Grand Council.

SM: Yes, the learnings from the annual consultations were recognized to be the way church was for us. That was really how we could be the church. We knew we could make important decisions by consensus. I still remember our identifying the four regions (presbyteries) of the conference, making decisions based in part on identity and on the political realities of groups of churches.

We met for two or three days after the apology in 1986 for some debriefing. Already there were two or three "political animals" saying, "The next step is obvious. Now that the apology is made we need to move to our own decision-making." So in 1987 most of the council meeting was about the selection of a name for the conference. In All Native Circle Conference, the most powerful word is *circle*. That was the symbol of the church. The circle and the cross. Those were the symbols for this developing image.

By 1988 the name had been chosen, the ANCC had been structured, and the first two leading elders had been chosen. Basically it was established in 1987, before General Council approved it. Then the drafting and formation of the conference went in a formal proposal to the 1988 General Council in Victoria, British Columbia. While the national church was preoccupied with other issues (debating the ordination of gay and lesbian persons), the All Native Circle Conference was approved and came into existence.

JS: The inauguration of the All Native Circle Conference did have a lot of meaning for many people present. I remember commissioners returning from the 1988 General Council talking about getting up early in the morning and gathering for ceremonies at the sacred fire.

Occasionally the All Native Circle Conference has been labeled a form of apartheid in the church. Some non-Aboriginal people are confused by this all-Aboriginal structure within the United Church. The striking difference from apartheid, though, is that the ANCC developed from Aboriginal people saying, "We need to govern ourselves."

SM: This again lifts up traditional spiritual themes and values. When Keewatin Presbytery was formed, the decision was made not as much on a strictly theological basis as on how we were the church in terms of polity: how we made decisions by consensus, how we sat in the circle, how we respected each other. Those were the issues at the heart of the decision. The motivation was not about cultural values in an open way, or about traditional ceremonies, but it was about traditional values, about respecting everyone and giving everyone voice.

In a sense, the ANCC is a form of apartheid in the church. In the 1990s the question continues to be whether there is a place within any of the historic mission denominations for the values First Nations people see as central to their spiritual expression. Is there room for them to be people of God, to be Christian in terms of Aboriginal understandings?

We have come an interesting circle here of self-government in First Nations churches. The question of self-government also is being raised in the Anglican church. Some congregations in the Roman Catholic community have pulled away from diocesan structures to form their own church life, to have self-governance within the congregation. All of that may move further, I expect, but at the moment it certainly is raising the question of what it is to be Aboriginal Christian.

In a sense these moves to self-government in the church are a separation, but in another way they are about survival. The values of the people are reflected in language and in respect for elders, respect for everyone in the circle. If you are going to maintain these values, then you cannot operate by a polity that says: "You win by fifteen to fourteen; it is too bad if fourteen people lose, because the majority has carried the day." That polity does not fit in the Aboriginal Christian community, the kind of polity that does not support the life of the community.

We are in an interesting time and, as we talk about it, I am quite amazed that the move to church self-government has happened. For some of us, the issue now is also about spirituality, about the traditional ceremonies, about the openness of our denomination's general population to our cultural realities. Yet it all started because we could not live any longer under paternalism, where others spoke for us and refused to hear our stories.

JS: What do the parallel struggles for Aboriginal self-government in the historical mission denominations say about gospel and culture? About the extent to which the gospel has been inculturated in the Anglo-European church systems brought to this continent?

SM: It raises a question about the structure of the church globally and how it fits the pattern of oppression of the marginalized. It will be important for indigenous people all over the world to look at their own tribal histories, which may mean going back a century or many centuries. The colonial idea imposed throughout the world is that you structure the church around rules and dogma which deny people a place as children of God and which pronounce judgment on them. I think the structural question is alive for us here because of our attempts to change the historic oppression done in the name of the gospel.

I know that corporate structures have influenced the church greatly, the dominant social and economic powers that dictate success and control and "good order." All of those things are elements of a modern culture that denies so many people dignity and good news. It may be *gospel* that we in First Nations communities here have learned that we are not going to accept foreign structures and values anymore. We are not going to submit to the obvious oppression in the name of gospel, not when our own understanding of the gospel tells us we must be liberated from this oppressive church system. We are going to give our church a shape which makes the gospel real to us in the context of our understanding of the Spirit of God. For me, that is a fundamental learning.

JS: The learning itself can be seen as gospel, as good news. If the container that carries the good news is broken, then you have to change the container. That is an extremely threatening revelation, because I think many people would like to see the gospel and culture question as something "out there," or something that can be discussed simply as "pure theological reflection." But it has to do with a critical evaluation and transformation of the very structures of the church; with who has the power and authority to define the gospel, to determine what is true and good, to draw the lines for who is in and outside the fold. The challenge is not only for people on the margins, but for the centers of ecclesiastical power.

SM: This is one reason we would be so interested to talk with theologians in other parts of the world. In the momentous changes in South Africa, for instance, where until recently the majority of society has not had voice in government. What does that say about the church, not only in South Africa, but in all of Africa? It is a very large question.

JS: In Korea people now have *minjung* theology, the suffering people's theology. As I understand it, part of that theology is looking at indigenous religions in a new light. Previously some theologians have acknowledged "the great world religions," such as Buddhism and Islam, yet looked down on tribal religions, which is ironic when you consider that Jewish, Christian, and Muslim roots are in a tribal religion. I have heard Chung Hyun Kyung speak of how shamanism was viewed as the lowest form of religion, yet that is often where women have found the most comfort and power. We seem to be on the verge of a global reawakening of the value and wisdom in these previously considered "low forms" of religion. I think there has been tremendous spiritual arrogance in the theological enterprise of church and academy.

SM: It certainly gives us much work in our small Aboriginal theological school because the process of liberation is such an important part of identity, of being a people under God. This was important for the Hebrew people, too, a tribal people following the teachings given them by God. It is a challenging and sometimes dangerous place to be. We hear of the ethnic conflicts in Eastern Europe and the Near and Mid-East around identity, so we need the spiritual teachings in the context of identity. The two—tribal identity and spirituality—stand somehow in tension. The traditional elders' teachings about balance and respect parallel the gospel commandment to love one another. That can lead us to the place where we work, The Dr. Jessie Saulteaux Resource Center. As the ministry program developed and as we literally faced opposition and persecution—in searching for a home and being rejected because we were Aboriginal—we recognized our need for healing. Being a circle of learning and respect was already there, but it was after we found a home here in Beausejour that some students in the circle identified it as a healing place. Looking back, I see this as a process of reconciliation. In some ways, reconciliation with oneself is a First Nations phenomenon. Repentance is a form of reconciliation with God and with oneself. Being victimized, marginalized, disenfranchised, is our special starting place for the process of reconciliation.

JS: We often think of reconciliation as between oppressor and oppressed. But we are saying here that it also is the internal process of the victimized finding wholeness of self, wholeness in community and as a people. It strikes me that the All Native Circle Conference and the Dr. Jessie Saulteaux Center both provide the *space* in which to find wholeness, a sacred space in which to reclaim identity. I think of our students' ongoing project of discerning their identity. "How can I be Christian and Cree?" for example. It is a painful struggle, often surfacing rage that strikes both outward and inward. All of this is necessary in the process of healing and critical for any process of reconciliation with the dominant culture.

True reconciliation can only happen from the personal and communal place of *strength*. The rejection of our Aboriginal theological center in the city of Winnipeg and elsewhere is an indication that the dominant culture is not prepared for reconciliation. What is critically important, however, is the transformation of Aboriginal people and leadership. Even if the dominant society were not as racist, and more prepared to reach out in reconciliation, without the healing process among Aboriginal people themselves reconciliation could not happen.

To be honest, reconciliation as a word is often problematical to me. Who is asking for the reconciliation, or even demanding it?

SM: There often is a ring of "peace, peace, when there is no peace." Another question is, What happens as people start to deal with some of the pain and the anger, and begin to grow out of it? They may come to fit into this community of learning but go back to their homes and not be able to relate anymore to their family or community. There is a cost in moving to increased self-understanding and self-worth. The student can see possibilities in the wider world, and the family at home feels that person is not as available to them. It can cause tensions.

JS: That reminds me of the elders' wisdom in setting up our ministry program. They decided on a field-based program of students working in their own communities between classes, so that they would not become alienated from their communities. But I know that does not totally solve the problem. I think of one student who essentially ministers to her whole extended family of about one hundred people. With strong communal values, if there is extensive brokenness in the family and one person with more wholeness, that person's sharing her wholeness with others can drag her back down. A traditional teaching is that healing is from the inside out, to your family and to your community. It is not the same as in an individualistic society, where you say, "I've got it together now. You go away, because you don't."

SM: That is one of the natural things of the tribal community, with people connected to one another, which modern society would have us move away from as being untenable with the aggressive, materialistic, individualistic society. It is difficult to know what the next step is, because people who are sharing and generous with their time and resources often slide down and find themselves depressed and overwhelmed. It is a challenging process. The way we learn in the circle—with each person valued for his or her experience and wisdom—is an attempt to affirm the sharing of learnings, of insight. There develops a very deep level of trust. When we sit in the circle and refer to one another as family in times of sharing, and when both Aboriginal and non-Aboriginal people experience the Center as a place of healing, all of that is about reconciliation. But how do we practice it beyond the walls of our community? The real challenge is to take that reconciliation out into the world when the world doesn't want to have any part of the process.

JS: It amazes me when students do develop circles of healing and reconciliation in their ministries. I think of a particular student who has developed a wonderful worship/healing/sharing circle in the midst of all kinds of brokenness and pain in a predominantly white inner-city congregation that doesn't even really understand her Aboriginal culture. I see in it the work of the Spirit. It speaks to the power of the indigenous spiritual traditions, the resources that are within the people and the people's connection with their God. This student has come a long way in reconciling her Christian faith with her traditional Aboriginal ways, and the result is a reconciling ministry. Creative power in the midst of brokenness. . . . This thing called reconciliation—it is a problematical word. (laughter)

SM: Especially if you hold it in a theological context of moving to some ideal . . . speaking of repentance and other acts of faith, called to love our neighbors as ourselves, to do unto others as we would have done to us, "what you do for the least of these." All of these profound ways of living are about reconciliation, about justice. Reconciliation is not only an abstract theological image, but has to do with practical applications of faithful living.

I think another element is that of geography, the reconciliation to place as well. Sacred land. Sacred place. It is not simply a human reality. Going to the [sweat] lodge [for a prayer ceremony] is in many ways a reconciliation of humans to one another, to the Creator and to the earth and other creatures.[5] As Jules Lavallee says, it is "a celebration of life," an expression of the whole-

ness we seek. To my mind there isn't much in the church that is about reconciliation in terms of ceremony. I guess regular worship is supposed to be that
for us, but I find there an absence of symbolism, an absence of ceremony.

JS: Yet there are a lot of words, like *reconciliation*, that have been dissoci-
ated from any reality. Words that float as ideas without substance or action. It
seems to me that there is virtually an idolatry of worship, where the words are
seldom connected with any lived experience.

If we return to the experience of The United Church of Canada and the
Native apology, was that truly a process of reconciliation?

SM: Where you mentioned the White Bear image of, "You teach us the way
of church politics and we'll teach you the Native spiritual way," I think there
is a potential for some sharing of power. It hasn't happened yet, but the potential is being worked on in some aspects. Also a sharing of spirit, of sacred
ways. At the apology that evening, Art Solomon—always the elder of insight
beyond the bullshit—said to the church, "Get real or get lost!" (laughter) And
that is reconciliation. Not the pretense, but the struggles for the fullness of
human life shared. The ongoing struggle to be fully human.

JS: I often think that Jesus' saying that in order to save your life you need
to lose it is best directed at the church itself. It always has been interpreted
more individualistically, but I think that it is a call to the church to give its life
and then it will receive it, to give up its power and control. This is very hard
for the leadership of the church to do, especially in the dominant culture where
control and power and wealth are reigning gods. Some people within the Canadian church have a sense of that call. There had to be enough supporters in
solidarity with Aboriginal people for our mainline denomination to come as
far as it has, to offer the apology and entrust the All Native Circle Conference
and our center, for example, with their own self-determination.

SM: The reconciliation begins in that will to be involved, but if you are
unwilling to struggle with the realities of the history and with the dreams of
the people, that is one of the reasons that "receiving," but not immediately
"accepting" the apology was so important. In Canada many people within the
structure of the church have not yet analyzed the historical breaking of spirits,
the crushing of the people in order to maintain the institution at all costs, and
they still are hanging onto dreams that are our nightmares. If that history is
not dealt with, there is a hollowness about the apology. The expected reconciliation is forever delayed because peoples still do not understand each other.
The talk of reconciliation is too soon, because the inequity, the status quo,
really hasn't changed. If part of the church can have all the benefits of the
land's resources, and others go wanting, reconciliation cannot happen. Justice
and the image of being the people of God aren't being acted out. This is true
both for First Nations relationships and the global church context.

JS: That reminds me of the Apostle Paul's great collection, where the collection is for the Jerusalem church. In 2 Corinthians Paul says to the Gentile
congregations, I'm asking you to do this as "a matter of equality," that you
share what you have with them now so that in the future, when they have and

you do not, they can reciprocate. He repeats "as a matter of equality" twice, that is, justice. Justice and love are one. Charity was never a matter of giving left-overs. If one part of the body suffers, everybody suffers. Reconciliation is within that sphere, that circle.

So the challenge is still before us. With rapidly shrinking financial resources in the mainline Canadian churches, the crunch is coming. For some, it is going to come down to dollars and cents. What is the cost of reconciliation? Can the church enter into the pain of the healing process? The next few years will reveal how far we are on this road to reconciliation.

Notes

[1] The United Church of Canada comprises thirteen conferences, twelve of which are geographical regions across Canada. In 1988 the thirteenth was added, the All Native Circle Conference. The story of its creation is recounted in this article. Each conference has staff, councils, and committees that are responsible for major areas of church life within its boundaries.

[2] The work of The United Church of Canada at the national level is carried out by five divisions, one of which is the Division of Mission in Canada. The broad mandate of the D.M.C. includes areas of justice, peace, and the environment, as well as the production of educational and worship resources. Historically it has had primary responsibility for Native United Churches across Canada.

[3] General Council is the body that develops policies for The United Church of Canada. It normally meets every two years, with lay and order of ministry representation from across Canada. Between its meetings a smaller body, the General Council Executive, meets to make decisions regarding the interim work of the denomination.

[4] Presbyeries are composed of the United Church congregations and ministries in given geographical areas. Each presbytery has work similar to that carried out by bishops in other denominations. The presbytery is the major link between local churches and the national United Church.

When The United Church of Canada formed in 1925, it instituted a church government that adopted various aspects of each founding denomination's polity (Methodist, Presbyterian, and Congregational). This has given it a relatively complex structure.

[5] The sweat-lodge ceremony is now practiced across North America by many different First Nations peoples. It is an ancient traditional ritual in which people gather in the heat and darkness of a small lodge to offer to the Creator prayers of thanksgiving, supplication, celebration, and renewal.

15

A Theological Afterword

GREGORY BAUM

Reading the essays of this collection, essays written in different parts of the world and dealing with different church-based enterprises, the theologian finds that they have much in common. They share several theological positions. What I wish to do in this Afterword is to spell out in greater detail the common convictions implicit in these essays and offer my own theological reflections on them.

1. The authors of this book take for granted that the Christian gospel summons the church to exercise a ministry of reconciliation in situations defined by strife and hostility.

The editors did not ask the authors to reveal the theological reasons why they hold this conviction; they were simply invited to report and analyze a particular church-based project of reconciliation. Since the authors belong to different denominational traditions—Protestant, Catholic, Orthodox, and Mennonite—it is likely that they would defend their conviction with different theological arguments. While they may disagree in their reading of the scriptures, they are fully united in the faith that Jesus is the savior of the world and that his disciples are to be agents of reconciliation and promoters of love, justice, and peace.

The only strictly theological essay of this collection is the one written by my co-editor, Protestant theologian Harold Wells, exploring the biblical meaning of reconciliation. He offers a persuasive reading of scripture in the light of the classical Protestant tradition with an emphasis on Christ's atonement, the forgiveness of sins, and justification by faith. Harold Wells rescues these biblical teachings from a purely private or personal interpretation and brings out and develops their public or social significance. He has chosen these particular teachings because they play such an important role in the self-understanding of Protestant Christians. Addressing himself to them, Wells shows that the faith they have inherited summons them to foster the reconciliation of peoples.

The Catholic self-understanding, I suggest, focuses on slightly different doctrinal themes. As a Catholic theologian I would be inclined to explore the public meaning of love of God and love of neighbor and stress the role of sanctifying grace in the salvation of the world. The new life of faith, hope, and love is summoned forth by Grace spelled with a capital G, or God's redemptive presence. Relying on several texts in the Pauline letters and the Fourth Gospel, Catholics tend to emphasize God's immanence in people's lives, in their loving interaction, and in their quest for truth and justice. Where sin abounds, grace abounds even more. Revealed in Jesus is God's reconciling action in the world. Today Catholic theologians speak of a "reconciling Transcendent" operative in human history that *precedes* the church's preaching—which Christians must discern, for which they must give thanks, and which they want to serve in the name of the message they have received. Harold Wells is likely to agree with this, yet addressing a different readership he focuses on different texts.

A theology of reconciliation also wants to listen to a point made by liberation theology and acknowledged in Wells's essay. When interpreting the salvational meaning of Christ's death on the cross, we must not separate this death—as traditional theology has done—from its concrete, historical circumstances. Jesus was persecuted and condemned to death by the secular and religious establishment of his time—because he spoke the truth, demanded justice, and showed compassion. The crucifixion reveals both the nature of the world's sins and the boundlessness of Christ's love.

Yet whatever differences in their theologies, the authors of these essays are in total agreement that Christians in the church are called by the gospel to be agents of reconciliation among groups and peoples caught in a history of conflict and enmity.

2. All the authors of this book recognize that the churches have rarely exercised their ministry of reconciliation.

The efforts at reconciliation described in these essays were initiated by groups of Christians who were minorities in their own churches. Only occasionally were these efforts endorsed and supported by ecclesiastical authority. We learned that in Chile the Catholic bishops often exercised the role of reconcilers, and that in Canada the moderator of the United Church acted in a ceremony of reconciliation with the Native peoples.

Absent from the pages of this book are the stories of Christians and their churches that refused to act as reconcilers in their societies. Because Harold Wells and I, the editors, believed that it was useless simply to bewail the church's inability to mediate between hostile groups, we looked for authors able to report on positive efforts made by Christian groups to foster reconciliation. We wanted the essays to be sources of encouragement and possibly offer models of action that could be imitated elsewhere. Fortunately there exist many other such positive efforts that deserve to be recorded and read as signals of hope.

Still, the theologian is obliged to reflect on the church's inability to act as reconciler in conflicts between groups and peoples. Why is it so difficult for the church to play a mediating role? It is possible to explain this in sociological terms. Churches are often so deeply identified with their own people that they are not considered credible mediators by the "other side"; and when churches do put forth gestures of reconciliation, they are often suspected of treason by their own people. This phenomenon has been studied by Ralph Premdas, one of the authors in this book, in his doctoral thesis at McGill University on the role of the churches in ethnic conflicts in several third-world countries. In many instances, the churches even intensify the conflict. It is no exaggeration to say that the successful "incarnation" of the church in a given community makes it difficult for the church to stand at a critical distance from it and take a nonpartisan view of the conflict in which it is involved. Studies on the preaching in Christian churches during the First and the Second World Wars reveal the extent to which the clergy were identified with their countries and their political aspirations.

Yet sociological reflections are not sufficient to explain the churches' reluctance to act as reconcilers in situations of conflict. Theology has to speak its own word in regard to this phenomenon. It is necessary, it seems to me, to confront the enormous ambiguity of scripture in dealing with the attitude of God's people to outsiders, whether individuals or collectivities. Passages proclaiming universal solidarity are few in comparison with the many passages that restrict solidarity to the believing community. The generosity toward strangers within this community is rarely extended to strangers without. For theological reasons, mindful of the divine election, the Bible encourages a "we-they" discourse that excludes "them" from participation and creates a negative rhetoric of otherness. This ambiguous theological heritage has prompted the church to look upon "the others" simply from its own perspective. The church has tended to define "the others" in its own terms, instead of first listening patiently to how they define themselves and then only reflecting on who they are in the light of Christian faith. The church's attitude throughout its history toward the Jewish people symbolizes the church's near-inability to respect the otherness of others. This tragic heritage, it seems to me, has made the church unable to teach its members to respect outsiders, discern among them the quest for the true and the good, and search for common bonds of solidarity. Yet this is precisely the spiritual orientation required for exercising a ministry of reconciliation.

The texts of the Hebrew and Christian scriptures proclaiming universal solidarity—Harold Wells mentions several of them in his essay—have come fully into their own only in the twentieth century. The shift in the church's official attitude toward the Jews is symptomatic of a new openness toward outsiders. Listening anew, in the contemporary context, to God's Word in the scriptures has urged many Christian communities to become reconcilers in situations of conflict and foster a church-transcending, universal solidarity, beginning with the poor and oppressed.

3. The authors in this book speak of the ministry of reconciliation as a pioneering activity.

This ministry is a bold undertaking that irritates the more traditional-minded members of the church. The authors realize that the church's theological tradition offers very little wisdom on the social meaning of reconciliation. It is symptomatic that even in the most recent *Handbook of Catholic Theology*, published by Crossroad in 1995, the long, scholarly article on reconciliation makes no reference whatever to the reconciliation between peoples. *The New Dictionary of Catholic Social Thought*, published by Liturgical Press in 1994, contains no article on reconciliation. Reflection on this topic is only beginning in the church.

Donald Shriver's book *An Ethic for Enemies: Forgiveness in Politics*, published by Oxford University Press in 1995, makes an important contribution to this topic. Shriver shows that the ancient Greeks and the ancient Hebrews were fully aware that justice alone was not enough to secure peace in society; they recognized that justice had to be tempered by forbearance. Since inflicting just punishment on evildoers cuts new wounds, creates resentment, and lays the foundation of future conflict, a peace-loving society must have laws that allow for tolerance through institutions such as amnesty and juridical pardon. Shriver presents texts drawn from two Greek authors, Aeschylus and Thucydides, that make this very point. Greek wisdom acknowledged the need for forgiveness in the life of society.

More emphatic is the emphasis on forbearance in the biblical books. Shriver offers an original reading of scripture texts that reveal that justice is not enough. While in Near Eastern societies the legal punishment for murder was death, we read in Genesis that after the murder of Abel, God forbade that capital punishment be inflicted on Cain. God put a sign on Cain's forehead to protect him from execution, that is, from receiving his due in accordance with the law. Shriver reads this as a signal that justice must be tempered by forbearance.

Of special interest, though not discussed by Shriver, are the biblical accounts of conflict and reconciliation between two brothers in the history of salvation, between Isaac and Ishmael, and later between Jacob and Esau. Here the enmity between the two brothers, caused by antecedent acts of injustice, is eventually resolved by a joint recognition of the unjust deed, the willingness to leave the past behind, and the desire to live in mutual respect. What takes place is not a full reconciliation but the entry into peaceful coexistence. Since the dramatis personae in Genesis refer to tribes and their interaction, these biblical texts communicate wisdom for the reconciliation of peoples.

Shriver attaches great importance to the long story, told in Genesis in great detail, of the reconciliation of Joseph and his brothers. The biblical text informs us about the crime against Joseph committed by his brothers, the position of power Joseph achieved in the land of Egypt, his ability to help his brothers in a situation of great need, the ritual punishment he imposed on them during their visit in Egypt, his discovery that the brothers repent of their crime, and finally the forgiveness he offers them. According to Shriver, this story had an important social message: it was written at a time when the twelve tribes of Israel were in conflict, in order to offer them a model of repentance, forgiveness, and reconciliation. Yet the message was not heeded. What actually happened was the break-up of the realm into two separate kingdoms, Israel in the north and Judah in the south.

Shriver studies the teaching of Jesus in the New Testament that presents forgiveness as an essential characteristic of the *ekklesia*. The community of disciples is to distinguish itself from secular societies by its wish and readiness to forgive and be reconciled. Even in the New Testament, Shriver shows, forgiveness had a public function. It would be worthwhile to study the biblical account of the conflicts in the early Christian community and the steps taken to overcome them in the hope of finding guidance for today's church in its effort to become a community of reconciliation. Shriver encourages us to think that the biblical tradition has much more to say about the political praxis of reconciliation than the silence of Christian theologians has made us believe.

4. The authors of this book agree that reconciliation *is an ambiguous theological term.*

Harold Wells reminds us that the message of reconciliation can be used ideologically to protect the privileges of the powerful. This was one of the points made by the *Kairos Document* of 1985 mentioned in John de Gruchy's essay. This declaration of protest, made by a group of South African Christians against the institution of apartheid, accused the liberal churches of their country of preaching reconciliation as a subtle way of avoiding resistance against evil. The liberal churches opposed injustice and discrimination, but they still believed that generosity, mutual understanding, and forgiveness on all sides would lead to a better, more reconciled society. Rejecting this theology, the *Kairos Document* advocated resistance and struggle in the present, and promised reconciliation only after apartheid had been abolished. The essays of John de Gruchy and Charles Villa-Vicencio reveal that in the new South Africa reconciliation has become an urgent political and social issue, a cause to which Christians want to make their contribution.

In Latin America conservative Catholic bishops have accused liberation theology of setting the poor against the affluent and thus sinning against the unity of the church. They propose instead a theology of reconciliation. They have the idea that since all people are sinners, the rich as well as the poor, all are called to repentance and forgiveness and to find their unity in Jesus Christ. They preach a reconciliation that does not demand structural change in the social order; their theology allows the rich to keep their power and privilege.

Feminist theology and the theologies of the Third World have reminded us that all the magnificent words of the Christian message—such as trust in God, love, forgiveness, humility, and patience—can be used ideologically to reconcile the victims of injustice to the social situation in which they are caught. In recent decades Christian theology has learned to be critical of its own discourse through an extended dialogue with secular thinkers, the so-called masters of suspicion, who have revealed the hidden agenda of domination in many high-sounding phrases lauding virtue and exalting divinity. The authors of this book agree that Christians engaged in social projects of reconciliation must be willing critically to review their own Christian tradition, its teaching, language, customs, and social patterns.

5. The fifth point on which the authors of this book agree is that the process of reconciliation demands metanoia, conversion, a change of mind and heart.

Whether people are religious or secular, reconciliation transcending a history of enmity is a spiritual process. It is the work of the Spirit. Many contemporary theologians hold that since in Jesus Christ God has reconciled all things with God, all things on earth and in heaven, a spiritual, reconciling thrust is graciously operative in human history, offering people the power beyond their own brokenness to enter into self-recognition and overcome the barriers erected by sin.

In *Reconciliation* Robert Schreiter makes the important point that a process of reconciliation must not be equated with the practice of conflict resolution. Conflict resolution is a useful administrative skill, taught in many schools of management and public administration, that enables a practitioner to gather the conflicting parties around the table and lead them along carefully planned steps into a conversation that will ultimately result in an agreement. The ethics involved in this process remains utilitarian. The contesting parties learn to recognize the justified interests of their opponents and through carefully managed negotiations reach a compromise that allows each party to protect the essential element of its own interests. Conflict resolution does not involve conversion and forgiveness. Conflict resolution may in many instances make an important contribution to the process of reconciliation, but it is not identical with it.

Reconciliation demands that the groups or peoples at enmity with one another review their own history and in a leap of faith redefine their path into the future. If the groups or peoples are related to one another as oppressor and oppressed, as was the case in the apartheid state, the oppressors must recognize the evil origin of their power and privilege, repent, and be willing to make reparation. When the oppressed, conscious of their history of suffering, see that the oppressors are ready to repent and make restitution, they must be willing to forgive and start out on a new path. Liberation theology insists that since victims have for the most part internalized the contempt in which they were held, they are in need of a new self-understanding. The oppressed will also have to forgive themselves for the destructive acts among their own, committed out of anger, frustration or despair. Conversion must take place for both master and slave, even if the nature of the conversion is different for each.

In many cases discussed in this book the relations of injustice and hostility cannot be accounted for in terms of oppressor and oppressed. Not all conflicts between groups or peoples correspond to the oppression of the Hebrews in the land of Pharaoh. While the relationship of the dominant Canadian society to the Native peoples may be understood in terms of oppressor and oppressed, this is not true, for instance, for the conflict between Canada and Quebec, discussed in the essay of Harry Oussoren. Nor is the Pharaoh/Israel model applicable to most of the conflicts examined in this book, in Fiji, Korea, Northern Ireland, and contemporary Chile. In each of these cases, the conflicting parties were both in one way or another victims of stronger powers. Here both sides speak from a position of vulnerability. Here the process of reconciliation demands that each party sort out its own story of wounds received and wounds inflicted and then repent and forgive in appropriate proportions. Without this kind of *metanoia*, reconciliation is impossible.

6. This leads us to the sixth agreement implicit in the essays of this collection, which I shall call the need for a common story.

According to the brilliant analysis in Schreiter's book *Reconciliation*, peoples' peace and security require not only material factors such as land, economic resources, and political institutions, but also ideational factors, especially their collective identity, that is, a commonly accepted story that defines their place in history. Schreiter argues that injustice and violence inflicted upon a people or a community are not adequately understood if they are restricted to the material damage and do not take into account the attack on its collective identity. Humiliating a people or a community is a form of aggression.

At the same time, in a sinful world, peoples and groups tend to tell their stories and define their identity in a manner that serves their collective self-interest and justifies an alleged superiority over others. Victorious nations integrate into their story the conquest of nations supposedly located on a lower cultural level. The histories written by empires justify the colonization of tribes and peoples in terms of their alleged inferiority. At the same time, the victims often tell their stories in a manner that demonizes the conqueror, refuses to recognize the victor's humanity, and sees the conqueror as incapable of changing and becoming a friend. In a sinful world each community inherits a distorted self-perception either by arrogance or by self-contempt—arrogance over against those deemed inferior, and self-contempt before those deemed superior. Thus it is possible for a group or a people to be exposed to racist contempt in their society and at the same time to harbor racist prejudice against others more vulnerable than they are.

Reconciliation demands that the parties involved be willing to examine their own history critically, recognize the distortions of their self-understanding, and humbly acknowledge the place assigned to the opponents in their own story. Conversion should enable the two parties to rewrite their histories and enter upon a new path that allows both of them to discover themselves as partners or even friends. Reconciliation demands that the two parties try to write a common story, that in the definition of their own self-identity they make room for the self-definition of the other.

This has been clearly recognized in the process of reconciliation between Germany and France after the Second World War. A joint French-German school commission was set up by the two countries; its task was to write the history of French-German relations in a manner acceptable in France and Germany. Only when history taught in French and German schools communicates a common story will friendship and collaboration between the French and the Germans become a stable reality. In my essay in this book I mention that a similar school commission was appointed to produce a common account of Polish-German relations in European history.

The churches had, until fairly recently, no awareness of the ideational dimension of violence and thus left no room for the self-understanding of "the others" in the account of their own history. I mentioned above that I regard this as a great weakness of the Christian tradition. It is the important achievement of the ecumenical movement, which—as acknowledged by Vatican Council II—was inspired by the Holy Spirit, to have opened the churches to the recognition of "the other," impelled them critically to review their own history, made them recognize and mourn their unjust words and deeds, and urged them to produce a common history of Christianity, acceptable to all Christian traditions. In the ecumenical movement, it is worth noting, none of the churches was asked to compromise its own self-understanding. There was a common recognition that a community's self-identity is not a static but a dynamic historical reality, one that constitutes itself by responding to new challenges in a spiritual process that introduces change or even self-correction and, at the same time, assures continuity and fidelity to the past.

7. The final agreement I find in the essays of this collection is the importance assigned to leadership in the process of reconciliation.

In all the accounts reconciliation between groups or peoples is promoted by a few Christians with strong convictions surrounded by many who remain indifferent or are even hostile to the idea. I mentioned earlier that the authors present the efforts of reconciliation as a pioneering activity. Since reconciliation calls for conversion, the leaders exercise a prophetic ministry; they mediate God's Word to a reluctant community. Their effort becomes successful only as an increasing number of people enter into the new spirit and offer their support for the movement of reconciliation.

It would be interesting to know what human experiences have prepared the initiators of reconciliation for their task. From the dialogue between Janet Silman and Stanley McKay we learn that it was a First Nations woman, Alberta Billy, who had herself many times experienced the humiliation of her people, who confronted the church's leaders about historic injustice and initiated the request for an apology. In the essay on Polish-German reconciliation, we read that the Polish bishop Boleslaw Kominek, who pleaded among his colleagues for reconciliation with the German Catholic Church, was brought up as a Pole in a German culture, faithful to his Polish heritage. He too participated in two cultures.

Other ardent reconcilers do not have this special background. Yet they must have had certain religious or cultural experiences that produced the inner urgency to engage themselves in such a controversial enterprise. The massive crimes against humanity in this century, which provoked the United Nations to promulgate the Universal Declaration of Human Rights (1948), have summoned forth among the churches an urgent sense of solidarity with "the others," especially the vulnerable and marginalized others. In Catholic theology this is often called the option for the poor and interpreted as a gift, a dimension of faith, the contemporary form of discipleship. This is a commitment widely spread in all the churches. One aspect of this faith option is the commitment to read one's own society from the perspective of its victims. The option for the poor demands that we review in critical fashion the history to which we belong. Men must be willing to read their civilization from the perspective of women. This faith option gives rise to spiritual experiences that urge many Christians to labor for reconciliation across the inherited boundaries, religious, ethnic, cultural, and sexual, and to yearn for a world pacified in love and justice.

Contributors

José Aldunate, S.J., is professor emeritus at the Catholic University of Chile in Santiago. He was a lecturer in moral theology and an activist in the labor movement and the struggle for human rights. He is the founder of the Jesuit periodical *Mensaje* and has published articles and books on human rights, especially the rights of the poor.

Gregory Baum is professor emeritus at the Religious Studies Faculty of McGill University in Montreal. Over the years one of his special interests has been ecumenism, meaning reconciliation among the churches. He is the editor of *The Ecumenist*. His most recent books are *Karl Polanyi on Ethics and Economics* (McGill-Queen's University Press, 1996) and *The Church for Others: Protestant Theology in Communist East Germany* (Eerdmans, 1996).

John W. de Gruchy is professor of Christian studies at the University of Cape Town, South Africa. He is author of many articles and books, including *Liberating Reformed Theology* (David Philip and Eerdmans, 1991) and *The Church Struggle in South Africa* (Eerdmans 1979/1986). With Charles Villa-Vicencio he is co-editor of volumes 1 and 2 of *Theology and Praxis* (David Philip and Orbis Books, 1994).

Jim Forest is secretary of the Orthodox Peace Fellowship and edits its quarterly journal *In Communion*. He is author of *Living with Wisdom* (a biography of Thomas Merton) (Orbis Books, 1991), *Love Is the Measure* (a biography of Dorothy Day) (Paulist Press, 1986; rev. ed. Orbis Books, 1994), *Pilgrim to the Russian Church* (Crossroad, 1988), and *Religion in the New Russia* (Crossroad, 1990). His next book is *Praying with Icons*. He lives in the Netherlands.

Michael Hurley, S.J., an Irish Jesuit priest, taught systematic theology at Milltown Park in Dublin from 1958 to 1970. He then became involved in the establishment of the Irish School of Ecumenics and was its director from 1970 to 1980. In 1983 he was involved in the foundation of the Columbanus Community of Reconciliation in Belfast and remained a member there until 1993, when he returned to Dublin.

Andrea Koch studied human geography in developing countries in Amsterdam. She worked for the Development Service of the Protestant Church in Germany before starting to work for Aktion Sühnezeichen Friedensdienste (ASF) in 1994. At ASF she is responsible for the volunteer program in Great Britain and the United States as well as for the evaluation seminars of long-term volunteers.

Ian Linden, a former university teacher in Malawi and Nigeria, is the author of a number of books on Christianity in Africa, including *Church and Revolution in Rwanda* (Manchester University Press, 1977). Later a professor of African Studies at the University of Hamburg, he moved to the southern Africa desk of the Catholic Institute for International Relations (CIIR) in London in 1980 and since 1986 has been CIIR's director.

Stanley McKay is former moderator of The United Church of Canada. Born in Fisher River, Manitoba, he is Cree, an ordained minister, and presently director of the Dr. Jessie Saulteaux Resource Centre, an Aboriginal learning center for ministry in Beausejour, Manitoba.

A. H. Harry Oussoren is a minister of The United Church of Canada serving Erin Mills United Church, Mississauga, Ontario, in a community created in large measure by the exodus of Anglophones from Quebec after the election of a Parti Québecois government. He holds a doctorate in theology and served on the national staff of the United Church as secretary for theological education. He was founder and longtime chair of the board of the *Journal for the Practice of Ministry in Canada*.

Catherine Peck served with her husband as the peace development team for the Mennonite Central Committee on the West Bank in Israel from 1993 to 1995. They live with their two daughters at George School in Newton, Pennsylvania.

Ralph R. Premdas is professor of political science and sociology at the University of the West Indies, St. Augustine, Trinidad, and Tobago. He is author of *Ethnicity and Development: The Case of Fiji* (London: Avebury, 1996). He is engaged in an ongoing project on the role of ecclesial institutions in ethnic and communal conflict, a topic on which he did a Ph.D. in religious studies at McGill University.

Brigitte Scheiger studied German literature, philosophy, and political science. For many years she taught and did research at the Freie Universität in Berlin. Since 1992 she has been working at Aktion Sühnezeichen Friedensdienste (ASF), where she is responsible for the volunteer program in the Netherlands, France, and Belgium as well as the preparation seminars for long-term volunteers.

Janet Silman is an ordained minister of mixed-blood ancestry (English/Cree/Scottish), Bible study columnist for *The United Church Observer*, and responsible for biblical studies and curriculum at the Dr. Jessie Saulteaux Resource Centre, an Aboriginal learning center for ministry in Beausejour, Manitoba.

Charles Villa-Vicencio is professor of religion and society at the University of Cape Town, South Africa. He is the author of *Civil Disobedience and Beyond* (David Philip and Eerdmans, 1990), *A Theology of Reconstruction* (Cambridge University Press, 1992), and *The Spirit of Hope* (Skotaville Publishers, 1994). With John de Gruchy he is co-editor of volumes 1 and 2 of *Theology and Praxis* (David Philip and Orbis Books, 1994).

Harold Wells is professor of systematic theology at Emmanuel College in the University of Toronto. He has served many years in congregational ministries of The United Church of Canada and as a lecturer in theology in Lesotho (southern Africa). It was his experience amid the conflicts of that region that stimulated his concern for the theology of reconciliation. His most recent book is *A Future for Socialism: Political Theology and "The Triumph of Capitalism"* (Valley Forge, Penn.: Trinity Press International, 1996).

Erich Weingartner, a graduate in theology, has worked at the Lutheran World Federation in Geneva, the International Documentation Centre (IDOC) in Rome, and the Commission of the Churches on International Affairs in Geneva, where from 1978 to 1986 he guided the World Council of Churches' policies on human rights. Since 1987 he has worked as a consultant on international affairs. His most recent publications are *The Pacific: Nuclear Testing and Minorities* (Minority Rights Group, 1991), *The Tragedy of Bosnia: Confronting the New World Disorder* (Commission of the Churches on International Affairs, 1994), and *Protecting Human Rights: A Manual for Practitioners* (1995).